Night Owl Fighter Pilot

To Dave
Best wishes to a
good friend
Take Care
Val

Night Owl Fighter Pilot

Val Ross Johnson

iUniverse, Inc.

New York Lincoln Shanghai

Night Owl Fighter Pilot

iUniverse books may be ordered through booksellers or by contacting:

iUniverse
2021 Pine Lake Road, Suite 100
Lincoln, NE 68512
www.iuniverse.com
1-800-Authors (1-800-288-4677)

ISBN-13: 978-0-595-41676-9 (pbk)
ISBN-13: 978-0-595-86020-3 (ebk)
ISBN-10: 0-595-41676-4 (pbk)
ISBN-10: 0-595-86020-6 (ebk)

Printed in the United States of America

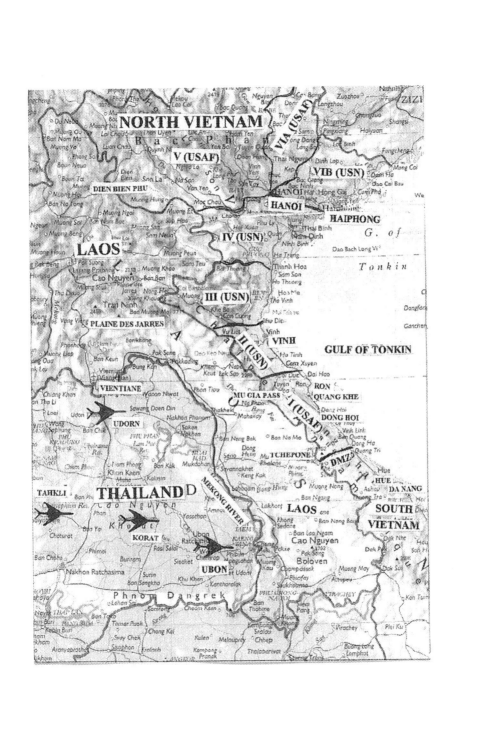

This book is dedicated to all the Night Owls in the 497th Tactical Fighter Squadron and everyone at Ubon, Thailand during the Vietnam War. A special tribute to exceptional friends: Dayton Ragland (Rags), Edward Collins Jr., Allen Pollard (Crash), Doug McCarty, and Denny Scarbough, who lost their lives in the F-4 Phantom II while serving their country.

Contents

Acknowledgments

Many special people have contributed to the completion of this book. I would like to thank my two sons, Dr. Andrew S. Johnson and Dr. Charles E. Johnson for their extensive editing efforts. My daughter, Dr. Ashley Wernli, and wife, Dr. Karen H. Johnson, provided many hours of proof reading and excellent suggestions.

I would like to thank Richard L. Penn, Lee M. Brazell, and Robert J. Frasier for their contributions and interest in this book.

I am grateful to William E. McGourin for helping me survive in the skies over North Vietnam.

Prologue

A man is fortunate if he is blessed with even one true talent—a physical or mental skill that he can perform as well as anyone in the world. Discovering such a talent, honing it, and then putting it to use may be one of the most satisfying experiences in life. I was blessed with two talents in my life—the ability to hurl a baseball 60 feet and to fly a jet aircraft faster than the speed of sound. Unfortunately, life demanded that I choose between my talents at an early age. Baseball allowed me to find my way from a small town in Northern Idaho to the University of Idaho where I received financial assistance from the athletic department and a ticket to qualify for flight training in the military. In 1959, professional baseball offered much less of a reliable future when compared to the $400 a month that the military had to offer. More importantly, I might be able to achieve a mythical dream to fly fighter aircraft that had been my focus as far back as I could remember. To think that the military would actually even pay me to fly the most advanced planes in the world seemed better than any World Series scenario.

To date, I have never seen a movie or read a book that adequately conveyed the essence of flying high performance jets in a combat environment. Those books that I have read by military pilots mainly detail historical events without capturing the spirit and emotions involved. I believe that the world of a fighter pilot is remarkably unique and it is difficult to impart the intensity of it in words—especially without having witnessed it first-hand. For eighteen years, I flew many different planes, including the F-102 and the F-4 (B, C, D and J series). During that time, the brotherhood I forged with fellow pilots was much more important than any award, pay, or promotion I may have received. Few people realize or appreciate what combat fighter pilots are subjected to during their military career.

Flying high performance jet fighters is one of the most hazardous professions in the world—yet pilots are somehow often perceived as insulated from the horrors of war. Most civilians do not realize that fighter pilots entrust each other with their lives on a daily basis, while flying just a few feet apart at high speeds and during any type of weather conditions. Most combat experiences are told from the perspective of the ground combatant, as though no other bond could be

1

as strong as between brothers-in-arms. I would argue that a pilot would go down in flames rather than fail to fiercely defend a fellow fighter. Each pilot enters a fight knowing it may be his last but is bound by honor and duty to defend his country with his life. Unlike the foot soldier, fighter pilots know that it may not even be enemy fire that frequently brings them down. In fact, I have lost several of my closest friends to mishaps that never involved a single round of enemy ammunition. My closest friend in the U.S. Navy, Lt. Doug McCarty, also a star football receiver who teamed with Roger Staubach at the Naval Academy, was lost when his F-4J fighter inexplicably crashed into the ocean as we returned from a mission. My best friend while I was serving at the Pentagon, Lt. Col. Denny Scarbourgh, disappeared into the Gulf of Mexico on a mission and was never found. Even those who had survived tours in Vietnam were not immune to daily hazards of flying. Ed Collins survived two tours flying over North Vietnam, only to be killed in the air traffic pattern when returning to land at his base. Finally, Al (Crash) Pollard survived flying missions with me in Vietnam only to be killed during a routine take off. The pain of losing such close friends in the service of your country is as strong as any loss I have ever felt. Only the grace of God has allowed me to try to describe my experiences and dedicate this book to those fellow pilots who can no longer tell their stories.

I want to reiterate that despite the somewhat glamorous image the media world has attached to fighter pilots, the military pilot has joined for one purpose: to defend his country. There is no significant monetary reward for flying combat missions. I received an extra sixty-five dollars a month for combat pay in Vietnam and flight pay in the Air Force is equivalent no matter what type of plane is flown. Military pay pales in comparison to the compensation packages of commercial airlines. In addition, fighter pilots have no special military benefits when it comes to retirement or promotions. The top graduates from military pilot training schools continue to select fighters for their military assignments. I strongly believe that the United States continues to produce the elite pilots of the world. Fighter pilots are fully aware that they will be the first to be called upon for combat operations in any hostile action and are willing to risk their lives on a daily basis. I am writing this non-fiction account in an attempt to bring recognition to all the fighter pilots that I have served with during the time I flew with the Air Force and the Navy. Specifically, I wish to recognize those courageous souls who lost their lives in Vietnam, a conflict I still have trouble understanding.

During my military career, I was fortunate to have served with both the Air Force and the Navy. I would like to give special thanks to Rear Admiral Peter Booth for allowing me to attend and graduate from the Navy Top Gun Fighter

Weapons School. Other memorable experiences include becoming day and night carrier qualified on the USS John F. Kennedy, as well as the first Air Force pilot to land on that carrier. Lt. General Joseph G. Wilson allowed me to become the commander of the 614th Tactical Fighter Squadron in Torrejon AB, Spain, with deployments to Incirlik, Turkey, and Aviano, Italy. Major General Yancy was instrumental in my assignment to the Special Crisis Response Team under the Joint Chiefs of Staff. Our team worked closely with the leaders of all the military services as well as the Secretary of Defense.

What follows is a detailed account of my experience as a combat fighter pilot during my assignment to the 497th Tactical Fighter Squadron, part of the 8th Tactical Fighter Wing. I have attempted to use the extensive daily records and notes I maintained while flying 100 missions over North Vietnam and 14 over Laos to describe my subjective and objective observations. As a prelude, I have given some background on the pathway I took to eventually become a fighter pilot, a route that required both skill and serendipity. However, the majority of my account will detail the journey I began on the day I left Travis Air Force Base on March 6th, 1966, until I returned from Ubon, Thailand, on August 28th, 1966.

1

MARCH 6, 1966
TRAVIS AIR FORCE BASE, CALIFORNIA
DEPARTURE FOR THE WAR

From my seat inside the terminal, I watched the waves of heat emanating off the tarmac. A feeling of restlessness made it difficult for me to find a comfortable position in the hard plastic seat. It was as if the heat waves were continuing to radiate up through the windows and into the pores of my skin, eventually bubbling through my blood vessels. I am not an anxious person by nature. In fact, my demeanor is probably one of my greatest assets when it comes to flying, but I could not help but feel uneasy about my deployment to Southeast Asia. I would soon be on my way to rejoin the 497th Tactical Fighter Squadron, which was part of the 8th Tactical Fighter Wing that was ordered to Ubon Royal Thai Air Force Base (RTAFB) on December 6, 1966. As I sat and waited, one of the quintessential military pastimes, I tried to put a finger on exactly what was causing this uncomfortable feeling.

For a start, I knew it was not the upcoming flying that had me worried. Not that flying my first combat missions was reason for concern, but I had spent the past six years preparing for this moment. I was confident that I was physically prepared for what lay ahead and was by no means afraid to enter a hostile environment. On the other hand, I was still trying to chew my way through the whole "domino" theory that my Commander-in-Chief was promoting as the rationale for our deployment. Somehow, I had trouble swallowing the idea that a third world country such as Vietnam could be the linchpin to the rampant spread of Communism. I couldn't shake the feeling that Uncle Sam was disrupting what had been up until this point a certain balance to my life.

I began to recall my past life and the many significant events that had led me to this point in time. Destiny may be too strong of a term, but my life had followed a series of twists and turns that had convinced me that there was a purpose behind my existence. By today's standards, I would be considered an agnostic. Unlike all my American ancestors who were devout Mormons and were among the first pioneers to settle in Salt Lake City, Utah, I am not a religious person. My parents grew up in Provo, Utah, and never attended religious services. I was allowed to attend any church of my choosing. While not drawn to organized religion, I do believe in a higher power, God or the "Big Boss", who has brought me to this point in my life. In fact, there are several vivid visual memories emblazoned in my consciousness that stand out as omens from God that indicated I was following a destiny to become a fighter pilot. I thought back in time to the series of events that had orchestrated my current situation.

My destiny began on November 22, 1937, when Val Ross Johnson was born to Dezell Abraham Johnson and Doris Baum Johnson in Rigby, Idaho. It was during the Depression and times were very difficult with our family surviving on very little. I was not a planned arrival but sometimes I imagine that maybe my birth "was just meant to be". My sister, Virginia, is a member of the Mormon Church and provided me with a copy of our family genealogy.

My great grandparents arrived from Sodervidinge and Malmom, Sweden; Helenbourgh, Scotland; and Pinvin, England. My great grandfather, George Baum, was born at Brandy Wine, Chester County, Pennsylvania in 1829. He became acquainted with the prophet Joseph Smith when he was eighteen and described him as a jolly man of pleasing personality. George helped build the Mormon Nauva Temple and acted as a bodyguard for Joseph Smith against the mobs who sought the prophet's life; but he was unable to prevent his leader's death in December 1844. He then came west to Salt Lake City in September 1848 with Brigham Young, who advised him to settle in Provo, Utah, where my parents were born.

As for my pathway towards becoming a pilot, it might have begun when I was three. I recalled that my 13 year-old brother placed me in a small soapbox car, that he had constructed from scrap lumber, and instructed me to steer while he pushed it as fast as he could run. The thrill of my brother's spin gave me feelings of excitement and fear; it was one of my earliest and strongest memories.

I distinctly remember my introduction to the "Bad People!" After the Japanese bombed Pearl Harbor, I recalled watching my mother pull down all the blinds at night and sealing off any additional light that might have been escaping from our house. I had just turned four and asked her why she had taken this unexpected action. She told me that we had to be protected from the "Bad People" who wanted to bomb us. I had no idea who the Japanese were or why they would want to bomb our small home with an outhouse in the back. However, I have come to realize there were "Bad People" in the world from which we had to protect ourselves.

Our family moved from Rigby to St. Maries, Idaho, following the attack, and my father became a fresh water fisherman on the surrounding lakes. I was given complete freedom to play around the lake while my parents trapped catfish for shipment to Chicago on the midnight train. My father earned sufficient money to buy our first house when I turned five and it was wonderful to have indoor plumbing.

The catfish were shipped to the Chicago market in various sized wooden boxes that my father constructed. The boxes were eventually returned by the buyers and stacked by our garage for future fish shipments. I might have received some guidance from the Big Boss as I arranged several of the empty boxes into my first fighter by using different size boxes to simulate my fighter's wings, tail, and finally one for my cockpit. Then I found an old straw broom that my mother had discarded, and turned it into a trusty machine gun that knocked down a staggering number of German and Japanese fighters. Maybe I was meant to spend hours each day defending my country from the "Bad People" in a make believe fighter with a wooden machine gun. There were few toys available for children during the war; so, my parents were happy that I could enjoy myself by sitting all alone in an empty fish box with an old broom handle while uttering weird noises.

I never realized it at that point in time, but maybe my fish box fighter was an omen of my destiny—to become a fighter pilot and protect my country from the "Bad People". However, I lost some of my interest after the war ended, as the fighter pilot exploits at the local movie theater ended. My father also broke up many of the fish boxes after the war when the State of Idaho halted fresh water fishing.

I was faced with a considerable dilemma when my Third Grade teacher, Mrs. Meroney, asked each student to tell the class what he or she wanted to become someday. I had to make an important decision between becoming an Idaho State Trooper, with my own patrol car, or a daring fighter pilot who would defend his country from the "Bad People". Now that the terrible war had ended, it seemed that becoming a courageous State Trooper would be the right decision; but for some unknown reason, I told the class that I wanted to become a fighter pilot some day. I believed this was a memory of some significance to me, as I could not remember the name of any other teacher in grade school.

I credit God with saving my life, during the summer of 1947, from a tidal river in California. My father decided to relocate to Bethel Island, California, to fish for catfish, after the war concluded. He stuffed our old GMC pick-up with numerous fishnets and then allotted a small area for our essential family belongings. We traveled for over two days from St. Maries to Bethel Island, where my parents leased an old one-bedroom motel with a tiny kitchen. Mother and I settled down in our new surroundings while my father explored the San Joaquin River Delta in a small wooden boat with a five horsepower Johnson outboard motor. He searched the numerous waterways for weeks before he determined the best areas to place his catfish nets and mink traps.

I retained a vivid memory of when I was swimming alone in the local river with a strong tide when I was nine years old. I had felt brave and discarded a large life jacket that I was instructed to wear whenever I played on a sandy beach area that boasted an old plank diving board. Being an aggressive future fighter pilot; I decided to dive off the worn wooden structure and quickly swim back to the shore. I had never performed that untrained maneuver, but future fighter pilots can do anything. I took my first daring dive off a very bouncy springboard and entered the dark water at an angle that flipped me over and caused me to become disoriented. I immediately started pulling myself with considerable effort to what I thought was the surface as fast as I could but I was actually heading straight to the bottom of the river. I was shocked when I finally reached the muddy riverbed and now I was almost completely out of air. I had become weak from my strong exertions and could feel consciousness slipping away. Suddenly an immense force took over my body, planted my feet in the muck, and propelled me upward with enormous strength. I recalled seeing a faint small dot of light, directly above my head, to swim towards. That glimmer of light gave me the strength that I desperately needed to hold my breath until I could reach the brightness of life. I can still remember the immense relief I experienced when my head broke water and I slowly dog paddled to the beach—completely exhausted. No one had witnessed my brush with death as I collapsed on the warm inviting sand. I never told my parents what had happened that day—now I believed that God might have assisted in my rescue. I am sorry to say that I never even thanked God for saving my life after I had returned safely to the beach.

However, the omen that is the most vivid and extraordinary in my memory occurred during a winter after we had returned to St. Maries. There was a steep hill by the high school that was excellent for sleigh riding, where you could build up a good head of speed. I was half way down the hill and going very fast when a large brown snarling dog came after me and tried to bite my leg. I kicked both of my legs as hard as I could, at the aggressive animal as the dog was trying to nip my right leg. I was very worried about the offensive actions of the dog and turned my head to look at the vicious animal. I was unaware that my strong kicking had propelled the sled to the left side of the road toward a parked car. I was not aware of my impending dangerous situation and never saw the automobile before I hit the bumper with my chin. I never saw or felt my collision with the vehicle but instantaneously found myself in the most vivid and brilliant dream that I have ever experienced. I found myself looking down at three dark figures standing in the snow not far from an automobile that displayed a boy sprawled in the snow by a sled. I could not clearly see the faces of the figures dressed in black cloaks with hoods, but they appeared to be intently looking at the collision. No one ever told me how long I had laid in the snow unconscious after hitting the bumper of the auto. I later became aware of a man trying to help me stand up out of the snow after I had finally become lucid. All I could cry out to the stranger was "I never realized that you could experience such a fantastic shining dream after you were knocked out". It was an experience that has never been repeated but is so solidly ingrained in my memory that it will never be forgotten. I might have broken my neck if my head had not been turned to catch the bumper on the only portion of my skull that would not have caused critical damage. I have always believed that some force stepped in to save my life—it was not my fate to die when I was 13.

I believed that the Big Boss might have helped me again when I turned fifteen. For some reason, I was blessed with a fastball that I called a "hummer"—a speeding object that may or may not be under control. I was pleased when I was invited to pitch for the town baseball team and later received notice in the local paper for my pitching success. The "hummer" changed my life as it opened doors to college and contributed to my destiny.

Pulled from my reverie, I realized that it was time to board the Continental Airlines Military Charter Flight from Travis Air Force Base, California for Bangkok, Thailand. The 707 departed for Hawaii with every seat occupied with new blood for the war to protect our way of life. Once seated, I returned to my memories that had led to this point in time.

I was seventeen when I departed St. Maries on 1 September 1955, for the University of Idaho at Moscow driving my prized 1941 Chevrolet coupe. I had very few belongings—all my clothes easily fit on the back seat of my small car. The only item that I had splurged on was a pair of nifty white buck shoes that seemed to be just what a college student would wear. The shoes sure looked neat and they even had a little bag of whitener that kept them looking groomed. I never let the fact that I needed at least one thousand dollars to complete two semesters of college bother me. After all, I had almost five hundred dollars in the bank and would figure out some way to make it through college. I was going to share a dorm room at Gault Hall with Clell Seelig, who was a good high school friend, and it was our first time away from home.

The University was a land grant college and required to offer, to all male students, either Air Force, Army, or Navy, Reserve Officer Training (ROTC) training. My destiny to become a fighter pilot was on track again as the Air Force ROTC allowed male students a chance to attend pilot training school if they qualified. Although signing up meant wearing an irksome uniform once a week, I believed I was back on track towards becoming a fighter pilot. However, I never wanted ROTC to interfere with my baseball activities as I expected to receive financial help from the Athletic Department if I made the team in the spring.

I was broke after the first semester despite washing pots and pans at the Student Union cafeteria after class. My mother came to my rescue—she worked in a small hot dog stand in St. Maries to help me during the second semester. I only had money for critical items and continued to work at the Student Union to help with necessities. Then the Idaho Athletic Department helped me to complete my next three years after I proved my mettle on the ball diamond during my frosh season. I received a partial grant in aid for baseball and the university provided a job in the dorm mess hall that paid for room and board. I also worked as a night janitor in another mess hall and graded papers for an economics course. I was pleased that AFROTC also helped by paying me twenty-two dollars a month during my last two years in college.

I excelled in baseball and thought I had an excellent chance to make it all the way to the Majors some day. I remembered that I had enjoyed a great summer playing baseball between my sophomore and junior years in a small town in northern Idaho. I was thrilled when I was selected to the Spokane, Washington, Twilight Semi-Pro All Star Team, while pitching for the Pack River Lumber Company in Sandpoint, Idaho. I returned to Idaho for my junior year with no intention of applying for advanced AFROTC, as it was not a requirement. Somehow my destiny intervened again and the next thing I knew, I had signed up for ROTC and even decided to take a test for becoming an Air Force pilot. The military required a commitment of five years if a student was accepted for pilot training and that obligation would dash my baseball career.

The advanced ROTC course also meant that I could not play semi-professional baseball, the summer before my senior year, due to Air Force prerequisites. I was not pleased that I had to attend Summer Camp at Fairchild Air Force Base in Spokane, Washington. I also had to turn down a marvelous offer to spend the summer in Canada playing high-level semi-professional ball and making good money. I questioned why I had decided to attend a miserable and demanding summer camp, where I was harassed, when I could have been playing high level baseball in Canada. I also let my college team down by not playing summer baseball, as the layoff was detrimental to my senior year pitching. Nevertheless, I took the tougher path towards my ultimate goal—maybe it was "just meant to be".

My confidence in becoming a fighter pilot was shaken when I became sick just before landing during my first jet ride in a T-33 fighter trainer at summer camp. It was embarrassing when I had to clean the cockpit—I had not gotten the oxygen bag off in time to use the barf bag. The Air Force also allowed me to fly in a B-52 during a routine training mission—I discovered that I never wanted to become a bomber pilot! It was a boring nine-hour mission, and I decided that I had no desire to fly in an aircraft that long. I had no ambition to fly unless it was alone in a fighter, and that might not be possible if I was going to get airsick in one. The Mickey Mouse crap at summer camp was also not enjoyable for an independent kid from the hills of Idaho who had run free for his whole life. Maybe the Big Boss had it all wrong! I speculated that I was really meant to play baseball and not become a fighter pilot.

I immediately contacted the ROTC Detachment office upon returning to the University of Idaho in September for my senior year. I informed them, with no uncertainty, that I absolutely wanted to be eliminated from AFROTC due to airsickness. For some mysterious reason, I let the ROTC instructors convince me that it was possible to overcome airsickness and I even agreed to take a long intricate written test for flying training. However, I decided to let a difficult test that was slanted towards engineers, be the final determinate as to whether to apply for pilot training. I was not especially pleased when the Air Force accepted me for pilot training with marginal scores. I only received a four on the pilot section along with a five for Observer and a six for Officer. I was concerned that the low pilot score might indicate that it was not my destiny to fly fighters after all.

My reminiscent thoughts were interrupted by the stewardess when she notified all passengers that "Never too Late" was the in-flight flick for the night. I decided to watch the movie, although I had seen the play in New York a few years before. The stewardess finally served a hot dinner and later the captain announced that our plane would arrive in Hawaii in a couple of hours. We were informed that our flight would only be on the ground for the time it took to refuel and no one would be allowed to deplane.

After dinner and the movie, my mind once more wandered back in time to the University of Idaho. I recalled that the Air Force allowed future pilots to receive thirty-five hours of training, at the Pullman-Moscow Flying Service—to qualify for a private pilot's license if the written and flying portions were passed. I was beginning to believe that my low score on the Air Force flying test might be in error, as I received my single engine land private pilot rating on 15 May 1959. I was also selected for the outstanding flying award from the Flying Service; more importantly, I was never airsick again.

I graduated from the University of Idaho on 6 June 1959, and received my appointment as a Reserve Officer in the Air Force. I wanted to attend pilot training immediately but the Air Force Academy graduates were granted the first choice of pilot training slots. I decided to return home and work at the local lumber mill while awaiting my entry into the United States Air Force the following December.

The St. Maries Chevrolet dealer, along with convenient bank financing, persuaded me to buy a new 1959 Honey Beige Chevrolet Impala for $3,000. I had previously upgraded my '41 Chevy to a maroon '51 model during my third year when I was working four jobs at the University of Idaho. The dealer allowed me a five hundred-dollar trade in, if my friend, Boyd Leonard, would immediately buy my old car. The bank was aware that I was entering the Air Force in December and would have a reliable income for the future payments. I could manage the monthly hundred-dollar car payment by working at the lumber mill but I would only receive about three hundred a month as a second lieutenant without flight pay. However, I would receive an extra one hundred dollars flying pay, when I started flying, which would just cover the monthly car payments. I realized that I would probably have to sell the new Chevy if I flunked out of pilot training. I decided that I would take the risk, confident that I was fated to become a pilot.

I departed St. Maries, Idaho, on December 7, 1959, in my '59 Chevy with all my worldly belongings in two leather suitcases that my parents had given me for college graduation. I recalled listening to KOMA in Oklahoma on the radio during the trip from Idaho to Lackland Air Force Base in San Antonio, Texas. My favorite song on the radio was "El Paso" by Marty Robbins and I heard it many times during three long days of driving to finally reach the Texas border. I was shocked to see all the barren country in west Texas that harbored a plethora of oil wells—I had never been in such a dry desolate area with few signs of anything green. My memories of Texas were interrupted when the Captain informed us that we were descending to land and refuel in Hawaii.

We departed on time, after refueling, and our plane finally leveled at 35,000 feet. Our captain announced that it would require eleven-hours to reach Clark Air Base in the Philippines. I decided to relax and watch the movie, "Oklahoma" though I had some reservations—it was a musical with a lot of singing. I learned that our flight would be crossing the International Date Line—another first for me. After the movie, I let the hypnotic hum of the jet engines lull me into a semi-conscious state. I again thought back and reflected on why the Big Boss wanted me to become a fighter pilot.

I recalled my initial entry into the Air Force in San Antonio, Texas—it appeared to be located in the middle of a desert. However, I was happy to have finally arrived at my first Air Force base and was ready to begin pilot training. I was pleased that the Air Force granted each new officer a three hundred-dollar allowance for new uniforms but I immediately squandered my windfall at a local uniform store. A polished salesman convinced me that he knew just what clothing a newly minted Second Lieutenant from Idaho needed to purchase. I found out later that it was not necessary to have purchased all the custom made uniforms that ate up my whole allowance. I was again broke and outfitted with expensive clothing that I seldom wore.

I have always thought that the Big Boss might have been aware and sympathetic towards my bankrupted situation. For some reason, I won a special Bingo card at the Officers Club that granted me five hundred dollars worth of goods at a local store. I was thrilled and thankful—it was just what a future fighter pilot that had squandered all his money needed. I had the good fortune to become the proud owner of a 35mm camera, a stereo system with two big wooden speakers, golf clubs, and a portable radio. I was even able to obtain some long-playing records that I had always wanted but could never afford. I was gratified to discover that my Chevy would hold all my newly won possessions along with two leather suitcases containing custom tailored uniforms.

My roommate, Will Hendrix, was from San Antonio and kindly showed me all the hot spots in the big city. I visited my first strip tease joint and experienced drinking margaritas that were delectable and very potent. We were delighted to find out that we had been assigned to Bainbridge, Georgia, to begin primary flying training on 21 January 1960. Will was a graduate of Texas A&M and the Aggie explained to a country boy from Idaho on how the military operated. He told me that he also desired to fly fighters but we probably had to graduate in the top ten percent of our class in order to select one. I received a final grade of 94% for the Officer Pre-Flight (Pilot) course at Lackland, which seemed to be a good start. As far as I was concerned, I was well on my way to fulfilling my destiny to become a fighter pilot. I happily departed San Antonio, in my packed Chevy, for the drive to Bainbridge, Georgia.

I had fond memories of Bainbridge Air Base—lots of trees and a pleasant river where we could water ski. However, we had to be watchful for cottonmouth water snakes that were ever present along the river. My new roommate, Andy

Holko, purchased a white fiber glass ski boat with a powerful outboard motor that we used on weekends when time and weather permitted. We enjoyed cruising around the small town in hopes of encountering some girls and even went so far as to attend church to meet the young ladies. Will was lucky and met a sweet girl that he eventually married after completing pilot training. We also had a great time driving to the large sandy beaches in Florida and visiting Florida State, in Tallahassee.

We first received 27 hours of flight training in the T-34, which was a prop job and great for acrobatics. Then we graduated to the small Cessna twinjet T-37 "Tweety Bird" that could spin faster than I ever thought possible. The "Tweet" also ruined some of my hearing in the high range due to the high pitched whine emitted from the jets during the 109 hours I spent flying the bird.

I was assigned a former Navy flying instructor who taught me how to operate jets although he could be a little temperamental at times. "'Daddy" Whitney would pound on the instrument panel, making you think that you were going to wash out at any moment, and then suddenly turn you loose for your first solo flight. When he felt the stress was getting to me, he let me blow off some steam by flying at tree top level from Bainbridge to his restaurant in Tallahassee, Florida. I received an 89% final training grade at Bainbridge and felt that it might keep me in the running for a fighter. However, I knew that I had to improve at Basic if my destiny was to be fulfilled. We graduated from Bainbridge on 18 July 1960, and left for Texas immediately as leave was not authorized between bases.

Will and I were both assigned to report to the 3561st Pilot Training Squadron, Webb Air Force Base, Big Springs, Texas, on July 26, 1960, for basic training in the T-33. I received 115 hours in the ancient T-33 that lacked nose wheel steering and, of course, I managed to cock the nose tire once, which was embarrassing. I was certain that the flying and academic competition would be fierce as class standing dictated your next assignment. I knew that I had to really study and fly right if I wanted any chance to select a fighter but there was still time for fun and games.

Will Hendrix was an excellent mechanic, who had his own drag racer, and convinced me that I needed to soup-up my 59 Chevy. Using my last few saved dollars, I purchased a used fuel injection system from a wrecked Corvette and we installed it on the Impala along with a Duntov cam. I discovered that Big Springs was a hot and dusty place with little greenery and fewer girls to date—the car was a nice distraction. We had some skillful basketball players in our class and I was lucky to win a starting position on a team that eventually won the Air Training Command Championship Tournament.

I received a 90% average for my final military training grade, which placed me in 14th position for our class of 61-E. Our future flying assignments were published after graduation on 27 January 1961, for our class to study. The top student was allowed the first choice of any aircraft and so on down the line by class standing. The hot century series fighters were usually the first to be chosen by the top students. The Air Force allotted seven F-100's, three F-101's and two F-102 fighters to Class 61-E. It was obvious that I would not complete my destiny unless two pilots, who had finished ahead of me, had no desire for fighters. I would need some help from the Big Boss or I would probably select a T-33 instructor assignment to Phoenix, Arizona. I would never stay in the Air Force if I had to fly a bomber or cargo aircraft. My best friend, Will Hendrix, finished second in our class and took the opportunity to select an F-100, which most pilots desired—it had a gun, dropped bombs, and fired rockets.

The top seven students selected the F-100 fighters, and the following three chose the F-101s, which looked very bad for me. The Big Boss might have still been looking out for me as the students ranked number 10 and 12 selected old C-118 cargo prop aircraft—an unbelievable break. This amazing assistance made it possible for me to select the last available fighter—an F-102 at Perrin AFB, TX. The Convair "Delta Dagger" was not armed with a gun, never dropped bombs, and only fired air-to-air rockets. Nevertheless, it certainly looked like a sleek fighter with its long nose and beautiful delta wing. I had watched the deuces that operated from an air defense squadron, stationed on the opposite side of Webb, and had thought they would be exciting to fly. I could not wait to report to the 3555th Flying Training Squadron, Perrin Air Force Base, Texas, to fulfill my destiny and finally become a fighter pilot.

Will and I had decided to celebrate our graduation on 26 January, 1961, after pinning on our pilots wings, by driving to New Orleans for the Mardi Gras festivities. Afterward he dropped me off at Hulbert Field in Florida so I could visit an old college friend and go deep-sea fishing. Will continued on to Bainbridge to visit his bride-to-be.

I was pleasantly surprised when I arrived at Perrin AFB, located between Sherman and Dennison. I was pleased to discover a base in Texas with numerous trees and a nice large lake. It was an impressive sight to see the Deuces in the traffic pattern when I arrived at the gate and received directions to the Bachelor Officer Quarters (BOQ). I was even happier with my new assignment when I discovered that I would continue flying the T-33 along with checking out in the F-102. The Deuce flew practice intercepts against the T-33 and students could volunteer to fly the trainer as a target when they had free time. I used all my extra time to fly missions in the T-33, as there were few distractions outside the confines of the base,

The F-102 was a sweet bird and I quickly fell in love with its sleek appearance, beautiful curves and smooth handling in the air. I thanked God for being so good to me and giving me the opportunity to fly the marvelous fighter of my dreams. I really hit the books and received excellent academic grades along with the best airborne intercept record in my class. However, I still had time to play on the squadron softball team and fly numerous extra T-33 target missions at night.

I completed the Interceptor Pilot Training Course in an outstanding manner and was qualified "Combat Ready". I managed to finish first in my class and was selected as the "Distinguished Graduate" of Class 62-A, Interceptor Pilot Training Course Number 112100D. I was informed that a Distinguished Graduate was eligible for a Regular Commission in the Air Force and I accepted this honor. Our class graduated on 11 August 1961, and we received exceptional class assignments, which was great as I had the first selection. I took time to recall my old Air Force written test that indicated that I would be a marginal pilot. It seemed that the little kid who had battled the enemy from the small wooden fish box fighter was finally going to become a real fighter pilot and protect his country from the "Bad People".

I had the opportunity to select an F-106 assignment to McChord AFB in Washington State that was tempting—it was near home and equipped with new Mach II fighters. However, the assignment to the 497th Fighter Interceptor Squadron, to fly F-102's, at Torrejon Air Base near Madrid, Spain, had to be the best assignment in the Air Force. I looked forward to living in Spain and maybe there had been a reason for the Spanish course that I was required to take at the University of Idaho.

I was required to attend survival training at Stead AFB, Nevada after graduating from Perrin, AFB and discovered that it was an arduous experience that I never wanted to repeat! I had to endure survival training in a simulated POW camp along with a week in the high Sierras evading instructors trying to catch us. I graduated from class 62-7 on September 6, 1961 with the knowledge that I never wanted to become a POW. I had lost ten pounds and discovered that the meat of a beaver was too tough for me to chew even if I was famished. I definitely never wanted to be captured in this lifetime—I could never live in a cage.

I had a great time visiting family and friends at home in St. Maries before driving back to Perrin AFB and getting ready for my departure to Spain. I traded my 1959 Chevrolet Impala for a new 1962 Corvair, after I arrived back in Texas, and drove it to New Jersey for shipment to Barcelona, Spain. I deposited the Corvair at the port in Bayonne, New Jersey and I caught a shuttle to McGuire, AFB, New Jersey for a very long C-121 flight to Torrejon AB, Spain.

I soon realized that the 497th Fighter Interceptor Squadron at Torrejon Air Base, Spain, was one of the best assignments in the world for a young single fighter pilot. I discovered that an Air Force Lieutenant could live like a millionaire in Madrid as the American dollar bought numerous amounts of pesetas. I was pleased that the 497th allowed pilots to fly the squadron's T-33 target aircraft to almost any airport in Europe on cross-country flights. We had the opportunity to spend weekends in Athens, London, Rome, Amsterdam, and various other locations using our squadron's aircraft. We enjoyed meeting Pan Am and TWA stewardesses, who had layovers in Madrid, and showing them the city when possible.

I thanked the Big Boss every time I flew the pilot-friendly Deuce—it was a thrilling aircraft to fly and I loved it. It was exciting to stand five-minute air defense alert and I looked forward to a possible scramble. It was a thrill to get a running start out of the alert barn and blast off the runway in less than five minutes. My flight commander let me fly the slot position in a diamond formation when our flight managed to get four birds in the air at the same time. Our squadron even allowed me to fly a Deuce to and from other bases on weekends when I was pitching for the Torrejon AB baseball team.

It was exciting when our squadron deployed to Wheeless AB, Tripoli, Libya each year to fire missiles over their desert. We found time to visit several spectacular Roman Ruins on the large sandy beaches in the North African country. I discovered that Spain was a beautiful country to observe during low-level missions and I enjoyed flying over the islands of Majorca and Ibiza. I upgraded to the highest operational ready status of "Expert" in the F-102 on 27 February, 1964, when Captain Francis J. McCarthy Jr. certified me after an extensive evaluation in the air and on the ground. I felt that I had really found my place in life and could not have been happier with my awesome freedom. I wished that God would allow me remain in Spain and fly F-102's for the rest of my military career, but that was not to be.

My ideal life was shattered when the 497 Fighter Interceptor Squadron in Spain was inactivated by the United States Air Force in 1964. Pilots were allowed to transfer to F-102 units in Germany, if they had sufficient time remaining on their overseas tour, or return to George AFB, California, to become part of the newly formed 8th Tactical Fighter Wing. I considered the option of moving to Germany, where I could continue to fly the deuce, but I was aware that the flying conditions in that northern country were terrible for many months of the year. I realized that I would miss Spain—I loved all the bright sunny days and delightful beaches.

I was aware that the Torrejon Base Commander had the power to grant bachelor officers a special exemption to transfer furniture to the States at Government expense. Having purchased many pieces of furniture from a small factory outside the entrance to the base, I requested this exemption. I made a command decision to transfer to Germany and then get out of the military unless I received this special consideration. My obligation to the Air Force would be completed if I extended for the tour in Germany and then I would be free to fly deuces with the Air National Guard in Boise. However, the Base Commander finally approved my special furniture transfer—I decided that my time in the Air Force was destined to be continued.

The squadron asked volunteers to fly our F-102s from Germany to Boise, Idaho, via Scotland, Iceland, Greenland, and Newfoundland, an assignment I readily requested. It was exciting to fly the deuce over the beautiful blinding white icecap although you would freeze to death in 30 minutes if you had to eject over the frigid waters. I was pleased for the opportunity to visit my former college girlfriend in Boise before departing for New York to await delivery of a friend's Alfa Romeo from Spain. I enjoyed visiting New York for a few days and attended several amusing Broadway plays with some friends. I took command of the Alfa at the Brooklyn docks on 26 June 1964 and started my long drive for Idaho. I had been granted thirty days leave before reporting to George AFB, which allowed time to visit friends and family in Idaho.

I enjoyed traveling to California but was pleased when I finally arrived at my new airbase. I checked into the BOQ at George AFB and immediately ambled to the flight line to inspect a couple of new F-4C's stationed on the ramp. The ugly gray bird with a drooping tail, funny wings, and a nose that looked as though it sported a long wart had not impressed me. I had no idea why the Big Boss wanted me to fly the Phantom—it was not a sleek fighter or even armed with an internal gun. However, it was advertised to be a Mach II fighter that could drop tons of bombs and fire many canisters of rockets. I had never dropped or fired ordnance on targets and was confident that diving at the ground would present an exciting challenge. I hated to leave the F-102, as it was a beautiful flying machine and looked like a sleek fighter. I would have to overlook the fact that it was an ugly aircraft and realize that it could do more than just fly intercepts. Nonetheless, I was impressed that it had two powerful jet engines and was one of the fastest planes in the world. I speculated that Big Ugly was "meant for me"—now I could accomplish everything the World War II fighter pilots had done on the RKO newsreels of my youth.

The 497th Fighter Interceptor Squadron (FIS) had now become the 497th Tactical Fighter Squadron (TFS) when it transferred to George AFB. Our unit had not received any F-4C's but squadron pilots were approved to fly T-33s on cross-country flights to obtain the required monthly flight hours. Our squadron was scheduled to deploy to Davis Monthan AFB, Tucson, Arizona in December to check out in the Phantom. However, the Air Force was not going to let us relax around George AFB as our military leaders had other strenuous missions for us.

The Commander of the Tactical Air Command (TAC) decided that it was essential for each TAC squadron to provide four pilots to the U.S. Army, when required, and they had to be jump qualified forward air controllers. The squadron pressured me into attending the airborne course at Fort Benning, Georgia, for three weeks in September 1964. I recalled completing five jumps from old C-119s that I thought were lucky to get off the ground.—I was happy to abandon the old under-powered bird. Then the Air Force ordered me to attend the Deep-Sea Survival Course at Langley AFB, Virginia, for five days in October. Finally it was on to Eglin AFB, Florida to attend the three week Combat Operations Special Course for Forward Air Controllers. I was now contemplating that I had made a huge mistake by returning to the States to fly the F-4—maybe I should have gone to Germany and remained in the deuce.

The 8th Tactical Fighter Wing was originally organized at George Air Force Base, California, on July 10th, 1964, and started receiving new F-4C Phantom's directly from the factory in St. Louis on the 1st of November. It was a memorable experience to fly commercially to the McDonald Douglas Aircraft Corporation to accept the delivery of a newly minted Phantom—I had never flown a new aircraft before. I recalled that I had done my best not to scratch the new bird by flying too low and striking any trees or power lines on the return flight to George, AFB

The 497 TFS was assigned to Davis Monthan AFB in December, for the 9 day F4C Familiarization course that was followed by the 8-week USAF Operational Training Course. I teamed with Lt. William E. McGourin as my back seat pilot, and we successfully completed the course in February 1965. Bill was from Washington State and I was pleased to be flying with a fellow Northwester. He was a rated pilot but had to fly in the rear seat as the Air Force had more pilots than airplanes. Bill was an excellent pilot and I made an effort to share our flying time with him whenever possible. We operated effectively as a crew, passed all our training requirements easily, and became operational in June 1965. However, my operational training came to a halt when I was ordered to attend Squadron Officers School (SOS) at Maxwell AFB, Alabama, from September through December 1965.

I was pleased to receive orders to join my squadron in Thailand after completing SOS. I had been worried that I might be assigned temporary duty (TDY), with the Army, as a Forward Air Controller operating in South Vietnam. I had not flown the F-4C since August except for one flight while I was in school. The new 8th Tactical Fighter Wing Commander, Colonel Joseph G. Wilson, flew a Phantom cross-country to Maxwell and permitted me to fly it during the weekend to remain current.

It was necessary to return to George AFB, after graduating from SOS, to place my furniture in storage and pick up my flight gear before departing for Thailand. I had not flown any training flights in the last six months and thought it would be appropriate to fly a few practice missions before entering combat in a hostile country. The Tactical Air Command listened to my request for a few refresher flights and allowed me to fly several missions before leaving for Ubon. I really appreciated the 68th Tactical Fighter Squadron for allowing me to fly with them and even allowing me to wager a few dollars on the ordnance scores at the gunnery range. The squadron commander, Lt. Colonel Bruce Hamilton, went out of his way to make sure that I received adequate stick time in the Phantom before shipping out for Thailand.

I was awakened from my reverie when our pilot announced that we were landing to refuel at Clark Air Base in the Philippines before continuing on to Saigon where most of the passengers were scheduled to depart the aircraft. The captain indicated that we would land at 0400 and passengers were allowed to take a short break. The pilot sounded bored—I questioned how he could endure the many unchanging hours on the big transport plane.

I discovered a discarded TIME publication in the terminal and read about an interview with Robert F. Kennedy—he mentioned that we might end the war by guaranteeing the guerrillas a seat in the next government in Vietnam. A fellow passenger let me read a current U.S. News & World Report article that painted a rosy picture of the war and indicated it was taking a noticeable turn for the better. The magazine stated that the U.S. was now employing 1,600 warplanes and dropping 150,000 bombs, a month on Red targets in Vietnam and the Ho Chi Minh Trail in Laos. The article went on to say that B-52 bombers could carry 51 bombs weighing 750 pounds each, yet there was no indication that the bombers were flying over North Vietnam. Maybe, if all was going so well, the war would be over before I flew my first mission, but I would not hold my breath in anticipation.

Our charter flight departed Clark on time and I finally got some sleep on the way to Saigon. We landed at the Saigon airfield for a short time and the numerous passengers were allowed to depart. I noticed that there was an abundance of heavy construction in progress with numerous men stripped to their waist and working in the red dirt. Wrecked aircraft and helicopters littered the field, which made for a depressing sight. This was my first taste of the ongoing war and I speculated that I might be in for a long tour with death and destruction entering my life on a daily basis. The base was a beehive of activity, with scores of planes, helicopters, and trucks operating all around the field. The captain announced that we were number ten for takeoff in a long line of departing birds—I was ready to leave the commotion.

As we waited for departure, I mused that too many unlikely events had occurred for me to believe that my becoming an F-4 Phantom pilot had been anything but destiny. As a military officer, I readily accepted my combat orders and was now nearing my destination of Thailand. On the other hand, the whole Vietnam conflict seemed to be rife with muddy unanswered questions. For the first time since I had gotten sick during my initial training flight, I had a sense of disequilibrium in my life. I could only pray that I would be able to find good omens in the cockpit; the one place I always felt confident and sure.

I arrived in Bangkok and settled into a US Government leased hotel that even had air-conditioning, which I considered essential in this hot humid climate. It had not taken long to in-process as they had the monotonous clearance system down pat for new guys. I decided that it was time to find the Officers Club for a cold beer and see if I knew anyone at the bar. I discovered three other pilots at the bar that were happy to discuss the madness of this war. After much bitching, we agreed to share a cab for the ninety-minute ride across town to the Navy Exchange but we were very disappointed to find the Exchange had closed just as our taxi arrived. By closing at 1500 hours, the only people that were able to use the services were store employees, while the military personnel stuck on duty during the normal work day were unable to buy goods; a typical military policy.

We all decided to keep the cab and had the driver take us on a tour of the city as the American dollar went a long way in Bangkok. I decided that the city was the dirtiest and smelliest place that I had ever seen—Libya had been at the top of my list until today. The buildings appeared to be built similar to ones I had seen in Spain, with stucco and white washed walls. By comparison, the neighborhoods of small pueblos in Spain had not reeked of sewage and the residents had kept their streets clean.

After a while, we decided to depart the hot cab and tested our ability to tolerate the strong smells and swarming flies when we walked through an open-air market. The flies had to have been the happiest in the world as they covered every item in sight and appeared to have overwhelmed any resistance to fighting them off. I had never seen such a collection of goods for sale in an open-air market as they included a multitude of snakes, birds, and strange looking live animals, along with fruits and vegetables.

It was interesting to note that we had not seen any other Caucasian people on our tour of the city, or, for that matter, anyone that even looked like a tourist. I saw no reason to visit this country as a tourist but had to think there might be some beautiful areas away from the teeming stench and chaos of the city. Personally, I soon had my fill of all the smells, noise, crowds, squalor—I would be glad to depart at 06:15 in the morning for my final destination.

2

MARCH 9, 1966
UBON, THAILAND

I was awake early and had time for coffee with sweet rolls before calling a taxi for the trip to Don Muang, a civilian airport outside of Bangkok, where my military transportation to Ubon was stationed. I had an exciting ride to the airport—my taxi driver enjoyed weaving in and out of all the colorful trucks that had heaps of fresh produce for the local markets. I was pleased to find a small complex at the airport with signs directing me to the appropriate passenger desk. I located a staff member who directed me to my departure gate where I encountered a two-man aircrew that flew the daily flight to Ubon. I was very surprised to see that our transportation was an ancient C-47 that looked as if it had come out of an old black and white World War II movie. Time seemed to stand still in this part of the world—I felt that I was going to war as men had over twenty-five years ago.

The plane was loaded with numerous boxes for the Base Exchange at Ubon, with scant room for the only passenger, and I smiled at the irony of the situation. Yesterday I was unable to shop at the exchange, and now I had a multitude of new items for the Ubon exchange right next to me. The flight was harrowing as the weather was choppy and the cargo had not been well secured. I spent my flight time trying not to become an early casualty as I dodged the boxes shifting about the cabin. It would have been a hell of a note to lose my life going to war in an old C-47 that belonged to another era.

The old cargo plane finally arrived safely at Ubon as scheduled at 0900 and slowly taxied to base operations. The transit aircraft ramp appeared completely deserted and no one met our plane. However, it must have been business as usual because it never concerned our crew. The captain waited to shut down the second engine until the copilot deplaned and found some chocks for the wheels. I grabbed my old green Air Force issue parachute bag that contained my K-2B green flight suits, G-suit, gloves, and boots. A military issue canvas B-4 suitcase

23

contained all my underwear and personal effects. I carried several 1505 khaki uniforms and a few civilian clothes in my canvas hang-up bag on the off chance that I was allowed military leave.

The luggage was heavy and I was pleased that it was a short walk to an ancient base operations building that also housed the control tower. It was strangely deserted with no security personnel in sight, making it hard to believe that a deadly war was going on across the border in Laos and North Vietnam. I had expected to see the fiery dual afterburners of Phantoms blasting off every few minutes heading to the war carrying heavy loads of bombs and rockets. The small shabby building also housed a resident Thai who was managing a small gift shop in the back section. I speculated as to who his customers might be—probably, the rare curious visitor from the States who would definitely be in a big hurry to depart.

I was surprised to see Australian F-86's at the end of the runway standing five-minute alert in case of a surprise attack by hostile aircraft. The Russian MiGs in North Vietnam were not believed to have the range to attack Ubon, but it was good that we had some protection. We were fortunate that we had the Aussies pulling this duty, as otherwise F-4's would probably have to be on alert, which might extend our tour. Looking at the Australian F-86's on alert made me think back to my three years in Spain, where I had to stand five and fifteen-minute alerts, along with Spanish F-86 aircraft. I knew that it was boring to sit around an alert barn knowing the chance of scrambling was slim to none. I was content to realize that I would soon be operating differently, even if it meant being subjected to enemy fire.

I finally found a telephone to call the base transportation section for a driver to pick me up at Base Ops. An Airman with a pickup truck arrived ten minutes later and drove me to the Bachelor Officer Quarters (BOQ). I located the BOQ office and signed for my room before walking over to the Officers Club that was a single story wooden building. I quickly grabbed my cap off my head as I entered the club in response to a loud roar from Captain Dave Condit. I was unaware that the front entrance of the building opened directly into the Officers Club bar room. It was an old Air Force custom to buy drinks for everyone in the bar if you were caught entering wearing any sort of head covering. Dave was alone in the room, certainly feeling no pain at this early hour, and now I owed him another drink. He was happily sitting at the bar, wearing only his underwear, and enjoying a concoction of some kind. I learned that he had been drinking since his mission had been completed many hours ago. He explained that he had sold his flight suit to some unknown person during the night. Dave was enjoying his life at Ubon while he could and having a hell of a good time until he had to fly another mission. His festivities, however, were cut short when the Base Commander arrived on the scene. The Colonel was not amused to see a drunken fighter pilot sitting at the bar half-naked—he kicked poor Dave out in his skivvies and raised hell about his conduct. It appeared to me that the officer was an old Strategic Air Command (SAC) navigator and a slave to military rules.

The OClub was better than I had expected when you considered we were in the middle of a strange country with a completely different way of life. I was pleased to find that the OClub had air-conditioning in the dining room, which was a great luxury in this hot place. The dining room had about fifteen tables with clean white napkins and Thai waitresses—someone was always on duty to take your order. I learned that the Officers Club was in operation twenty-four hours a day and it was always Happy Hour at the bar. The booze was a bargain—we were only charged two bits for a shot from a huge selection of expensive name brand drinks. The OClub had a large game room at one end of the building with two pool tables and several card tables. I was pleased to see that there was a serving bar and grill in the rear of the dining room where customers could always get breakfast with eggs cooked as requested. It was a lot nicer than I had expected, as I assumed we would be fed chow from a cafeteria serving line.

No one else was hanging around the club, which seemed strange, as I had expected to see many aircrews at this time of day. I wandered back across the narrow dirty street to look at my new sleeping accommodations. My assigned back seat pilot, Lt. William E. McGourin, had a bed reserved for me in his hootch (open-air plywood building that housed four officers). The hootch was built on blocks about two feet high—probably to help keep out the numerous cobra snakes that frequented the area and the heavy monsoon rains. The building had been constructed to allow air to flow freely in and out of the screened air vents on each side. I imagined that this concept might work as advertised if there was ever any wind in this hot humid place.

Bill had just awaken and appeared pleased to see his old aircraft commander again. He and the squadron had been wondering when I was finally going to arrive and get to work. I had not seen Bill since leaving for Squadron Officers School last summer. He explained that he had become the 'bastard' GIB, after I had departed for school, and was required to fly with many different aircraft commanders. The Air Force had too many pilots, and not enough airplanes, so they had put newly trained pilots in the rear seat of the F-4. Someone started calling these pilots GIBs, which stood for guy-in-the-back and it had stuck. The GIBs were not happy to be in the back seat but had no choice in the matter, as it was always the "needs" of the Air Force that were adhered to in our life. Someday they wanted to be upgraded to the front seat, but only time and luck would determine their fate. I speculated that the Air Force might be short of fighter pilots in the near future, as it appeared that more were being killed or captured than could currently be trained in the States.

Bill explained that each officer had his own little cot surrounded with mosquito netting and an old metal locker placed against a wall. It was obvious that we would all be sharing a small cramped area—the only storage space was located under the bed or on top of each pilot's locker. I had just enough room in the locker for my hang up bag and the small number of uniforms from my B-4 suitcase. Then I placed everything else into the parachute bag for storage under the cot. I needed very few clothes—I expected to enjoy life in a flight suit for the complete tour. Bill explained that I would be able to find an inexpensive houseboy to do my washing as they had a place down at the local creek to wash clothes.

We walked over to the OClub to get a cup of coffee, and then he brought me up to date on what had transpired in the squadron during the last three months. Bill told me that two F-4C Squadrons were operating out of Ubon with very little flying activity during the middle of the day. He had completed a number of missions with the Wing Safety Officer but finally refused to fly with him after pulling him out of some dives. Bill told me that this Safety troop had finally plunged his Phantom into the hostile jungle near Dien Bien Phu. It was rumored that he was strafing some bizarre enemy supply transporters that his surviving wingman called elephants. Bill explained that he had completed thirty combat missions over North Vietnam since the squadron arrived in Thailand last December.

I learned that our squadron flew mainly night missions over North Vietnam and Laos. It was difficult for the squadron's aircrews to sleep in these hot quarters during the daytime hours. The other squadron, the 433 TFS, conducted late afternoon and early night missions. That explained why the base was so quiet with little activity when I arrived. It appeared that some of the jocks were now calling the 497th the "Night Owl" squadron due to all the night missions. The squadron never had a nickname before and the original squadron patch was a conglomeration of colors that RL Penn likened to a worm crawling out of a sewer. Bill had designed a 100 mission Night Owl patch that I might purchase to keep for a souvenir if I managed to complete the magic number of flights.

The 497th had been very fortunate to date and only lost one Phantom, in Laos, during a night flare mission. Bill explained there was a lot of burning going on in the Laotian jungles which that made it very difficult to fly night flare missions in the smoke and haze. The unfortunate aircrew had become disoriented during their mission and stalled the bird at a low altitude from which it was impossible to recover. The F-4 was not a user-friendly aircraft—it usually required about ten thousand feet to recover from an out-of-control position and that was in the daytime. The aircrew had to eject into the hostile jungle and spend the night avoiding an enemy that was hot on their trail. The aircraft commander, Captain Jack Moore, injured his back during the ejection that was followed by a difficult jungle landing in rugged mountains. His pilot, Lt. Mike Peters, was able to locate Jack in the dense jungle and helped him avoid the bad guys during the rest of the night. They were very fortunate, as the Jolly Green troops rescued them at dawn with the enemy in hot pursuit.

The Air Force HH-3 "Jolly Green" helicopter was manned with an expert recovery team and was acclaimed for timely rescues in dangerous situations. The chopper crews were very efficient at swiftly extracting downed aircrews from the jungle, which was critical when under enemy fire. The chopper was equipped with a petal-like heavy metal implement that went through the heavy jungle foliage to reach downed aircrews. The chopper also had a rescue man aboard who could descend to the ground and assist disabled men. Jack's back injuries were so extensive that he had to be airlifted back to the States for medical treatment. However, Mike was not injured and living in our hootch with a tale for his kids if he could just complete one hundred missions over North Vietnam.

Bill enlightened me about the current regulations that allowed a pilot to return to the States upon culmination of 100 missions over North Vietnam—missions over Laos would not count toward this magic figure. Our night missions were usually divided evenly between targets in Laos and North Vietnam, which made it difficult to get the counters. In addition, the weather was extremely unfavorable at this time of the year over North Vietnam, which resulted in numerous sorties diverted into Laos. Everyone wanted to fly counters and get back to the States as soon as possible—I had the impression that very few aircrews were enthusiastic about this war.

Missions had also been difficult to attain due to numerous political bombing pauses that allowed the enemy to easily replenish their guns and surface-to-air missiles (SAMs). The pauses had been very bad for our aircrews—the enemy defenses were at full strength and waiting for us when missions resumed over the North. Bill indicated that the Wing allowed us to have five days off after every sixty days in Thailand. We could use the time for rest and relaxation (R&R) or we could save the days and take fifteen days off after six months.

The 497th was usually tasked for about 16 sorties a night and it varied as to where each flight would operate. During March, the squadron was usually sent to

Laos, Route Package One (RPI), or Route Package V (RPV), in North Vietnam. All missions in Laos were called Barrel Roll and missions in North Vietnam were named Rolling Thunder. We would be operating in the following Route Packages during our tour.

RPI was an area that originated along the 47-mile demilitarized zone (DMZ) that separated North and South Vietnam, and then continued north about 65 miles up the coast to Ron Ferry. The northern border extended from Ron Ferry to the Laotian border near Mu Gia Pass. The eastern border extended from just north of Mu Gia Pass back down to the DMZ. The major targets were the ferries at Quang Khe and Ron and near the city of Dong Hoi. The main choke point on the Ho Chi Minh Trail in RPI was Mu Gia Pass.

RPV was in the northwest portion of North Vietnam, extending from Laos toward Hanoi. The northern section ran along the Chinese border with a 30-mile buffer zone. It included the Red River Valley and a section of mountains called Thud Ridge. Thud Ridge was a ridge just North of Yen Bai that extended along the Red River towards Hanoi, with mountains that exceeded five thousand feet.

RPVIA was a pie shaped area extending from Hanoi along the northeast railroad to the Chinese border and then west to a point almost directly north of Hanoi. The northern border with China had a 25-mile buffer zone. It was necessary to fly through RPVIB, which was assigned to our Navy, to reach this area when attacking from the coast.

RPVIB was a pie shaped area running along the northeast railroad on its western border to the Chinese border and then east to the coast. The southern border extended from Hanoi east to Haiphong.

I finished stowing my gear and caught a ride to the flight line with the squadron duty driver. The 8th Tactical Fighter Wing (TFW) had allotted each fighter squadron two panel trucks and our Squadron Commander, Lt. Colonel James McGuire, had been assigned a jeep. These were the only vehicles that we could use on base, so most of the aircrews had bought bicycles from local vendors.

The 497th TFS was located next to the flight line and shared the same large wooden building complex with the 433rd TFS. The 8th TFW Headquarters was also located in the same complex between the two squadrons. Each squadron had an operations area with a large scheduling board and sign in/out counter. There was also a large briefing room and two small flight planning rooms that were air-conditioned. The 555th (Triple Nickel Squadron) was also part of the 8th TFW but was currently located 200 miles due north of Ubon at Udorn Air Base. It was interesting to note that the U.S. Government never allowed any publicity about our activities or acknowledged that our Wing was based in Thailand. It appeared that the American people had no right or need to know what was going on. I felt uncomfortable about this deceit, but maybe I just could not see the big picture.

There was a fence surrounding our complex of buildings with a guard positioned at the gate but he was not checking any of us. It appeared that security was not a factor—there were few defenders in sight around the base. There was an outhouse located outside the rear of the building that had a reputation for housing cobras—several had been killed there. I imagined that the snakes were simply catching the resident rats that infested the outhouse. I quickly decided that I would only use that outhouse if I was truly desperate, carried my pistol, and used a good strong flashlight.

I reported to Lt. Col. McGuire and informed our Commander that I was ready, willing, and able, to assume my Night Owl duties at the first opportunity. He appeared pleased to see me again after my long absence and welcomed me back into the squadron. He then turned me over to Major Ralph A. Hoyt—the Squadron Operations Officer and responsible for all the new guy indoctrination procedures. I was an old head in the 497th but would now be an F—ing New Guy (FNG) until I had completed several missions over North Vietnam.

My first step was to visit the personal equipment sergeant, whose shop was also located in our squadron building, where I could obtain all the required combat gear. Each crewmember had the choice of wearing survival equipment in a vest or in chaps around the legs. I decided to wear the chaps, as all the bulk around my chest made me feel uncomfortable. Every crewmember personally carried a RT-10 hand-held survival radio and there was another radio in the aircraft survival kit located under the seat cushion of each cockpit. The radio was both a voice transmitter and a beeper that provided a radio fix for search and rescue planes to home in on. We were issued a 38-caliber pistol and leather holster with two types of ammunition—solid hard nose bullets for defense and others that could shoot red tracers for rescue purposes. Crewmembers carried standard day and night flares, and a small tube about the size of a pencil that could shoot a small flare up about 100 yards. Finally, I was issued a standard military knife in a holster, and a new apparatus that consisted of a rope system to enable you to descend from tall trees. Bill also recommended that I carry a plastic baby bottle full of water, as your throat could become so dry after bailout that it was impossible to talk right away.

Major Hoyt then sent me next door to Wing Headquarters for a briefing on the ground rules of the war and to study photos of selected targets in our designated areas. I decided to pay a visit to Wing Intelligence after the ground rules briefing to obtain information on the enemy defenses. I located a non-rated briefing officer who informed me that Route Package One had a multitude of enemy 37/57mm guns that were effective up to around 17,000 feet. The majority of them were deployed around the town of Dong Hoi and near the ferry crossings at Mui Ron and Quang Khe. All three of the areas were located on the coast just north of the DMZ—approximately 200 miles east of Ubon. I learned that many of the truck convoys were protected with SU-23-2 quad 23-mm guns that could fire 1000 rounds per minute up to 10,000 feet. It appeared that most of the enemy ground units were equipped with 12.7mm machine guns that could fire 600 rounds a minute—they posed a threat up to 2500 feet. The majority of the 85/100mm big guns were located around Hanoi and Haiphong and capable of firing up to 15-20 rounds a minute.

The SA-2 surface-to-air missile sites (SAMs), consisting of six launchers arranged in a star pattern, were mainly positioned in RPVI. The missiles were 35 feet long, weighed 5,000 pounds, and contained a 286-pound warhead that had a 200-foot kill pattern. The launchers and radar van were advertised to be very mobile—they could be repositioned over night. I assumed that the enemy would soon have SAMs and the big guns in RPI before long so I had to be alert—there was no radar or missile warning gear in the F-4s. We had to rely on our eyeballs for protection against SAMs and MiGs, and I questioned why the Air Force had not seen fit to equip our birds with warning gear.

It was apparent that I had little experience in night warfare—the Air Force had never given me any training in the States for bombing under flares. Major Hoyt and Lt. Col. McGuire thought that I should fly my first mission as an instructional flight in the rear seat since I had never bombed at night. They noted that I had only flown a few flights in the F-4 since last September and it might not be rational to start out flying my first mission at night. I knew that I was rusty and had little experience with night bombing but no fighter pilot would ever admit that he was not ready to get the show on the road. A little thing like flying under flares, for the first time, over hostile jungle was no problem for any fighter pilot worth his salt.

I convinced them that this first mission would be a piece of cake if I could fly an early evening mission in Laos with Bill in the rear seat. I was very fortunate to be flying with Bill, as he was a combat experienced GIB who would be of immense help in understanding the layout and rules in the war zone. I had great confidence in his judgement and skill in flying the Phantom during day or night conditions. Bill also voiced his opinion that he could keep me out of trouble during my first night combat mission. Major Hoyt told me to hang loose and he would work me in on a twilight bombing mission in Laos. This would be an opportunity for me to see the area in the day and taste my first experience at night bombing. Major Hoyt told me to take a few days to become acquainted with the base and then the squadron would schedule us for an evening mission.

MARCH 10, 1966

During my tour of the base, I was pleased to discover a small library and hoped to visit it often, as I loved to read. It was also one of the few air-conditioned build-ings on the base which provided an added incentive for going there. The library received several current newsmagazines, that were recent, and a small supply of novels. I was gratified to see they received TIME and U.S. News & World Report along with the usual "Stars and Stripes" newspaper.

I noticed that the old wooden Chapel also doubled as the base motion picture theater with a different free movie each night. It appeared that the movies con-sisted of a recent production once a week with the other flicks possibly coming from the ancient archives of a military warehouse. I was delighted to see that there was a concession stand selling fresh popcorn and cold soda pop, just like in the States. The same movie was repeated all night to allow anyone on base to view it no matter what time they worked. Maybe it was a blessing that the hard wooden straight back bench seats looked uncomfortable as some of the older movies could be very boring and easily put a tired person to sleep.

The base had once been the proud possessor of a decent sized swimming pool but now it was in a sad state of disrepair. I was sorry to see that the long neglected pool had deteriorated into a stinking mixture of dirty water and several feet of mud. It had obviously seen better times in the distant past, but I was told that someday it would actually be reconditioned. The Base Exchange was a very small wooden building consisting of a single room with a few shelves that contained some of the necessities of life, such as toothpaste, razor blades and other personal items. However, the shopkeeper had managed to find space for local souvenirs, jewelry, and small gifts, to send back home for special occasions.

There was obviously a big building boom going on all over the base with extensive construction activities and stacks of plywood everywhere. It reminded me of those old western movies where they were building a gold rush town in a hurry. It appeared the base construction crews were building quarters for the enlisted troops so they could get out of their hot tents. Bill explained that the 497th aircrews would get air-conditioned quarters in the future so we could sleep during the day and fly at night. I noticed that every building on base appeared to be constructed from plywood. I wondered if this was how they had constructed bases during WWII—it brought up old memories of the war movies I had seen in Idaho as a kid.

I decided to test the food at the Officers Club that operated around-the-clock and was the only mess hall for officers on the base. It was interesting to note that the bar mainly stocked high quality brand named booze—Jack Daniels or Johnnie Walker only cost twenty-five cents a shot. It was questionably praiseworthy of the Air Force to provide expensive cheap booze for fighter pilots to swig before flying North to face hundreds of guns and missiles. It was also the custom for each crewmember to buy 100 free drinks when they completed the magic hundred missions—there would be many free drinks in the future if everyone survived this tour.

I had lunch with Lieutenant Ed Collins, a good bachelor friend, who had been part of our recreation crew at George AFB. Ed was a member of our group that had driven to Los Angles each weekend to enjoy the Manhattan Beach nightclubs. He joined Tom Boyd, Al Pollard, and me, when we had flown to Hawaii and stayed at Fort Derussy—an old military hotel located on the beach. We rented a car to tour the island and had a wonderful time exploring all the beautiful beaches and trying to meet girls. The hotel maintained a nice expanse of green grass between their complex and the beach, along with an open-air handball court where we played for hours. We enjoyed taking our dates to a nice nightclub where Don Ho was singing. I wanted to return to Hawaii if I could get leave during this tour—it was a neat place to unwind while sipping a Mai Tai and watching the sun set in the ocean.

Ed was the proud owner of his own small single engine plane that we had flown to the gunnery range at Cuddyback dry lake when we were stationed at George AFB. His plane was a blessing as it was a long hot dusty drive for many hours across the Mojave Desert to the isolated complex when we had the mandatory duty every few months. We were very fortunate that our Wing Commander let us fly his bird to the short runway and avoid the miserable trip.

Al (Crash) Pollard, another good friend, joined us later and I was pleased to see him again. Ed and Crash had flown in the rear seat of an F-4C to Ubon from George AFB when the Wing deployed last December. They were both back seat pilots and desired to upgrade to the front seat as soon as possible. It was enjoyable to remember and relive all the notable times we had on the beaches in Hawaii and LA. It was difficult to believe that such a beautiful world like that once existed for us in another time and place. Ed had a good-looking Continental stewardess that adored him, but Crash had not encountered a steady girlfriend. We all agreed that it might make more sense to be flying safe commercial airliners with friendly stewardesses instead of experiencing enemy fire each night over hostile country.

After lunch, I returned to my quarters to locate my personnel records for processing at the Base Personnel Office and I needed to examine my financial records. I learned that the Air Force paid me about eleven hundred dollars a month and congress had authorized an extra sixty-five dollars for combat pay. I weighed the fact that I was going to get an extra two dollars a day to be fired upon and possibly shot down over enemy territory. I questioned the rationale of the token combat pay all the way to the flight surgeons office, where I had to get the required in-country shots, which also pissed me off. I had not even flown my first mission and I already disliked this war—it was going to be a long hundred missions!

I tried not to focus on my hostility and decided to head to the OClub for dinner where I joined two good friends that I had known in Spain. Captain Lee Brazell (Braz) and Captain Dick Wade had lived in the BOQ, at Torrejon, when we were flying deuces. Braz later married a delightful Spanish girl from a nice family—he always had to have a member of his future wife's family with them on a date until they were married. Braz had found some dates for me with several nice Spanish girls but I preferred to date American women. I was thrilled when Braz allowed me drive his new Alpha Romeo convertible, from the port in Brooklyn, to Idaho, and then to George AFB in Victorville, California, when the 497th returned from Europe. I treasured driving my first ragtop and I kept the top down for the entire trip so I could attain a nice tan along the way. Braz must have thought that he would never get his car back as I spent a few additional weeks in St. Maries visiting my mother and old friends. The freedom that I enjoyed with the Alpha Romeo provided me with memories to remember for the rest of my life, which might not be long, if I was unlucky over here. I tried to reciprocate by letting Braz pick up my new XKE Jaguar, after it arrived at the Long Beach Port in Los Angles, and drive it while I was at the Army Jump School.

Captain Dick Wade was single when he first arrived in Madrid and had joined us when we visited the reverberating Casa Blanca nightclub. We also enjoyed the Officers Club in Madrid where Dick met and fell in love with an attractive flamenco dancer who performed several nights a week. I recalled that he dated Mari Carmen for a long time before he finally convinced her to marry him.

After we settled down for dinner in our plywood box of an officers club, we discussed how different this was from Spain. A steak dinner with wine and all the extras, in the finest restaurant in Madrid, only cost five dollars. Custom-made suits at the Castillana Hilton men's store were only $25 for labor, and we had a great selection of high quality, inexpensive materials, from Hong Kong or Britain. I had taken Spanish in college and managed to converse, in the present tense, if everyone spoke slowly. It seemed that I was always more fluent after drinking sangria in one of the ancient bodegas under the Plaza Mayor that had been there long before Columbus sailed. However, all my wonderful experiences ended when the 497th Fighter Interceptor Squadron left Spain and moved to George AFB to become part of the 8th TFW.

It was interesting to note that I had now completed three permanent base changes on three different continents in the same squadron. Our old deuce squadron had traveled far, changed aircraft, and now called the "Night Owl" squadron. However, right now I wished that I could be enjoying dinner at the Jockey Club in Madrid. If I could do it over again, I would have extended in Europe and gone to Germany to fly the Deuce. Maybe God wanted me in this war for some reason but it was still a mystery to me.

Most of the guys had their own method of keeping track of each mission that would eventually take them out of this war. I noticed Bill had put a bomb on his ball cap for each mission that counted towards the magic one hundred counters and a chance to depart on the freedom bird. I decided to take some time to think about how to keep track of my missions over North Vietnam; each one would be very important to me.

MARCH 11, 1966

I survived my night under the mosquito netting and enjoyed a nice hot shower with no cobras in sight. I relished a tasty breakfast at the OClub and was pleased to see that it was a nice sunny day. I took a short walk to the 497th Squadron Operations building located next to the F-4 ramp. I questioned why all the Phantoms were neatly lined up close together in rows and no revetments to protect them from an assault. It appeared that no one was concerned that the base might be attacked from the air or on the ground. Maybe our leaders had a mutual agreement with North Vietnam in that no one would raid each other's air bases. We were all upset and confused by the fact that we could not strike the enemies airfields or ports.

I returned to the personal equipment (PE) section to see if they had my flight gear ready for my first mission. I was always impressed with the PE enlisted men—they were always very professional and took great pride in their work. The sergeant in charge of the shop was on the ball and had my helmet and parachute harness ready to be fitted. I placed my G-suit and checklist bag on my equipment rack—I had carried them from the States in my parachute bag. I inspected my survival radio, revolver, and was shown how to operate the long nylon cord used for descending from the top of a tall tree, if you ended up there, after ejecting. I was given a plastic baby bottle for water that I filled and placed in the bottom pocket in my G-suit. I was shown how to operate the test equipment for checking the headset in my helmet and for proper oxygen flow before each flight.

I then met with Major Hoyt for more info on our squadron's nightly operations. He explained that the 8th TFW received the daily operations order (FRAG) from 7th Air Force that was located at Tan Son Nhut Airbase, Republic of Vietnam. The frag designated the ordnance load, takeoff time, route to recce and even a target (usually a suspected truck park) if no valid targets were located. The Wing then issued the designated mission assignments to each squadron where the operations officer paired the crews with the tasking. The Squadron duty officer immediately posted all the nightly missions on a large scheduling board, which allowed the aircrews ample time to study and prepare for their mission briefing. Major Hoyt had us scheduled for an evening mission with him leading the flight. It would start in the late evening, which allowed me a chance to start with daylight attack, and then continued into the night. It would be the first night flare mission that I had ever experienced and over the hostile jungle of Laos.

Bill joined me at the squadron and was pleased to see that Major Hoyt had placed us on the schedule for the following night. I learned that the 497th was operating mainly in Laos as the squadron was only scheduled to fly between 4 to 8 missions over North Vietnam each night. The desired counters were usually missions flying on the wing of a B-66 light bomber and dropping on the bomber's signal tone while flying at a high altitude. All the unguided iron bombs were assumed to accurately strike a dirt road in Mu Gia Pass. However, I questioned if the bombs would successfully hit a small dirt trail in a narrow canyon. It looked like a complete waste of time and bombs but no one seemed to care—it was an easy counter. This war was already looking suspect to me and I had not even flown my first mission.

Our schedule indicated that we were fragged for a mission in Laos on the Ho Chi Minh Trail near a town called Tchepone. Most of the missions in Laos were 'no sweat" types unless you got careless and lost control of the plane. I was aware that it was difficult, if not impossible, to recover from a spin when under ten thousand feet. Bill explained that there was little to fear from the manual tracking guns in Laos at night—the biggest problem was flying into the ground. The only areas that we needed to be concerned about were on the Plain of Jars and around Tchepone

Bill said that the Wing kept a map displaying the location of every aircraft shot down in the war and it was easy to identify the hot spots. There were numerous pins around Tchepone and I learned that a deadly accurate gun crew was located there. The Tchepone resident gunner was very selective and extremely accurate when he fired at an unsuspecting bird. It was interesting that no one could locate the deadly AAA site. I speculated that the murderous site immediately disappeared into a cave after firing a salvo. The gun crew was racking up numerous kills on Air Force, Navy, and Marine fighters along with Army helicopters. Bill told me that this bloodthirsty site had been shooting down aircraft almost every day since he had been at Ubon.

Bill took me to one of our small briefing rooms to show me where we would be flying tomorrow night and to discuss the hazards of night flare operations. He explained that our squadron had arrived at Ubon with little if any training in operating with flares at night and there were no experts available in the Wing. It seemed bizarre that the Air Force had never trained for night operations using flares. Maybe the ingenious experts at the Pentagon never assumed the military would need to attack the enemy at night.

The ground rules were currently being written and everyone had their own ideas on the best approach for employing ordnance at night. There was still a great deal of controversy in our squadron over the best way to accomplish the mission. It appeared that most of the pilots had agreed on one simple rule—never attack under the flares or get close enough to the flares to illuminate your aircraft. The squadron's old heads also recommended starting your pull out early enough to keep the aircraft from descending below 3500 feet above ground level (AGL). I was informed that it was critical to fly above 3500 feet during the day to avoid the automatic weapons fire.

Bill helped me prepare maps for all areas in Laos and then we completed additional maps for all of North Vietnam. He showed me the main roads traversing through Laos and Route Package One. We also annotated our maps for the route we were ordered to recce during my first mission in Laos. The Wing Intelligence shop had photos of some of the suspected targets, which were usually so-called truck parks that looked like a few acres of jungle. I had no idea how we were ever going to find a particular piece of jungle at night but I just nodded my head as if I understood all that they were feeding me.

Our flight was ordered to flare the designated routes and immediately strike any vehicles sighted on the road and to expend any remaining ordnance on the suspected truck park designated in the frag. I was informed that our Commander in Chief never wanted any bombs dropped over 100 yards from the Ho Chi

Minh trail going through Laos, which brought a smile to my face, but I held my snicker. I later informed Bill that I would be lucky to get any of my bombs within 300 feet of a target at night when dropping high above the flares. However, I speculated that I might be able to hit a road with one of my bombs if there was no wind and I released them in a long string. Bill said it was difficult to find a road at night in the heavy jungle much less hit a truck; so, this rule had to be taken with a grain of salt. This conflict was getting more interesting all the time but I questioned what the hell was really going on.

Next I walked over to the 8th TFW Intelligence shop that was located next to the squadron building and received the standard FNG briefing on local flying rules and combat regulations. I was told in a loud and clear proclamation that each aircrew was responsible to do exactly as directed by the seventh Air Force in Saigon. They explained that aircrews could only strike military targets along specified highways, railroads, and coastal routes. We could only hit rolling stock such as military trucks, locomotives, railroad cars, or road repair equipment. Hostile water vessels were also fair game but I had no idea how I was supposed to judge if they were aggressive. The High Rollers had recently expanded the ground rules to include ferries, bridges, and barges, which was big of them. I was gratified to learn that we could also crater roads or choke points. I thought that it might be better to interdict a road than trying to find a truck park in the middle of the jungle at night.

The tasking designated exactly which routes we had to fly and where to drop our ordnance if a target was not found—I could not believe that our missions were so restricted! I questioned why we were not authorized to fly search and destroy missions like those that the Army Air Corp flew during WWII. Intelligence explained that the frags, with mission details, were sent to Ubon the day before the night sorties were scheduled. I learned that it was possible for our Wing to change the main mission and go to a secondary target if the weather was bad in the primary area.

I was informed that President Johnson made the final decision as to which targets could be struck; it seemed fitting that I should start calling LBJ the Target Master. Bill explained that challenging the target coordinates was almost blasphemy. However, they had to challenge the rules once when they were being sent into China as someone somewhere had screwed up. I realized that it was going to be very difficult for me to accomplish an effective mission using these unreasonable ground rules. It was hard to believe that I had been enjoying a free enjoyable life less than a week ago in California.

3

I arrived at the squadron well before briefing time to inspect all my personal equipment and then visited Wing Intelligence for the latest war news. Intel narrated the latest enemy air activity with the location of suspected guns in my flight area—automatic weapons and possible 37mm cannons. The helicopter rescue procedures were covered along with correct code words to radio to the rescue troops in case you had to be recovered from a hostile area.

Major Hoyt conducted a very detailed briefing on bombing under flares since it was my first night mission in over eight months and I had never bombed at night. He explained that I was the flight shooter and had to be in position to immediately strike any valid target that he flared. It would be unlikely that he would have time to reposition and strike a target before it disappeared into the jungle.

We had about thirty minutes of daylight for our tour of Laos and the Ho Chi Minh Trail that snaked through the jungle always heading toward South Vietnam. I was lucky that Lt. William E. McGourin would be in my back seat as he was very familiar with all the Seventh AF procedures since he had been flying missions since December. I was pleased to be flying with Bill, as it would be our first flight together since I had gone to Squadron Officers School last summer. I felt that I had wasted valuable time in a boring school. I should have remained at George AFB and prepared for a conflict that was still a conundrum to me.

Our Phantom would be loaded with six M117 general purpose bombs, wing fuel tanks, and two Sparrow missiles. The 750-pound bombs would leave a crater approximately 26 feet in diameter and 9 feet deep in medium soil. Major Hoyt was assigned to carry two pods of flares, centerline fuel tank, and 6 pods of 2.75" rockets. We concluded our briefing and scrawled our aircraft numbers on our

38

briefing cards before signing out. We ambled down to the personnel equipment room, to don our equipment, and checked the helmet's radio and oxygen mask. The equipment was bulky, uncomfortable to wear, and seemed antiquated for the richest country in the world. I wondered if the Air Force made the bomber troops wear this old equipment or was it just reserved for fighter pilots who might be shot down.

We stripped off the removable 497th TFS patch, nametag and Tactical Air Command insignia from our green Air Force flight suit before departing. We could only fly with military identification (ID), dog tags, and a Geneva Convention Card, which I placed in a small pocket on the upper arm of my flight suit. I felt it was a waste of time, as North Vietnam never adhered to our ground rules. However, I played the game and followed the local procedures as required. Each pilot was apportioned a small bin for their valuables until they returned from their mission—with any luck at all.

The 497th duty driver took us to our aircraft in one of our two allotted panel trucks. Bill indicated that we could usually expect to find our bird parked on the ramp in front of the squadron or out between the taxiway and runway. All the birds had been carefully lined up in rows, which made them sitting ducks for sabotage or an air attack. A conscientious crew chief waited at our assigned F-4C and voiced a quick briefing on the status of the bird.

It was good to see the massive Phantom, as I had missed the rugged bird that just might take me through this war. It would be interesting to see if Big Ugly could accomplish all that we had trained for at George AFB. I tended to compare the F-4 to an immense deafening and rugged dump truck that turned badly. The Phantom had gobs of power but burned tons of fuel while emitting a steady stream of dense black fumes. However, it was a workhorse and could carry most any kind of garbage for a reasonable distance, depending on the fuel load. At times, it was beneficial to have two engines, but the big JP-4 guzzling flame-throwers were loud and smoked like an old movie star. The Phantom was a large aircraft; 62 feet 11 inches long, 16 feet 5 inches tall and with a wing span of 38 feet 11 inches. It weighed 28,958 pounds empty, 51,577 pounds gross, and had a max takeoff weight of 59,380 pounds.

The big bird contained up to 3,230 gallons of fuel but tonight we were only carrying 1260 gallons of internal fuselage fuel plus 630 gallons in the internal wing tanks. The Night Owl Shooter normally carried two 370-gallon external wing tanks while the Lead Owl carried a 600-gallon center line fuel tank and two flare pods. The Phantom could carry 16,000 pounds of external ordnance but you would be lucky to get to the local supermarket and back since there was now no room for external fuel tanks.

Bill inspected the six 750-pound bombs and the two AIM—7 missiles while I conducted a preflight for chinks in the bird's armor. The Air Force still required fighter pilots to carry a checklist around in their hand and opened to the correct page although no one ever looked at it. I inspected the aircraft form, number 781, to validate that our bird had been inspected by maintenance and was ready for flight. The aircraft commander had to verify that he was aware of any conditions noted in the form and made sure the aircraft was not on a red X status.

We usually had a few minutes, after the external checks, to relax before we climbed up the ladder to check the cockpit switches and complete a thorough preflight of the ejection seat. For obvious reasons, I felt that I had better check my ejection seat more closely than usual. I climbed into the cockpit and connected my harness to the Martin Baker rocket ejection seat after inspecting a multitude of checklist items and pulling many pins. The seat worked well and you could even eject safely when on the ground but it had numerous sequences that had to function before it finally fired. Each aircrew member had a choice of using a handle between their legs or a face curtain, located on top of the seat, to initiate the ejection sequence. There was a survival kit attached to the seat that contained an inflatable raft, additional survival radio and various other items that would be essential if you ejected. An emergency beeper was triggered after ejection to assist the rescue helicopters in locating your position on the ground. I wondered if the enemy also had direction finders that might allow them to discover my location before the rescue troops could arrive.

We completed all the cockpit inspections and then checked in with Major Hoyt on our squadron ground control radio frequency. Owl Lead radioed back that we were cleared to start our engines, as he was also ready to roll. We gave the crew chief the crank up signal by turning our finger straight up in the air and he applied high-pressure air to the number one engine. The ignition button was depressed at ten percent RPM and then the throttle was advanced around the horn. The fuel flow, exhaust gas temperature (EGT) and nozzles were monitored for proper readings as the turbine ignited. The button was released at 45% RPM and then the engine stabilized at 65%. The oil pressure, fuel flow, and hydraulic systems were also checked to make sure they were stabilized in the "green". The number two engine was then started and air disconnected before the aircraft flight controls, flaps, and speed brakes were checked for proper movement. The crew chief also had to check the boundary layer air control over each wing before buttoning up all the panels. We gave the chocks out signal to the chief after radioing Major Hoyt that we were ready to roll.

Lead called us to change to ground control frequency which we acknowledged and then switched on the taxi light as we left the ramp for the arming area at the end of the runway. I acknowledged leads check-in call and received taxi instruction from Ubon ground control. We took spacing behind lead on the way to the departure arming area. We were required to remain 300 feet behind lead to avoid any ground fodder that might be blown up into the air. Upon reaching the arming area, we followed the ground crews directions. They had to see your hands out of the cockpit before they handled the bird. The arming crew never wanted us to touch any switches while they were pulling pins on the ordnance.

The ground crew pulled the numerous arming pins on the bombs, flares, wing tanks, and the sparrow missiles. Two AIM-7 Sparrow low drag missiles, carried on all missions, were always tuned in the arming area before takeoff. The semi-active radar homing air-to-air missiles were located in semi-recessed slots in the forward fuselage belly. Another ground crew gave us a final check for leaks and general aircraft appearance. We then switched from ground to tower frequency and Owl Lead requested takeoff instruction with 30 seconds delay between aircraft. It was not smart to make a wing takeoff at night on a short runway with armed ordnance. The tower cleared us onto the runway for the engine run up but instructed us to hold for further release.

The Ubon runway was very short as it only had about 5,800 feet of useable concrete with no overruns. It also had a drainage ditch around the runway, which created a lip at each end of the landing strip. It was obvious to me that a short touchdown would probably wipe out the landing gear. There was plenty of room for our takeoff but very little to play with when landing on a wet runway. We were fortunate that the F-4 had been designed for low speed landings on an aircraft carrier. It was highly improbable that a Thud could operate from this runway safely, even when it was dry.

I ran each engine up to 100% and inspected the EGT, hydraulics, nozzles, fuel flow, and oil pressures, to see if they were within the green markings. We never checked the afterburners (A/B's), as the brakes would not be able to hold the Phantom in place. The flap lever was lowered to the one half position and indicators noted, along with a final flight control check. Bill read the before take-off check list, and I acknowledged that the three stability augmentation switches were engaged, trim was set two units down, pitot heat and anti skid were on. We both confirmed that our seat pins were out, shoulder harness locked, and no warning lights were illuminated. We were finally ready to roll after checking that the canopy was down and locked.

The tower cleared our flight for takeoff with thirty second spacing. Lead acknowledged the instructions and then released his brakes while selecting both afterburners. We released our brakes and engaged both blowers after watching to make sure that lead had rotated. We had to make sure that lead was off the runway, before we blasted off, in case we had to abort. My EGT and afterburner nozzles were quickly scanned and airspeed monitored for correct acceleration. I had computed our nose lift-off speed at about 165 knots but mainly relied on my own instinct for correct acceleration while watching the runway markers stream by.

I had decided in my own mind that it would be impossible to stop a heavily loaded "Hummer" on the runway once it had reached one hundred knots. I instructed Bill to eject both of us if we had not become airborne by the time we reached the end of the runway. I believed the Martin Baker's advertisement that the seat would safely eject aircrews at ground level. One of my good friends had tried to stay with a bird that had not lifted off the concrete and he bought the farm. The "Hummer" had tremendous power but I still got concerned when the speeding object was accelerating down the runway attempting to reach 170 knots. It always made me feel better if I pumped the stick a few times just to convince myself that I truly had full back stick while eyeballing the rapidly disappearing runway markers.

The landing gear was quickly raised, after becoming airborne, as the Phantom had a maximum gear down airspeed limit of 250 knots. I retracted the flaps a few seconds later but they would automatically blow up, when the airspeed increased, if I forgot the flap lever. Bill continued to read the after-takeoff-check-list items while I monitored the wing fuel tanks for correct transfer into the internal fuselage tanks.

I imagined that I might experience butterflies and a dry mouth when we departed on my first combat mission. However, it felt like a routine training flight, but I knew that the night was young and I had a long mission ahead. I realized that I had better be sharp tonight, as I had to fly my first night flare mission over a dark hostile jungle, instead of a safe training range in the States.

We established a 4-5 mile trail position on Lead Owl as he turned for Tchepone and switched us over to our combat frequency. We soared up to 15,000 feet to save fuel, as we were not worried about enemy missiles or AAA in this area. Bill tuned in the coordinates of our target area in the Litton AN/ASN-48 inertial navigation system that may or may not be accurate. I had discovered the hard way in the past that the system appeared to be working well but you ended up many miles from your target. The TACAN navigation system, located at Ubon, was an effective accurate aid in locating your target in some parts of Laos.

It was still twilight and I could see the wet terrain and rice patties of Thailand far below our bird. A few minutes later we could see the Mekong River, which was about fifty miles away, as it came into view off our nose. Bill instructed me to select the inboard stations and bombs ripple on the armament panel (nicknamed "dog bone" because of its shape). He explained that our squadron normally used the Mekong River as the arming line for our ordnance. Laos appeared to be dark and desolate with no lights to be seen except for numerous fires that were burning in many areas. The smoke from all the fires had contributed to a dense and terrible haze layer that extended up in the air to over 20,000 feet in some areas.

We started our descent over Laos after Owl Lead located the Ho Chi Minh Trail that meandered through the Laotian jungle, winding its way to South Vietnam. I was surprised to see that the jungle road appeared to be in excellent shape with no evidence of bombing. It resembled one of the reddish dirt roads that I had seen in Florida while attending the Forward Air Controllers School at Hurlburt Field near Fort Walton Beach. I had expected to see at least a few bomb craters and several destroyed vehicles but there was nothing in sight. There had to be numerous worker bees down fixing the trail overnight or else no bombs were even hitting the road. I speculated that the enemy had efficient road crews that could maintain the trail no matter how many bombs we dropped. It would be interesting to crater the small dirt road and see just how fast they could repair it.

It was time to get to work and locate our designated recce route on the trail. The sun had set and the jungle was slowly becoming an eerie dark black carpet. Major Hoyt ordered us to extinguish our external position lights—now we had to keep track of each other's position by radio calls. Lead radioed "flares away" when he released four eight million-candle-power parachute flares. They had an ignition delay of approximately 20 seconds and burned for four minutes, over the suspected target area. We watched them twinkle as they were ejected from the flare canister and illuminated just before we reached them. The haze was terrible tonight and both of us were having a hard time trying to make out what was on the ground below. All I could see was a very dark area of jungle with no sign of a road in any direction. I let Bill fly the bird when I was looking or I would take over the controls and let him look as we always wanted one pilot on the gauges at all times.

It seemed logical that any truck driver would have heard our noisy jets long before we arrived over the trail. I assumed that the drivers would hide their trucks in the dense jungle until we had to leave due to fuel limitations. It appeared to me that the only way that we would ever catch a truck on the road was if it had broken down or it was a flak trap. I decided that this Night Owl was not going to hold its breath while waiting to catch a truck hunkering on the Ho Chi Minh Trail at night.

We radioed our position to lead as we approached the flares and then took spacing on him as we both circled the flare pattern looking for a small dirt trail. There was nothing in view, so we continued searching as lead dropped more flares farther to the north. Again we circled the flares but the elusive trail still never appeared to us. The third flare drop was the charm as lead finally illuminated an empty dirt road below us. I never expected to see any trucks sitting in the middle of the trail for us to bomb, as the enemy could not be that stupid.

We continued down the road until lead owl radioed that they had seen the flash of some automatic weapons fire. It was not logical for the enemy to be firing, as they could not see our aircraft though they could surely hear us. The suspected sighting of weapons fire gave our flight an excuse to unload the ordnance in this area as we were down to the end of our flares, fuel and ideas. It was necessary to climb up to 8,000 feet if we wanted to release our bombs above the flares. I popped up to eight grand and initiated an easy roll down toward the jungle while attempting to acquire the desired 30-degree dive angle. We had computed a release altitude of 5,000 feet on the altimeter with a reading of approximately 480 knots indicated airspeed. Bill then voiced a "Pickle" call to me when the desired parameters were reached on his rear cockpit instruments. This was the command for me to push the little red button on top of the control stick of the front cockpit. Depressing the weapons button initiated the release of all six bombs that I had previously armed. We felt the bombs rippling off the Phantom and heading for somewhere down below into the dark hazy jungle.

I immediately started a four to five G pull that would bring our bird's nose up to wings level and then we would climb back to a safe altitude. I had to instantly reverse my full attention, from outside the cockpit, to the aircraft's artificial horizon instrument. I had to immediately recover from the dive, level our wings, and get the "Hummers" nose above the horizon by using aircraft instruments. My recovery in the haze was abnormal and discomforting to me as I attempted to get my bird's nose away from the ground. I had no outside references and it appeared to me that we were flying on the inside of a dark tunnel with no definite horizon. Bill repeated his "pull out" call until our artificial horizon instrument indicated that we were ascending. All my senses kept telling me to level out but Bill was urging me to continue the climb and our instruments agreed with him. I relied on Bill's instructions and our attitude instruments while I continued to pull back on the stick to attain additional altitude. It was high pulse rate frequency (PRF) time for me until we were safely back above the flares.

I had attempted to avoid any possible ground fire by staying out of the flare light during my attack. I noted that I had only attained a 25-degree dive bomb angle and Bill had to add power to reach the desired airspeed. Those parameters indicated that my bombs would strike the jungle well short of the target. It was going to be very difficult for me to obtain a thirty-degree dive angle at night using only flares with no horizon. I realized that I would have to compute my bomb mil settings and release altitudes for 25 degrees dive angles if I was going to get my bombs anywhere close to a truck. I was certainly not capable of flying 30-degree dive patterns at night but maybe I would improve over time.

I now realized that bombing with flares at night, under very hazy conditions, was going to be extremely difficult. The abnormal night attack, using unfamiliar flares, created many extraordinary and unnatural effects on my mind. I realized that it was critical to rely wholly on the aircraft instruments—your senses were useless in this environment. It was a great relief to get away from the flares, as they tended to disorient me with weird vertigo effects.

I had never been trained to drop ordnance at night and found it extremely difficult to manipulate the correct switches in a dark cockpit. I discovered that it was necessary to improvise and use various floodlights or even use my flashlight with red lens to read the ordnance switch settings. Maybe the engineers at McDonald Douglas never envisioned dropping ordnance off Big Ugly at night or maybe they would have provided adequate lightning for the armament panel. I was not pleased that I had to learn how to attack the enemy at night, over hostile terrain, and experiment with ordnance switches in a dark cockpit. A mistake could get us killed if I lost control and we had to eject in an area that was hostile to fighter pilots. I questioned why our leaders never trained us for night attack operations on the training ranges in the States. However, maybe our astute Air Force training experts never expected the Phantom to drop ordnance at night.

Lead radioed that he was rolling in, for his final attack, to fire all of his rockets in the same general area. Lead Owl's rockets appeared as beautiful red streaks hurling to the ground as they discharged from the rocket pods. It was the first time that I had ever seen rockets fired at night and I was surprised to see that his aircraft was clearly highlighted by the blast. I realized that the enemy would know exactly where to aim when the aircraft was exposed to their gun emplacements. In addition, the flight path of the rockets showed the gunners where the Night Owl was heading which could not bode well for any bird. It appeared to me that firing rockets in a heavily defended area at night could cause a disastrous situation for the shooter. I expected to see some ground fire coming up toward his exposed aircraft but no gunners fired at him. I was disappointed that there were no secondary explosions resulting from our bombs or his rockets. We had to leave the dark jungle without knowing where our ordnance had struck the earth.

Major Hoyt radioed that he was climbing to angels 15 and heading toward Ubon. I turned the controls over to Bill and illuminated our position lights again. We were required to join with lead and complete a hung ordnance check before landing. Bill closed with our leader and then flew in close formation while I used my flashlight to verify that their rocket pods were jettisoned. We then assumed the lead position so they could verify that there were no bombs remaining on our triple ejector racks. Lead Owl then reassumed the lead for our return to base.

Each aircraft was required to make an individual approach to Ubon, as wing landings were not authorized at night. Lead switched us over to approach control, where we each received holding instructions before our clearance for separate approaches. I took the aircraft controls back from Bill so I could become familiar with the TACAN approach at Ubon. I also needed to complete the radar ground controlled approach (GCA), as I had only flown several approaches in the last six months.

I was not pleased that Ubon only possessed a single 5,800-foot runway! However, the base had installed new arresting gear that was positioned at the middle of the runway. This gear was similar to the arresting gear on a navy aircraft carrier and was definitely a real help during emergencies or wet runway operations. I was elated to see that the runway had strobe lights on the approach end. I speculated that the bright lights would be a real aid during bad weather. Our main divert base was about 200 miles eastward at Korat, where the F-105 (Thud) drivers hung out.

I completed a standard TACAN approach to Ubon with a full stop GCA landing on the very short runway. I immediately deployed the drag chute and tested the brakes, as we would have to take the barrier if they failed. Bill read the after landing checklist after I had determined that the "Hummer" would stop safely on the runway. I switched off the anti skid, pitot heat, Stab Aug, and raised the flaps, while setting the trim two units nose low. We turned off at the end of the runway into the dearming area where the ground/arming crews were waiting to replace the external tank and ordnance safety pins. It was always a relief to open the canopy and feel the night air on your face. Bill switched us to ground control, and I requested clearance to taxi back to our line on the ramp. I was pleased to see that our crew chief was waiting with his flashlights to direct us into our parking spot. We completed our engine shut down procedures after the crew chief had placed chocks around the main landing gear tires. I concluded the cockpit shutdown checklist, replaced the ejection seat pins, and raised the lower guard handle on the ejection seat.

Our squadron's panel truck was waiting to give us a ride back to the squadron, but Bill said it was seldom there when it was pouring. We returned our flight gear to the personnel equipment shop for cleaning and storage and recovered our valuables. Then we had to complete our required sign in at the operations counter with our flight time and mission code. We logged 1+15 hours of combat time that included thirty minutes day and forty-five minute's nighttime. The mission code was 1.3, to designate a mission in Laos, and was not a counter towards the magic one hundred missions.

It was mandatory to go next door to the Wing Intelligence shop for debriefing the mission. I tried to explain what we had accomplished to a non-rated officer who appeared to have no concept of what was required of an F-4C aircrew during night operations. There was not a great deal to explain tonight, as our flight had only seen possible light automatic weapons fire. I stressed that we had attempted to drop our bombs on the road in an area where our leader had seen automatic weapons fire but we were unable to obtain visual results concerning where or what our bombs had hit. I never bothered to explain that our bombs had probably landed somewhere in the middle of an indescribable jungle. I felt that our mission was a complete waste of our time and had not helped our troops in South Vietnam.

I was pleased to have lived through my initial combat mission and my first night dive bombing attack under flares. It had been a routine mission until I attempted my first engagement at night and then I had my eyes watered. I realized that night attacks under flares would require excellent instrument work and insidious vertigo would be a deadly hazard. The flares and haze had combined to make the mission extremely difficult but I felt it would get easier with additional experience. I concluded that the odds of my hitting a truck at night with bombs were "slim to none". It was very difficult to obtain consistent dive angles and the releases were too high if you wanted to avoid the flare light. I speculated that I would have to fly low angle attacks under the flares to be effective. We also needed ordnance that provided a large kill or damage area.

I decided that it had been an illuminating mission for a new guy although it should have been conducted over a safe bombing range back at George AFB. I caught a ride with the duty driver to the OClub for a beer with Bill to celebrate surviving my first sortie. It felt good to have completed my first combat flight although it was only over Laos.

Mission Results: 0 trucks. (+30 day & +45 night)

Total Barrel-Roll Results: 0 trucks

Mission Notes:

-Vertigo was always present and dangerous during night missions.

-It was arduous and impracticable for me to attain 30-degree dive angles at night.

-Firing rockets at night exposed the aircraft to enemy gunners.

-F-4C armament panel lighting was marginal, as switch settings were difficult to see.

-It was extremely difficult to hit a small target using high altitude release parameters.

-It was impossible to obtain wind speed and direction for releasing ordnance.

-It was very troublesome to find the Ho Chi Minh Trail at night in Laos.

-The short Ubon runway would make stopping a "Hummer" difficult when it was wet.

MARCH 13, 1966
BARREL ROLL MISSION #2

Major Hoyt cleared me to start flying missions with my newly assigned Flight Commander, Major Claud A. Wilkins. The 497th scheduled Bill and I for another mission to Laos but this would be later at night. We would again carry six 750-pound bombs and two external 370-gallon fuel tanks located under the outer pylon of each wing. Major Wilkins bird was loaded with the standard two flare canisters, two rocket pods, and a 600-gallon centerline fuel tank.

The flight was fragged for the same general area as our first mission but now there was no daylight to make it easier. Major Wilkins was one of the "old heads" at Ubon and gave me another detailed briefing on how to stay alive in a dangerous night combat environment. He was in agreement with Major Hoyt on releasing ordnance above the flares. I realized that it was most likely safer, but I knew that it would be very difficult for me to hit a truck when releasing so high and never knowing the winds. Maybe I would be able to hit a truck if I dropped six bombs in the singles mode—I could obtain a long blast pattern over the ground.

We executed the standard Ubon departure procedure and then joined with lead owl at 15,000 feet to conserve fuel before reaching the Mekong. Bill flew our shooter owl to the designated Ho Chi Minh Trail section in Laos while I studied the terrain. I observed numerous fires burning in the jungle and the miserable dense haze was still horrible. It was going to be another difficult night trying to find a jungle road, much less any moving vehicles. I still could not imagine a truck stopping in the middle of the trail so I could try to bomb it.

Lead Owl located the road with his second set of flares but the trail was deserted as I had expected. I was appalled to see that the path again appeared to be in excellent condition with no craters or wrecked trucks in sight. Maybe there were hundreds of maintenance troops down there along with numerous trucks hiding under the trees but out of sight to us. I requested and received permission from lead to execute some practice dive bomb attacks on the road to become accustomed to the flares. The eerie reflections from the flares in the haze continued to bother me and I still had a tendency to level our bird too soon during the pull out. Bill was an invaluable aid in assisting me to stay focused on the pattern procedures and keeping us out of trouble. It was critical that one pilot always stayed on the instruments as vertigo was a constant danger while flying in this black void. I was very lucky to have an experienced pilot in the rear cockpit that had flown thirty missions over North Vietnam.

Our flight never discovered any trucks on the trail so lead decided to drop his last flares on the designated truck park—I never grasped how he found it! The dense jungle all looked the same to me, as it was just a mass of black foliage. I tried to drop my bombs near where his rockets appeared to go but it was just in the middle of nowhere. I questioned what in the world were we trying to accomplish in Laos!

I turned the controls over to Bill for the recovery and hung ordnance check. It had been an interesting mission but I had not expected to find any deaf truck drivers sitting in the middle of the Ho Chi Minh Trail waiting for us to bomb them. I could not understand how I would ever discover a truck at night. However, I was learning to complete attacks using flares and the enemy gun crews had not caused any problems.

Our birds recovered at the Ubon roost where we signed in at the 497th for a 1.3 mission. Then we completed the standard debriefing with Intel and told them that we had dropped our bombs on a truck park. I assumed that was the standard way of saying that nothing was accomplished.

Mission Results: 0 trucks. (1+25 night)

Total Barrel-Roll Results: 0 trucks.

Mission Notes:

-Enemy drivers could unquestionably hear Night Owls coming for many miles.

-The Ho Chi Minh Trail appeared remarkably well maintained with no visible ruts or craters.

-Trying to hit a truck with an unguided iron bomb at night was unrealistic to me.

-Designated truck parks appeared to be just a generic patch of jungle.

I checked the squadron frags before catching a ride to the OClub for breakfast and learned that there would be an increased number of sorties scheduled for North Vietnam the following night. The non—counters in Laos were fine for a practice missions, but I felt that I was now ready for the big time and wanted to get started toward the required 100 counters.

The 497th designated a Primary, Secondary, and Duty flight, for each night's flying schedule. Our flight was assured of getting a counter every third night when it was designated the Primary flight. The Secondary flight might also get a counter over North Vietnam but lately they had gone to Laos. The Duty flight got all the grubby ground jobs such as duty driver, tower recorder, mobile control, etc.

I enjoyed the breakfast meal at the OClub—they had a good selection of eggs, potatoes, meats, pancakes, and the cooks made an omelet if requested. There was a good chance that I would eat breakfast when I arose after dark and again before I went to bed at dawn. After breakfast, Crash agreed to be my partner playing bridge, and we found another pair to play for a tenth of a cent a point. Bridge was a good card game to keep your mind off the war, and it appeared that no one wanted to talk about their missions anyway. I noticed that there were only a few aircrews hanging around the bar, even though booze was just two bits a drink.

4

MARCH 14, 1966
FIRST MISSION OVER NORTH VIETNAM
ROLLING THUNDER MISSON #1

I arose after sleeping about six hours and decided to eat another appetizing breakfast—I always liked eggs when first awakening. Many aircrews tried to sleep as long as they could during the day, but by noon, the heat had become too unbearable to stay in a bed with netting over you. The shower facility for the hootches was located about 50 feet away from our beds and it really felt gratifying to stand under a nice cool refreshing stream of water. I took a short walk to the 497th after breakfast to see what missions had been scheduled.

I was pleased to see that Bill and I had been fragged for my first mission over the North, with my Flight Commander as Lead Owl. Our flight was tasked to search for trucks on the portion of the Ho Chi Minh Trail that wound through Mu Gia Pass. It would be a relief to finally fly a mission over North Vietnam and discover what was going on in Route Package One. The Air Force was resourceful to give aircrews a brass ring to reach for, as the hundred-missions for freedom rule made you want to fly every night. I might have had a very different attitude about wanting to fly over North Vietnam every night if I had to remain here for a full year.

Our designated route was a segment of Ho Chi Minh Trail that began north of Mu Gia Pass and progressed south through the pass toward South Vietnam. It was the main pass on Route 15 for material coming out of North Vietnam and designated as a major choke point on the Ho Chi Minh Trail. The canyon had very steep walls rising approximately two thousand feet on one side and 2500 feet on the other side. Bill described it as a narrow twisting pass, approximately 25 miles in length, with peaks over four thousand feet high and consisting of very rugged terrain. Our flight would fly north through the mountainous part of Laos and then turn east to meet the trail just north of the pass. It would be easy to find our target as we could paint the high mountain peaks on our Phantom's radar-scope. We would stay on the deck flying through Laos and possibly surprise a few trucks when we popped up over mountains and quickly dove into the valley.

Our bird was again loaded with six 750-pound bombs and lead carried rockets that were more effective for hitting trucks—they had a large damage footprint. We lifted off before sunset and it appeared that we should have a few minutes daylight remaining when we arrived at the pass. I executed a quick join-up on lead and then assumed loose formation for the flight across northern Laos with Bill on the controls. There were no SAMs to worry about in Laos, so we climbed to 15,000 feet to save fuel until we were close to the mountains. There was no visible sign of life in Laos after we crossed the Mekong River near Udorn. I figured that a conniving enemy probably had a lookout posted on top of every mountain in North Vietnam. The mountains in north Laos looked exquisite with a dense green covering that was imprinted with remarkable steep jagged granite colored rocks that Bill called karst. I resumed control of the Phantom—Bill needed to operate his radar controls to search for the mountain peaks near Mu Gia Pass. I glanced at my radarscope and noticed that Bill had painted a large peak just to the north of our target. Lead was also flying toward the same peak and had initiated a descent to bring our flight down to a few hundred feet above the jungle. The enemy radar sites would have a hard time tracking us at this altitude, but any mountain lookouts could see our black smoke from a long distance. I maneuvered to maintain a position about a mile behind lead and re-checked that our armament switches were hot as we neared the mountain pass

Lead Owl initiated an expeditious climb to clear the mountain peak and then quickly dove into the valley. We were just seconds behind lead and spotted a dirt road in the pass that was visible in the twilight. The mountain lookouts must have been sleeping as lead radioed that he had spotted a number of trucks on the road. I also detected vehicles that appeared to be a line of dark trucks speeding down the trail. We had surprised an enemy truck convoy but an accompanying gunner on a vehicle had spotted us and was firing. We observed a solid stream of brilliant bloody tracers rising from the convoy and they captured my full attention. The blistering red tracers were strangely beautiful but were also a deadly menace when they rose towards our owl and Bill was telling me to jink away from the murderous fireballs. I immediately turned to avoid the lethal spray and initiated a pop-up maneuver in order to execute a bombing attack on the trucks that were rapidly departing the road.

The trucks promptly disappeared into the jungle before I could commence my attack but we had the area spotted. Lead Owl initiated a low angle rocket pass and picked up heavy fire from the 23mm gun that had four barrels and the capability to fire 1,000 rounds per minute from each barrel. Major Wilkins fired all his rockets into the area where the convoy had left the road and then started his recovery to the west. I completed my high-speed pop-up and positioned our bird for a dive bomb attack on the right side of the road where the trucks had vanished. I hoped to hit several of the trucks and cut the road as that might delay the convoy for later flights scheduled into this area.

I started our dive and Bill called out the altitude while I carefully placed my piper on the side of the road where the trucks had departed. I depressed the little red pickle button and dropped the bombs one at a time after I heard the "Pickle" call. Our long release had taken us too close to the enemy gunner and a zillion sizzling fireballs were coming towards us. The solid red spray looked like it was coming from a fire hose and it was intent on washing us right out of the sky. We heard lead calling us to jink hard as the scorching fireballs were nearing our bird. I immediately started a hard five-G pull and jinked to the left as we flew up away from the gun and out of the pass. We departed the valley floor, banked to the West, and started searching for lead during out climb.

Major Wilkins radioed that our bombs had cut the road but they had not seen any secondary explosions. Maybe we had slowed the trucks down for a later flight but I figured road crews were already filling in the bomb craters, and the trucks would soon be on their way. An internal 20mm Gattling gun on the Phantom would have been the ticket—we could have fired into the jungle where the trucks were hiding. The six shooter was an excellent weapon that could be accurately directed to hit a target and capable of strafing a large area. I questioned why the Air Force had never acquired an internal gattling gun for the F-4C as even a dumb fighter pilot from Idaho could see that we needed the weapon.

It was sure that it would have been impossible for us to strike the trucks any quicker. I thought that we had been fortunate as we surprised the convoy with sufficient light to initiate an immediate attack. I was astonished that the trucks had been able to instantly disappear into the jungle before we could drop our bombs. It was obvious that vehicles could vanish, within seconds, when there was nearby jungle for them to drive under. I speculated that there were probably numerous turnouts available all the way to South Vietnam. I questioned if it would be possible to destroy many trucks along the Ho Chi Minh Trail due to the ever-present jungle

Bill took over the controls as we departed the pass and closed on our leader who was heading south toward Thailand. Major Wilkins radioed our squadron to alert later flights about the truck convoy we had spotted in Mu Gia Pass. He described the target area and relayed the coordinates of the trucks using the F-4C inertial navigation system. I relaxed and then realized that I had been fired upon for the first time in my life! However, it had been of little consequence to me as I was so busy maneuvering and attempting to execute a good bomb attack that I had no time to think about the deadly flak. Bill remarked that it was the heaviest firepower he had ever seen on any of his missions. It was obvious that I was going to experience a lot of flak over North Vietnam. However, I was thrilled to have finally seen some trucks on the Ho Chi Minh Trail! I hoped that I would never have to eject in Mu Gia Pass, as it was rough mountainous terrain and populated with hostile residents.

I was also acutely aware that the Big Boss had been riding shotgun with me—I had almost made a fatal mistake. I had been so excited to see the trucks that I started to execute a low altitude release next to the target. If the gunner had held his fire a few seconds longer, I would have been in range for a good hosing and blasted out of the sky. I was fortunate that it had been dark enough to see the red fireballs and jink away. I was sure that it would have been more difficult to see the tracers in the daytime. I was lucky to have been flying with an experienced flight leader and with Bill in the back cockpit. It might have been a disaster if I had tried to drop my bombs close to the target as we had inappropriately practiced at George AFB. I had lived through a rookie blunder that I would not repeat in the future! I now realized that it was critical to release my ordnance before we were within range of a four-barreled cannon.

We flew directly back to Ubon for a straight-in landing and then signed in at our squadron before debriefing. Major Wilkins observed that we had flown a good mission and he was impressed by the way we had rolled in on the trucks and ignored the steady stream of blistering fireballs arising from the rapid-fire cannons. He was pleased that we had not been deterred by the heavy flak and attacked the convoy in an aggressive manner. However, we provided little assistance to our troops in South Vietnam—we had not destroyed any enemy trucks.

We then debriefed the mission with Wing Intelligence, and I explained how quickly the trucks had vanished into the jungle, although we had completely surprised them. It was interesting to note that the truck convoy was protected with mobile 23mm high fire cannons to prevent low altitude passes on the trucks. I decided that it was going to be an extremely difficult challenge to find and destroy trucks unless we surprised them in an open area with no jungle to hide under. I wondered if there were any open areas along the Ho Chi Minh Trail—I had only seen jungle so far.

Mission Results: 0 trucks. (1+20 night time)

Total Rolling Thunder Mission Results: 0 trucks.

Mission Notes:

-Mu Gia Pass was a narrow 25-mile trail with dense jungle on both sides.

-We had surprised enemy trucks in Mu Gia Pass by flying across Laos on the deck.

-The trucks were protected by rapid firing 23mm cannons.

-23mm guns sprayed a solid stream of fire similar to water coming from a large fire hose.

-Low angle passes would be required to effectively strike trucks.

-Trucks could disappear off the trail in seconds.

5

NORTH VIETNAM LEAGUE DIRECTORY

It was now evident that I was involved in a deadly conflict with weird ground rules. I decided to compare it to other strenuous contests in which I had previously competed. However, now the stakes were immensely higher! This was a match where one error could be fatal, and you were always the visiting team that had to compete on belligerent fields. I learned long ago that it was vital to grasp all the essential ground rules when competing in sports on the road. I recalled the unusual directions we adhered to on the gravel fields in the mining towns of Kellogg and Wallace, Idaho. I realized that it was very important to always comprehend and adhere to the local discipline if one wanted to survive and win the engagement. I decided that it was consequential for me to perceive every facet of this dangerous contest or I could be scratched from the lineup.

The following Directory and Team Roster outlines this contest of life and death.

NORTH VIETNAM LEAGUE (NVL)

OWNERS: Millions of North Vietnam Residents.
 LEAGUE PRESIDENT: Ho Chi Minh
 UMPIRE: Ho Chi Minh
 FANS: Residents of North Vietnam
 CHEERLEADERS AND SUPPLIERS:
 China
 Russia

TEAMS:

Trucks (Moles)
 AAA Sites (Skunks)

Fighter Aircraft (MiGs)
Missiles (SAMs)

PLAYING PARKS for the visiting American League Teams.

-Route Package I: Park located north of DMZ extending to Ron Ferry and open to all visiting American Teams.

-Route Package II: Park located directly North of RPI that extended to Vinh. (U.S. Navy Teams)

-Route Package III: Park located directly North of RPII that extended from Vinh to south of Thanh Hoa. (U.S.Navy Teams)

-Route Package IV: Park located north of RPIII extending from Thanh Hoa to Hanoi. (U.S. Navy Teams)

-Route Package V: Park located in the Northwest portion of North Vietnam (U.S. Air Force Teams).

-Route Package VI: Park located due north of Hanoi and separated into sections A & B.

"A": Air Force Park located due north of Hanoi that extended to the Chinese border and then east to the Northeast Railroad.

"B": Navy Park that extended from the Northeast Railroad to the East Coast.

DESIGNATED PLAYING FIELDS:

Ho Chi Minh Trail
Mu Gia Pass
Dong Hoi
Quang Khe Naval Base and Ferry Crossing.
Ron Ferry
Dien Bien Phu
Northeast Railroad

EQUIPMENT:

Russian MiG 15/17/21 Fighters
100/85mm AAA
37/57mm AAA
23mm AAA
12.7mm Automatic Weapons
Trucks
SA-2 Surface-to-Air Missiles

GROUND MAINTENANCE:

All Residents of North Vietnam

ROLLING THUNDER LEAGUE (RTL)

ROLLING THUNDER: All League Games Played in North Vietnam
   BARREL ROLL LEAGUE: Exhibition Games played in Laos
   OWNERS: American Taxpayers
   LEAGUE PRESIDENT: President Johnson (a.k.a. Target Master)
   LEAGUE SECRETARY: Robert Strange McNamara (a.k.a. Edsel Kid)
   SENIOR MANAGERS: Generals and Admirals
   FIELD MANAGERS: Wing Commanders

MAIN TEAMS:

8th Tactical Fighter Wing (F-4C Phantom II)
   497th Tactical Fighter Squadron (F-4C)—Night Owls
   433rd Tactical Fighter Squadron (F-4C)—Day/Nighters
   555th Tactical Fighter Squadron (F-4C)—Triple Nickel
   355th Tactical Fighter Wing, (F-105)—Takhli Thuds
   388th Tactical Fighter Wing, (F-105)—Korat Thuds

SUBSTITUTES:

B-52 Bombers (Buffs) a.k.a. Heavy Hitters, Home Run Hitters
   B-66 Bombers (Sky Spot)
   KC-135 (Tankers)
   Helicopters (Jolly Green)
   AC-47 Gun Ships (Spooky)
   O-1 (Bird Dog)

EQUIPMENT:

F4C Fighter, a.k.a. Phantom, Hummer, Big Ugly
   F-105 Fighter (Thud)
   Aim-9 Heat seeking air-to-air heat seeking missile. (Sidewinder)
   Aim-7 Radar air-to-air missile. (Sparrow)
   2.75" Rockets
   500/750/1000# Bombs
   CBU-24 Rearward Dispensing Munitions

Napalm
SUU-16 20mm Gattling Gun
SUU-25 Flare Dispenser

MAINTENANCE:

8th Field Maintenance
   8th Armament & Electronics Maintenance Squadron
   408th Munitions Maintenance Squadron
   UMPIRE: Commander 7th Air Force located at Tan Son Nhut Airbase in South Vietnam
   CHEERLEADERS: None available except for long distance telephone operator (Bert)
   HOME PLATE: Ubon Royal Thai Airforce Base
   CLUBHOUSE: Ubon Officers Club.

TEAM ROSTER FOR THE 497TH TFS:

Head Coach—Lt. Colonel James McGuire, Squadron Commander
   Assistant Coach—Major Ralph A. Hoyt, Operations Officer

TEAMMATES:

Major Paul E. Blease
   Major John W. Vogt
   Major Claud A. Wilkins
   Major Dayton W. Ragland (Rags)
   Captain Daniel P. Warwick
   Captain Robert E. McKenzie
   Captain Phillip W. Offill
   Captain Lee M. Brazell (Braz)
   Captain John E. Keating
   Captain Robert J. Frasier
   Captain Thomas S. Dewberry
   Captain Val R. Johnson
   Captain Richard L. Penn (RL)
   Captain Rodger H. Jaquith (Jake)
   Captain Richard A. Wade (Dick)
   Captain John B. Olson (Ole)
   Captain Jack L. Moore

Captain William F. Mickelson
Captain Kenneth D. Robinson
Lt. William E. McGourin (Bill)
Lt. Edward M. Collins Jr.
Lt. John W. Newhouse
Lt. George H. Lippemeier
Lt. Joseph T. Kirkby
Lt. Ned R. Herrold
Lt. Michael J. Peters
Lt. Edward G. Marcato
Lt. Benjamin B. Finzer
Lt. George M. Hardwick (Mac)
Lt. Patrick F. Riley
Lt. Jimmy P. Roberts
Lt. Allen C. Pollard (Crash)
Lt. Wilson H. Parma (Willie)
Lt. Sammie D. Hoff

ROLLING THUNDER LEAGUE RULES

1. All contests are played in the NVL Parks and on their playing fields.

2. MiG Teams protected and never intervened with on their home fields.

3. The Target Master will designate all parks, playing fields, and targets.

4. NVL residents, buildings and large ships are not to be attacked.

5. RTL competitors are not allowed within 25 miles of Chinese border in Route Package VI or 30 miles in Route Package V.

6. A 30-mile prohibited flying ring protects Hanoi.

7. A 10-mile prohibited flying ring protects Haiphong.

8. Day and night engagements scheduled for every day of the year.

9. No time limits imposed for ending league competition.

10. The Hanoi Clubhouse and Haiphong Harbor are off-limits for visiting teams.

I decided that the numerous AAA emplacements would be treated like vicious skunks as I had learned years before in Idaho that you might be sprayed when you confronted the nasty vermin. It was almost impossible to see the little black and white critters at night and it was always a no-win situation when you tried to go head-to-head with a disagreeable skunk in the dark. I had learned the hard way to tread cautiously and always protect your rear when in the company of belligerent skunks, or you could be sprayed in a way never forgotten.

I resolved that searching for elusive trucks on small dirt trails was like trying to locate the miserable resident moles that had nearly demolished my stateside yard by employing a vast maze of underground tunnels. I could always discover where the devious moles were working or their trails, but it was impossible to catch the little bastards no matter what I tried. Once I was lucky and surprised a cowardly mole constructing an underground trail but the black nuisance disappeared in a heartbeat before I could attack him. I had to admit that I was never able to catch a glimpse of a timid mole, much less strike the critter, during many day and night missions to my yard. It had always been my fervent desire to kill one of those elusive pests, but they always disappeared down a trail or found a hiding place before I could attack. Very few things in life have ever upset me, but trying to destroy my resident moles was one of the most undesirable contests that I had ever attempted—it never failed to get me chaffed. I was positive that searching for elusive trucks was similar to hunting for shifty moles.

MARCH 15, 1966

My squadron granted me the night off with an exemption from all duties but I would rather have flown a mission for a counter. I walked over to the Officers Club, after sunset, for dinner instead of my usual breakfast and then tried to drum up a game of Bridge. I joined Major Dayton W. Ragland (Rags) and his rear seat pilot, Lt. Ned R. Herrold, for the evening meal and then enjoyed a scrumptious piece of cherry pie with tasty vanilla ice cream. I had known Rags from the good old days in Spain when we both lived in the Bachelor Officers Quarters at Torrejon Air Base. He was the only black fighter pilot in our squadron and maybe the entire Wing. I informed Rags that no one had stolen his Oldsmobile "98" because it was still sitting in the Officers Club parking lot at George AFB.

Rags and I had attended Army Jump School together at Fort Benning, Georgia last July. The Tactical Air Command had directed each F-4C fighter squadron to provide four jump qualified pilot forward air controllers (FACs) to the Army when required. The Squadron volunteered me to attend this tough, demanding school because I was single and had stayed in good physical condition. Rags had not been required to attend the school, he was a field grade officer, but he had volunteered to go anyway. I observed that Rags had always done more than was required of him and was always upbeat about life, with an exceptional sense of humor.

Rags was the only pilot that I had ever met who had flown against Russian MiG fighters—he had flown missions during the Korean War. He told me about a MiG 15 that had stealthily maneuvered into his deep six position and then shot him down during an air battle in Korea. He said that he had never seen the MiG that had destroyed his F-86 fighter with cannon fire and caused him to eject over enemy terrain. Rags was subsequently captured and compelled to spend 600 days as a prisoner of war (POW). It was not in his nature to be a complacent prisoner so Rags was placed in a "Recalcitrant Camp" and tortured. I personally felt that it was not appropriate for the Air Force to have ordered him to another war in the Far East—he had certainly paid his dues.

We enjoyed conversing about the uncomfortable days training at the Army Parachute Jump School together during a hot Georgia summer that was subsequently cooled by a hurricane. I had been harassed as though I was a buck private by all the enlisted drill instructors despite being an Air Force Captain. I recalled my last training jump where the Army required everyone to wear full field equipment and strap a rifle to your leg. I remembered that it had been such a relief to finally leap out of the ancient Air National Guard C-119—I had my doubts about its ability to remain airborne. It was just my luck to find that my chute had opened directly over a large bonfire that marked the center of the jump zone. I tried to maneuver the chute, as we had been taught, but I was never able to change the direction of any Army chute no matter how hard I tried. My descent was taking me directly down toward the fire and I was so concerned that I had forgotten to release the rifle, which could have resulted in a broken leg upon landing. It certainly appeared to me that I was going to be severely burned when I landed on the bonfire. However, the rising heat from the fire suddenly stopped my descent and carried me safely away from the danger where I touched down gently without even leaving my feet. That was my final day with the Army, and I had happily returned to George AFB, pleased to be free of the Army aggravations. We still had to retain our paratroop currency, by making additional jumps but now we leaped from a modern C-130 aircraft onto the soft sand at El Centro Navy base.

I left Rags and located several teammates in the Clubhouse game room that were amenable to a basketball scrimmage on a small cement court across the street near the contaminated swimming pool. It was a good feeling to experience a hard physical workout before the sun set and then to enjoy a long cool shower. I still wanted to find something to do for the rest of night—the movie in the old church was not worth seeing. I wandered back to the Clubhouse and joined five of my teammates from Spain for a poker game until the sun arose.

MARCH 16, 1966

Crash and Braz decided to show me the town of Ubon since we were free of squadron duties. They knew how to find a restaurant that was approved by the base flight surgeon, which meant he had inspected it. The restaurant might have met the medical sanitary rules but we had no idea about what kind of meat was served, it could have been dog, water buffalo or even snake. I was not interested in knowing what it was, as long as it tasted good and would not give me the trots. The town employed a daily bus system to transport Thai workers to and from the base, and it was available to us for a few baht. We only had to wait a few minutes for a colorful bus that stopped just outside the main gate. The motor coach was not crowded, and we each located a small seat before the driver set course for the town of Ubon, which was not far away. The bus route followed a small dirt road that was bordered by endless rice patties where numerous local farmers were tending their crops. We finally reached the small town after a dusty and bouncy ride on the rough thoroughfare.

The modest restaurant in Ubon was better than I had expected with a pleasant atmosphere and clean tables with metal utensils. The waiter was friendly and seemed happy to see us, or maybe it was just our American money. The restaurant was busy but the service was superb, and our meals arrived quickly. The food was hot and spicy with tasty rice and vegetables along with delicious tender meat. However, the meat was definably not beef or chicken but something left to the imagination. The restaurant even had an enjoyable floorshow, which we greatly appreciated, and we left a nice tip for the excellent waiters.

We spent the rest of the evening racing around Ubon in little Thai taxies called Samlars. They were three wheeled pedal cycles that were pumped by a young Thai with very strong legs. The Thai drivers probably thought we were crazy Americans from a different world with strange diversions but they also seemed to enjoy racing. The drivers really got into the competition when we bet on the outcomes and gave the winning Thai some of the loot. We also presented each of them with a very large tip after we finished our racing—it was probably more than they earned in a week.

We returned to our Base via the same multi-colored bus that had carried us to town. Braz observed that the passenger bus was similar to those we had seen and ridden on in Spain. We had both enjoyed all the wonderful diverse areas of Spain with its many delightful festivals. We also attended many bullfights together and then went Tosco hopping in old Madrid. The small rough road to the base also reminded us of driving on many of the ancient bumpy roadways in Spain for almost three years.

I recalled that I had purchased a new 1962 Corvair Monza, before leaving Texas for Madrid, in November 1961. I drove it thousands of miles around Spain on some of the roughest roads imaginable and never had a problem. The Corvair handled the uneven cobble stone roads of Madrid, and the numerous deep potholes of the rugged country roads through out Spain, with ease. It was a great time in my life when I motored to southern Spain and enjoyed the beautiful beaches near Marbella and Benedorm. It was also pleasant to drive north in the summer to the cool green mountains near San Sabastian. Dick Westerhoff and I had a noteworthy excursion when we loaded the Corvair with vino de casa and celebrated at the "Running of the Bulls" Festival in Pamplona. The little Monza also carried me safely in comfort to festivals in Valencia and Barcelona that were located on the East Coast of Spain. It was a sad time when I sold the trusty little Corvair to the Spanish Government, at the end of my tour in Spain, but I received more money for el coche than it had cost new in Texas. I changed the pesetas to English pounds and ordered a XKE Jaguar from the factory in England for shipment directly to California.

MARCH 17, 1966
ROLLING THUNDER MISSION #2

The 497th scheduled us for a Pack One contest near Dong Hoi on the coast just north of the DMZ. Major Wilkins would lead our flight on a route recce mission that started south of Mu Gia Pass and continued to the Dong Hoi on the coast. Our bird was loaded with six five hundred-pound bombs and our leader carried the standard two flare pods and six rocket pods. Wing Intel dug up some old photos of the area around Dong Hoi for us and then voiced a canned briefing that warned aircrews about multiple 37/57 AAA in the area.

The twilight was rapidly fading during the thirty-minute flight to the coast but it was sufficient to allow us to observe the little dirt road winding through the countryside on its way to the ocean. The trail was well graded and in excellent condition but there was no sign of vehicular traffic on the road. It seemed strange to know that we were in a war but there was no evidence of a single destroyed truck along the route. Bill assured me that both of our squadrons had been bombing the road every night but there were no craters to be seen. It was eerie to fly over unfamiliar darkening countryside and never see a glimmer of light or any indication of movement on the ground. It appeared that all the local residents were extremely well conditioned to nightly battles on their fields and they remained out of sight. Even the Skunk Teams seemed to be avoiding our Rolling Thunder League (RTL) event tonight as they refused to enter the contest by tossing a few sizzling fireballs.

Owl lead illuminated the road leading north from Dong Hoi that traversed through abundant rice patties. We were lucky as we saw a lone truck driving south on a small dirt road with no foliage for cover. Lead immediately cleared me to attack the speeding mole that had no tall grass to hide under and wisely decided to make a run for it. The driver instantly put the pedal to the floor and high tailed down the road like a startled deer in an open field heading for cover. I was mindful of the fact that it was going to be a challenge to get my pipper on a speeding truck—the winds were unknown and the vehicle appeared to be accelerating nicely. I had to give the surprised driver his due as he could have abandoned his truck and taken shelter in the rice fields. I might have had a slim chance of hitting the truck if the driver had stopped, but it was not possible to whack a moving truck at night with high unknown winds. I tried to extend our bomb pattern by dropping them in the "singles" switch setting that presented a larger kill area but the wind carried them far to the right of the truck. I speculated that there might be several fighter pilots in the world that could hit a speeding truck at night with bombs but I was most definitely not one of them. I may have had a chance to hit the truck if Big Ugly was equipped with an internal gattling gun that could be directed on a moving object. I felt that all our bombs should be delivered to the Thud Teams as the F-105s had a bomb bay and were armed with an internal gun for backup when the bombs missed.

The flares extinguished before lead could make a rocket pass, but I figured the accelerating mole had most likely reached a dark hole at the DMZ by now. Major Wilkins fired his rockets into a suspected molehill (truck park) as designated by the Umpire—I doubted if my swift elusive mole was hiding there. It appeared to me that the only way to hit a truck at night was to attack close to the target by flying under the flares with area coverage ordnance. I might have been able to destroy the truck with a 20mm gattling gun, but it was impossible for me to ever hit a running mole at night using unguided bombs.

I had no idea about what possessed the truck driver to keep hauling ass, but I was definitely impressed with his determined attitude. It might be a tough formidable task trying to defeat a country where the residents were willing to sacrifice their life carrying supplies to their troops in the South. I was dispirited to realize that we had not helped our ground fighters in South Vietnam, though I had tried my best using ordnance that was not designed for destroying trucks at night.

I signed our squadron score sheet after we returned and noticed that we had been scheduled for another league contest with Major Wilkins tomorrow night in the Pack One Park. We debriefed with Wing Intel and I explained that we tried to bomb a lone truck speeding through the rice patties but the driver had outrun my bombs. I had not been successful during my first two missions over North Vietnam.

Mission Results: 0 trucks. (1+40 night)

RTL Summary: 0 trucks.

Mission Notes:

-Speeding trucks could easily outrun bombs.

-Package One trails were maintained in superb condition with no craters visible.

-There was no evidence of any destroyed vehicles on the Ho Chi Minh Trail.

6

MARCH 18, 1966
LOW LEVEL ATTACK ON THE QUANG KHE FERRY
ROLLING THUNDER MISSION #3

The Squadron Commanders had recently briefed their aircrews that aircraft commanders were not being sufficiently aggressive during missions over North Vietnam. In response to this criticism, Bill and I decided that we would fly an extremely offensive mission, as we would have sufficient daylight for an attack on the Quang Khe Ferry. The ferry crossing was located in the Pack One Park north of Dong Hoi, where the coastal road crossed a river. I decided to take my 8mm Cannon camera, that I had purchased at the Torrejon Base Exchange in Spain, to record our exploits on this mission.

Bill and I convinced our Flight Commander that we should attack the Quang Khe ferry crossing on the deck, as our aircraft was loaded with a new low level ordnance—two cluster bomb units (CBU-24s). I had never operated this ordnance, but I knew that it was an expensive piece of equipment. The weapon was a streamlined canister with multiple tubes in the rear that dispensed 600 golf-ball size bomblets. Each deadly bomblet would explode and expel 300 lethal steel balls when they contacted the ground. The ordnance manual indicated that the ordnance could be employed at an altitude of 50 to 500 feet above ground level, with speeds up to 600 knots, that resulted in a pattern about 30X400 meters long. The manual recommended a release altitude of 100 feet at 450 knots but I decided to fly at a higher speed if we were taking fire. I figured that we would be flying at over 500 knots, if our "Hummer" would go that fast, with all the external drag from fuel tanks and ordnance. It was critical to maintain a straight and level attitude while dispensing the ordnance because it was possible for the bomblets to strike our birds tail if we experienced negative G's.

Major Wilkins decided that our flight would remain on the deck, after we crossed into Laos, so we might have a chance to surprise some trucks at the cross-

67

ing. Owl Lead indicated they would complete a pass on the ferry to search for trucks, and then maneuver to fire their rockets after we completed our low-level run. I looked forward to crossing Laos on the deck in the daylight but would avoid Tchepone—I respected the exceptional skill of the deadly resident skunk den located there. It would be delightful to fly in the daytime for a change of pace and not be in violation of some wretched Air Force directive for flying too low.

We blasted off from Home Plate on time and descended to tree top level once we crossed the Mekong. Our low level flight through Laos was exhilarating as the karst (vertical limestone rocks) were dramatic and not one sinister skunk attempted a quick spray shot at us as we cruised along at 360 knots ground speed. The spectacular mountains appeared to have granite rocks embedded in the steep sides that were covered with exquisite dense green jungle. I speculated that it would be impossible to travel on foot for even a few yards in such rocky impenetrable terrain. I decided to remain where I landed, if I had to eject, and hope that the rescue troops could quickly locate me. I would not attempt to move in such forbidding terrain! I had no idea about how the natives could travel in Laos unless they were using hidden trails.

We maintained a position about five miles behind lead using our radar to paint his bird. It was remarkably easy to locate Lead Owl visually by searching for the profuse black exhaust that emanated from his engines. The discernible dark smoke trail made me realize that we might not surprise any trucks. I speculated that lookouts were probably posted on hilltops and could see us coming long before we ever neared the mountains separating Laos from North Vietnam. We flew approximately 300 feet above the jungle until we reached the mountains on the border where we popped up to clear the ridge and then flew down the backside into North Vietnam. I immediately rolled inverted upon clearing the mountain peak and then pulled our nose down toward the valley floor in an attempt to remain close to the ground.

We received a rude greeting from the NVL residents when the valley erupted with white sparkling flashes from automatic weapons fire. It looked as though every hostile Fan in the area had a weapon and was letting us know that we were not welcome. I immediately climbed above 1500 feet, to avoid the small arms fire until we were ready for our bomb run. It was obvious that me that we had not surprised the angry farmers since every one seemed to have an automatic weapon to fire at us. I had never seen so many sparklers going off since the last Fourth of July and this dramatic show was just for us.

I lost sight of our leader after clearing the mountain range but I could still see his ever-present smoke trail. Bill voiced a heading that would take us directly to the ferry. A few minutes later I was able to see the ocean and the river leading to the Quang Khe ferry complex. I finally located our leader visually when the sky ahead erupted with red tracers followed by little black bursts of flak. It was obvious that our leader had arrived at the ferry because every pissed off skunk den was hurling sizzling fireballs at his bird. We were amazed to see the tremendous firepower unfolding before our eyes—we had thought there would just be a few gun emplacements around the ferry. The enemy had my full attention, as soon it would be our turn to compete with all those unfriendly skunk teams. I had always wondered what it would be like to fly through dense flak, like I had seen in the movies, and now I would have a precarious opportunity. There was no retreat; it was my conviction that a fighter pilot would rather go down in flames than have his peers think that he never had the balls to do his job. There was no place in the fighter community for a weenie that could not stomach whatever the enemy had to offer. Now it was our turn to take the field against the vicious Skunk Teams that wanted to strike us out. I was going to push our "Hummer" to its limit in an attempt to avoid the blistering red fireballs that the wicked stinkers were going to throw at us.

I pushed the "Hummers" throttles up to full military power, while slowly descending, we wanted to be at around one hundred feet AGL for the final run. The airspeed was over 500 knots when we leveled and visually acquired the road leading to the ferry crossing. All the Skunk Teams had now switched their attention to our lonely owl and heavy stinker piss flashed all around us. Wing Intelligence had not informed us that there would be so many gun emplacements but we had to face the situation—we were committed to our run. We planned to fly down the small road going through the village to the ferry. I would start dispensing our bomblets before we arrived at the ferry and continue dropping even as we crossed the river since there might be an underwater crossing. I would continue releasing ordnance on the other side of the ferry in case there were some concealed trucks waiting to cross the river.

The numerous 37/57mm skunk dens were certainly aware of our presence as flaming tracers sprayed past both sides of our speeding "Hummer". I tried to jink left and right in an attempt to confuse the offensive skunks and prevent them from pulling lead on us. It was very discouraging to see red and yellow fireballs coming up ahead of our flight path because that meant they were seasoned stinkers and pulling lead on us. I had never seen yellow flak before! I had no idea what kind of AAA site was firing them since I could not spy any gun emplacements. I remained directly over the small dirt road leading to the ferry crossing, while flying straight and level, so I could safely release the bomblets. It was time for a gut check! I knew that it was going to be very dangerous since the hurtful skunk dens now had a bird flying in a straight line. The enemy gunners could draw a steady bead on us—we could not maneuver while dispensing the bomblets.

I questioned if the CBU dispenser had been designed by an astute weapons engineer for firepower demonstrations in the States where no one shot at you. It was not possible to change our flight path once we started releasing the bomblets because they could strike our tail if I did not remain straight and level. Bill and I were in a quandary! We needed to avoid the flak, but it was impossible to maneuver or we would shoot ourselves down. I was not pleased with the crafty weapons expert who had designed equipment that made us an easy target for enemy gunners. I mused that we were also at fault for not considering what could happen when using CBUs in a heavily defended area! However, Wing Intelligence had not sufficiently informed us about the numerous AAA sites around Quang Khe. It was unfortunate that our experienced teammates had never warned us about using this weapon in a combat situation but maybe no one had ever used this dispenser in a war.

Our "Hummer" leveled and now I was using the radar altimeter to maintain about 100 feet AGL over the road-leading northeast to the ferry crossing. I depressed and continued to hold the bomb release button as we approached the ferry crossing. I had to avoid negative Gs because we could not afford to let a bomblet strike our tail. I was not pleased to see that the stinkers were walking their deadly fireballs close to our aircraft. It was disturbing to watch the murderous tracers flash by our canopy! It was necessary to grit my teeth as I really wanted to maneuver away from the flak, but we had to keep the wings level while the bomblets spewed out. Still it was comforting to realize that we could probably make it to the Gulf, if a vile skunk got lucky with a golden fireball. I was gratified when the lethal tracers started to fade away after we crossed over the river. I released the bomb button and turned sharply toward the ocean after I was reasonably sure the bomblets had stopped dispensing.

I popped up to five thousand feet to take us out of range of the hostile skunk dens and then we looked back to see the results of our attack. We could see black smoke rising from the road surface and over the water from the bomblets. We had not seen a truck, ferry, or any sign of life during our run but there had been a zillion AAA sites firing at us. I told Bill that I could not believe the number of sizzling tracers we had seen flashing all around us while we made our run.

I realized that I was electrified during our attack! Never in my life had I ever experienced such exhilaration and a sense of invincibility. It was fascinating to watch the murderous red and yellow fireballs flash by our canopy during our attack! I had not been scared during the battle, although the lethal flak was only a few feet away. It was like being in another dimension where I could just watch the action unfold and have no fear of being harmed. I had never felt such a profound rush that resulted in an ultimate high; an exhilarating and bizarre experience for me!

I found myself wanting to repeat this strange intense awesome feeling of elation again! I asked Bill if he wanted to go back for another attack, although we had expended all of our ordnance. Bill must have been feeling the same euphoria because he readily agreed to reverse course for another ferocious airing. We radioed Lead Owl that we were going back down, which caused concern, as he thought we had taken a hit and were plunging due to flak damage. We immediately informed Major Wilkins that we were OK and would fly along the river toward the west to hunt possible targets for him to strike. We again descended to 100 feet AGL to fly a low level run over the river, so we could search for ferries or barges

The ferry crossing was still delineated with blue smoke and it was even rising up from our expenditures over the water. We looked long and hard at the ferry complex, during our decent, but we never noticed any movement in the area. We thought that we might have noticed a few camouflaged trucks along the road, or maybe an underwater crossing, but we had not seen anything during our run. We flew along the river heading west and the wretched stinkers were anxious to have another go at us, but now we could maneuver to avoid their spray. The sun was setting over a river that appeared to be calm and peaceful. We ignored the numerous flashing tracers around us—they were of no concern because we felt invincible.

I could see a multitude of solitary fishermen in little dark wooden boats on the river that flowed from the mountains to the ocean. Sizzling fireballs continued to streak by the canopy, from dangerous skunk dens on both sides of the river, but we could not see the deadly sites—their camouflage was too effective. We continued to maneuver along the river looking for trucks or barges. I was forced to execute a steep turn directly over the river to avoid numerous red fireballs coming from a 23mm gun emplacement located ahead of us. We were approximately 100 feet above the water and in a precipitous steep bank to the right when I flew directly over one of the little black wooden boats. I found myself looking down into the calm face of a solitary fisherman standing erect in his tiny boat while pulling in a fish net. He appeared unafraid of us, continued to hold his little net, and stared up at our aircraft. He was looking directly at me. It had only taken a few seconds to complete my steep turn but there was ample time to behold his face. It appeared that he was looking directly at my head during our maneuver.

This was the first time that I had actually seen the enemy and it was an extraordinary experience! It was mysterious and fascinating that I could undergo such an unforgettable event during a steep high G turn while flying more than 500 knots. It was one of those inexplicable moments when God appeared to make time stand still. I was granted the opportunity to record a breathtaking scene that I would be able to relive forever. The tranquil fisherman's expression seemed to insinuate that I was just an uncalled-for nuisance, and not welcome. He seemed to imply that I had no right to frighten fish that his family needed. I could not see any anger or fear in his expression but simply a look of indifference that seemed to imply that he wanted to be left in peace. Our speeding aircraft was obviously an irritant to his way of life. We were affecting his ability to feed his family. I speculated that it might be very difficult to conquer a country with residents that were not threatened or concerned by our presence. The little fisherman indicated to me that I had no business stirring up a ruckus while flying over his country. I also questioned what I was doing here—he had not appeared to be one of the "Bad People" that wanted to harm our country. Maybe God was sending me a compassionate message that I might come to understand as this strange conflict unfolded. I departed the unruffled fisherman and continued our low level run up the river towards the west to look for ferries or barges. I was sure that I would never forget my encounter with the man and his boat.

We resumed our wild flight down the river. I spotted a large dark green truck parked under a tall tree, but it would have been impossible to describe the location to Lead Owl. Major Wilkins finally fired his rockets on a suspected gun emplacement, but I never caught sight of a single sinister skunk den. We popped up to ten thousand feet for the return to Home Plate. I radioed Major Wilkins that we would eventually join them somewhere over Laos. I turned the flight controls over to Bill as we slowly joined on lead for the hung ordnance check that would require a flashlight.

The euphoria from the mission was beginning to wear off, and I realized how lucky we had been. I remembered reading a book titled "The War Lover", about a pilot's love for war. I now understood how the adrenaline from close encounters with death resulted in feelings of euphoria. Maybe the Big Boss was riding shotgun because we had completed an insane mission without getting taking a hit from thousands of deadly fireballs. I realized that I had never used my camera and vowed that I would not carry it again—it might be a flak magnet.

I was gratified to relax while Bill executed our night approach to Home Plate. I was completely drained of all emotion and eager for a cold brew at the Clubhouse. I knew that I would never forget the expression on the little fisherman's face as he stood in his small dark wooden boat with his net. I decided that trying to achieve high rushes of adrenaline might shorten my life span. I conceived that it was not smart to be the proverbial "moth to the flame".

Major Wilkins had been very impressed with our aggressive attack on the ferry crossing. He was pleased as he watched us make our low level bombing run through dense flak without maneuvering. He was going to nominate us for a Distinguished Flying Cross for completing a dangerous low level attack while under heavy fire on a major ferry complex. I never mentioned that we had no idea there were so many gun emplacements around Quang Khe, as we had never flown in that region during the day. It was a real revelation and an exciting mission for Bill and me. We had thought it would be a routine day contest with minimal Skunk Team participation while hunting for moles.

We debriefed with Wing Intel and enlightened them with the fact that numerous 37/57mm-gun emplacements protected the Quang Khe ferry crossing. I pointed out that our Intel experts had briefed that we would only encounter light AAA fire near the ferry. Neither Bill nor I had realized, while planning this mission that flying a low level constrained pass might be very dangerous. Now I grasped the fact that Wing Intel would never have the latest information on enemy defenses as the situation was apparently changing daily.

Mission Results: 0 trucks. (1+00 day & +45 night)

RTL Summary: 0 trucks.

Mission Notes:

-The enemy probably used mountain lookouts to spot our highly visible smoke trails.

-It might be impossible to spot camouflaged AAA sites while flying very fast.

-Cluster bomb units (CBUs) were hazardous to employ in heavily defended areas.

-Adrenaline rushes during heat-of-the-battle contests are perilous to your health.

-Every resident in North Vietnam appears to possess an automatic weapon with plenty of ammo.

-It was not wise to fly low-level attacks in heavily defended areas during the day.

MARCH 19, 1966
ROLLING THUNDER MISSION #4

Our squadron assigned us a mission that required air-to-air refueling near Udorn before we flew into Pack Five. The battle was to take place in the Red River Valley north of Dien Bien Phu and west of Hanoi. I felt that it would be interesting to fly over this area. I recalled reading about how the North Vietnamese had defeated the French Army around Dien Bien Phu. We had to fly over several mountain ranges in our designated territory that extended from the Chinese border towards Hanoi. Bill implied that the Thuds used the far side of this ridge to help protect their birds from AAA when they attacked targets near Hanoi. The ridge, about 1700 meters high, afforded some protection to their aircraft—they had named it "Thud Ridge". I seriously doubted there would be any Thud teammates in the area because they preferred to leave the after dark conflicts to Night Owls.

We would hook-up with a KC-135 tanker near Udorn that had flown to Thailand from Clark Air Force Base in the Philippines. Years earlier, I recalled watching the weighty tankers stagger off the runway in Torrejon, Spain as our hangar was at the departure end of the field when we pulled five-minute alert. I felt that the Tanker Teams were gutsy teammates since a fully loaded bird was carrying l00, 000 pounds of JP-4. They also routinely applied water injection to their jets in order to become airborne before they reached the overrun. I had not participated with a KC-135 for over a year, but I was looking forward to refueling, though I might be a tad rusty.

Major Wilkins was loaded with the standard rockets, flares, and centerline fuel tank. Our Phantom carried the usual six 750 pound bombs that were always a challenge for me to drop anywhere within a mile of a truck. The refueling track was about 200 miles due north of Ubon, which allowed Bill stick time during our loose formation with lead Owl. The airfield at Udorn was also designated an emergency landing base, as the 555th TFS was flying day missions from the field.

We departed Ubon about ten minutes before sunset, which allowed time to locate the tanker before it was too dark. Lead finally called a radar contact on the tanker when we were close to Udorn. I noticed that Bill had also painted the KC-135 on our radar display. Major Wilkins requested the tanker to initiate a turn when we were less than ten miles away, which brought our flight to the stern position for a quick join up on the tanker's wing. Lead was immediately cleared into the refueling position; we took the tanker's right wing to await our turn. Owl lead had air refueled many times during the last three months and quickly topped off his tanks. I received clearance to the refueling position once lead finished and moved to the tanker's left wing. I activated the air-refueling switch and Bill acknowledged that our receptacle, located just behind his canopy, was open.

I had learned to stay in the correct stationary position by concentrating on the refueling operator's window. The boom operator (boomer) was usually an enlisted sergeant who lay flat on his stomach in a little compartment just under the tankers tail section. All the boomers that I had encountered were very proficient and took great pride in their ability to safely transfer fuel at up to 6,000 pounds a minute into the small F-4 refueling receptacle. The KC-135 also had indicator lights on the forward portion of their fuselage to help position refueling aircraft, but I never liked to use those indicators. Bill could also voice refueling instructions when necessary—he had a good view of the booms colored indicator markings from the rear seat. I looked forward to the challenge of refueling, after a long dry spell, and I was determined to do well.

I had discovered that I really enjoyed air refueling because it allowed me a chance to fly slot formation on the tanker. I recalled that my flight commander, during my tour in Spain, had permitted me fly the F-102 in the slot position when we maneuvered in a diamond formation. Captain Ted Fisher would gather three other members of his flight in a diamond formation for a low altitude pass down the Torrejon runway to provide a little "show time". The slot position was fairly demanding since you had to keep perfect position on lead and avoid hitting the other aircraft positioned on each wing. I loved the challenge of flying in a perfect position during this formation but realized that I would suffer sarcasm from my peers if I made an error.

I was pleased to get back into the air-refueling groove, and made contact without any problems. Our thirsty bird received a drink that consisted of thousands of gallons of JP-4 to refill our fuel tanks. We needed all the fuel that we could hold for this long mission. It was over 500 miles from Dien Bien Phu to Ubon and our flight would not be refueling on the way back. Lead moved back into the refueling position after I repositioned on the tanker's right wing. Major Wilkins topped off his tanks again as he had less fuel since he only carried a centerline tank—we had two wing tanks.

Lead completed his final refueling, thanked the Tanker Team for giving our parched owls a long drink, before calling us to the combat control frequency. Our flight crossed the border into Laos near Vientiane. We then continued across the Plaine des Jarres, en route to Dien Bien Phu. The sun had set and it was growing dark when we crossed into the northwestern portion of North Vietnam.

We finally approached the area known as Thud Ridge, but there was no sign of any lights on the ground or hostile fireballs from bad-tempered skunks.

Owl lead flared the road that extended from the Chinese border to Hanoi but the trail was deserted. I was not surprised since the drivers had plenty of time to clear the trail. We assumed the enemy radar had tracked our approach since we had remained at fifteen thousand feet for most of the flight. The terrain was completely black with no evidence of light coming from any of the towns in Pack Five. We had sufficient fuel to use the flares sparsely while we hunted for elusive moles along the road leading to Hanoi. Bill flew the bird and I concentrated on searching the road for trucks but there was no visible movement anywhere. The trail was in excellent shape with no evidence of any craters or damaged vehicles. We were possibly flying over many trucks, AAA sites, and road maintenance crews, but they were well hidden. It was almost disappointing that none of the Skunk Teams wanted to compete so we could at least drop our bombs on their field. I was troubled that I had not been able to spot any skunk dugouts.

We finally had to give up our search when the last of our night-lights illuminated with no sign of an elusive mole. We were forced to dispense our bombs and Lead's rockets on a suspected truck park that was designated by our Umpire. I felt that it was a huge waste of time and effort to come all this way to compete on a distant field and never even meet the opposing teams. I wondered if the opposing competitors were laughing at us when we dispersed all our ordnance on a deserted molehill, after hauling them for hundreds of miles. I tried to speculate on the cost of our ineffective contest, but the numbers were too immense for me to compute. The enemy probably thought that we were idiots without a game plan. How were we ever going to win a contest in their park?

We joined for the hung ordnance check before Bill flew the bird back to Ubon. I was disgusted after completing our long mission to hunt for trucks that remained hidden in the jungle. I thought that we would never discover any vehicles in Pack Five—there was too much jungle for cover. I mused that this was a strange conflict. I had no idea on how we were going to win any contests to help end this war. I was convinced in my own mind that it was inconceivable for any teammate to hit a truck at night with an iron bomb.

Mission Result: 0 trucks. (+10 day & 2+00 night)

RTL Summary: 0 trucks.

Mission Notes:

-I believed that it was extremely time consuming and expensive to compete in Pack Five.

-Our flight had not observed any targets of significance in the Pack Five Park.

MARCH 20, 1966

I was not placed in the lineup, which allowed me to play Bridge with Crash until the sun arose and won $1.25. It was too hot to stay in bed after 1000 hours, so I walked over to the Clubhouse to take advantage of the excellent air conditioning. I was pleasantly surprised to see the Club was serving an excellent buffet that offered beef, ham, and chicken. There was ice cream on the menu, which was always a nice treat because it was only served three to four times a week. The Club bakers were excellent and displayed an admirable assortment of pies, breads, and very tasty sweet rolls. The pineapple was not comparable to the sweet Hawaiian harvest, but I was pleased that fresh fruit was usually available each day.

It was St. Patrick's Day and the OClub was pouring expensive name brand hard liquor for ten-cents to relish along with the tasty buffet. I was not a big boozer but decided to sample several dime drinks since I was not on the flying schedule. I ordered a shot of Canadian Club mixed in a large glass of Seven Up with ice that I could sip on for a long time. I would never forget that I had a bad experience with vodka during an outdoor party when I was a sophomore in high school. One of my older classmates had gotten a fifth of Smirnoff for me and I had proceeded to show off by quickly drinking two large paper cups of the potent liquor. It was not long until I was seeing double and feeling no pain. My friends drove me home and placed me in my bed, which fortunately was in our basement with a private side entrance—it was a miserable long night! I had gotten very sick and tried to drink buckets of water until I finally fell asleep. That was the last time I had drunk any hard liquor in high school.

It was easy to avoid intoxicating beverages in college because I seldom had extra money for even a single beer. I had enjoyed drinking glasses of sangria in ancient bodegas that I discovered in the spirited caves under the Plaza Mayor in old Madrid. I was always delighted to pause at outdoor cafés for cheese and wine when I toured around Spain. I had drunk sumptuous wine in many commendable restaurants in Europe. The wine was excellent when I visited very old vineyards in Spain, France, and Germany. However, I preferred to order the house wine or a pitcher of sangria along with a serving of an appetizing local cheese.

I departed the boisterous buffet and walked to the unoccupied library to read the latest war news. The newsmagazines appeared to have various writers that were experts on all aspects of the conflict. I found it interesting to read about McNamara's views on the war—he indicated that it could go on for months or years. He stated that the air campaign in the North was mainly an effort to interdict lines of communication and military traffic in an effort to assist the ground war in the south. I was not aware of any lines of communication in North Vietnam unless he was referring to a maze of small dirt roads. I had the impression that no one was aware of the fact that it was very difficult, if not impossible, to halt trucks that quickly disappeared into the jungle. I speculated that McNamara never had a clue about hunting trucks on the Ho Chi Minh Trail or what was really taking place over here. I was not aware of a single Senior Manager that had ever visited our squadron to observe or hear what fighter pilots had to say about the war.

MARCH 21, 1966

I decided to visit the air-conditioned library again since I was still off the flying schedule and it was hot and humid. I found that it was impossible to get the vision of the little dark haired fisherman out of my mind. It was the first time that I had actually seen the enemy and the revelation was not going away. I tended to think of trucks as inanimate objects with no humans involved—no different from our practice targets in the States. It was difficult for me to rationalize what we were doing in this poor country—I was not sure that these were the "Bad People". Nonetheless, I knew that the resident farmers would most likely kill me if I had to eject. I was convinced that everyone in North Vietnam seemed to posses a weapon except the fishermen on the river. I realized that it was important to assist the ground troops fighting for their life in South Vietnam. I wanted to do everything possible to aid them during my tour. It was going to be a long miserable war that was too complicated for me to understand. Maybe I would figure it out when I had more missions under my belt.

I learned that RL Penn and Lee Brazell had volunteered to fly with our Thud teammates to make movies for the Fans back in the States. They flew from Ubon to Takhli Air Base, briefed with the F-105 Teams, and then followed a flight of Thuds to their assigned target. They chased the pointy nosed competitors in close trail formation to an assigned target and then took pictures of the bombs striking the ground. I could understand that RL would think that this was an important exciting contest, but I thought Braz had more sense. This was not the kind of sport that I would want to participate in, although all the missions were flown during the day.

I asked RL why he had volunteered for this mission that he labeled a "Kamarakazi" event. He told me that our Navy teammates had taken movies for the High Rollers that displayed all kinds of action and now the Air Force had to join the road show. The Umpire requested RL and Braz to take pictures of bombs actually hitting targets—aircraft dropping ordnance were unable to accomplish this feat without running into the ground. RL perfected his own method of film-ing the bomb's impact by attempting to delay his high-speed dive to allow his cameraman more time to film. He pulled his throttles to idle, extended the speed brakes, and performed a high-G barrel roll during his dive behind the Thuds. He indicated that this maneuver, performed during a 45-degree dive, actually gained additional movie time while not losing excessive altitude. The downside was that it really watered his eyes and those of the combat cameraman in the rear cockpit. The enlisted photographer in the rear seat had big balls to fly these missions! RL mentioned that the E-6, Arthur C. McGraw, was absolutely fearless and loved seeing all the action.

MARCH 22, 1966
ROLLING THUNDER MISSION #5

Bill and I flew with Major Wilkins again to Route Package One carrying the usual six bombs. Lead was loaded with the standard flares and rockets. Our flight managed to draw innumerable red fireballs from the resident stinkers around Dong Hoi. They were probably protecting trucks in the area but we could not locate them. It was a real spectacular Fourth of July celebration, with numerous offensive skunk dens spraying the black sky with sizzling red fireballs every time we released a flare. Lead received harassing attention from the competitors when his bird lit up while firing his rockets at a suspected storage site near town. The bad-tempered home team was throwing bean balls, sliders, curves and spitballs. The Skunk Team must have gotten a large supply of fireballs from China. It turned out to be an exciting night contest that ended with no hits or errors by either side.

We scattered our bombs along a well-traveled trail leading from town towards the DMZ because there might have been a few trucks hidden in the tall grass along the road. Several of our bombs actually hit the trail but the groundkeepers probably had it groomed before we touched down at Home Plate. I executed an expeditious straight in landing on a nice dry runway and was thankful that the weather had been pleasant. I was certainly aware that all our time and effort tonight had not helped the troops in South Vietnam.

Mission Results: 0 trucks (1+15 night)

RTL Summary: 0 trucks.

MARCH 23, 1966

The 497th had not placed me in the lineup or on the duty roster, which allowed time to read a novel that I checked out from the library. There were moments when I felt that I should be concerned about being used for live target practice by the Skunk Teams, but it had not yet overwhelmed me. I just hoped that God would see me through an uncomfortable series of contests that I had to participate in with miserable unfair ground rules. The Big Boss had been overly generous in the past and assisted me in fulfilling my destiny many times. I gave thanks each night for the wonderful opportunity to live the most exciting life possible. I treasured the freedom to have grown up in north Idaho, which I considered God's country. I appreciated the fact that I had the chance to become a fighter pilot and then to secure the greatest assignment in the Air Force. I was convinced that my life had been spared in the past. I felt that my freedom would only be taken away in God's own time. I was not going to worry about what may occur during this conflict—I felt that it was out of my hands. I could not imagine having a more exciting life than flying high performance jet fighters. I was not afraid to die for my country but was in a quandary about this war.

7

MARCH 24, 1966
EMERGENCY LANDING
BARREL ROLL MISSION #3

Bill and I had bad luck tonight with one of Big Ugly's flame-throwers. The oil pressure on our number two engine started dropping before we departed Laos for North Vietnam. I first noticed the problem when we were unable to maintain our trail position behind lead. I immediately analyzed the gauge on my right front instrument panel that displayed the position of our engine nozzles. I was dismayed to see an indication showing the nozzles of the number two engine were excessively open. I recognized that this unusual nozzle indication was a bad sign—we may be losing precious oil from the affected engine. I was forced to glance down, between my legs, to read the oil pressure gauge placed behind the control stick. My fears were immediately confirmed as the oil pressure had fallen almost to zero. It occurred to me that the cockpit designers had made a mistake in placing a critical gauge at the bottom of the instrument panel.

We were still flying over Laos, but only minutes from the North Vietnam border, when I decided that I had better follow the required Dash-1 safety procedures. I realized that I would have to declare an emergency, shut down the number two engine, and immediately reverse course toward Home Plate. I soon discovered that I had to judiciously light my remaining afterburner to maintain a safe altitude and airspeed during our return to base. Our Phantom was loaded with six 750# bombs that I was not authorized to drop at random in Laos since there might be friendly residents below. I radioed lead owl that he should continue his mission to North Vietnam for a counter. We would return to Ubon without any assistance from them. I then contacted Ubon tower, informed them of our intentions, and declared an emergency as directed by the F-4C Flight Manual. I was aware that our six bombs had to be dropped in the Wing designated ordnance jettison area.

The tower controllers were in a quandary! They had never experienced an aircraft returning at night with bombs to be released in the base disposal area. I had to fly around the field in circles while periodically cycling the operating blower to maintain altitude. The tower quickly tried to discover where the bomb disposal area was located. The Tower Team finally roused a helicopter for assistance, but they also had difficulty trying to find the disposal area. The Chopper Team finally decided to toss a flare towards a rice patty near the suspected drop area because we were running out of fuel. The tower then authorized us to drop our bombs on the flare and to confirm that they were unarmed. I rechecked the armament panel before assuring the tower crew that the switches were in the safe mode. I then maneuvered to obtain a shallow dive that would allow a low release on the red flare. Bill computed a safe release altitude that would keep us out of the frag pattern in case a bomb exploded. I dropped each bomb separately, so we could feel each release, in order to confirm that the aircraft was clean for landing. We were surprised to see the bright glare of three explosions behind our bird! We had not expected any of the unarmed bombs to explode in the soft rice patty. Our ordnance teammates would have to dig up the remaining three bombs to disarm them. I imagined that someone would have to pay the resident farmer for any damage. I finally positioned our tired wounded bird on final approach for a full stop landing that would end a very frustrating night.

There was no doubt that we had caused a commotion by following the 8th TFW directives for releasing bombs in a designated ordnance disposal area. It was obvious that the Wing participants needed to review their procedures on how to find and mark the drop area at night. The tower players probably used the FNG (F—ing New Guy) acronym many times and maybe they had good cause. An experienced competitor would have kept silent and continued the mission over the border into North Vietnam. The bombs could have been scattered on a suspected skunk den before declaring an emergency and returning home. I had flown over 1000 hours in a single engine fighter and flying around for a few more minutes on one engine in a "Hummer" was not a big deal. Next time I would ignore the Dash One emergency procedures. I would complete my mission over the border, even if I had to use the operating burner when required.

Another unfortunate aspect of this fiasco was that the mission had to logged as a non-counter since we had not flown over the border into North Vietnam. It would be a shame if either Bill or I were shot down on our 100th mission due to my stupidity.

Mission Results: 0 trucks (1+10 night)

Barrel-Roll Summary: 0 trucks.

Mission Notes:

-Never return ordnance to Home Plate during an emergency.

MARCH 25, 1966
ROLLING THUNDER MISSION #6

Bill and I flew the usual route recce through the Pack One Park without seeing a solitary mole. I noticed that the trails were in excellent condition, as usual, with no visible craters. I recalled that there were many dirt roads in Idaho that were not maintained in the same high quality condition as evidenced on the Ho Chi Minh Trail. We finally expended our ordnance on the usual designated Truck Park but we never observed any secondary explosions when the bombs exploded in the jungle. It appeared that our Umpire had not informed the Mole competitors on where to park their trucks during our contests. I questioned how our astute targeting experts had discovered these truck parks—all the jungle looked like the same piece of real estate to me.

Mission Results: 0 trucks (1+40 night)

RTL Summary: 0 trucks.

-Mission Notes: Mole Teams were not competing on the fields designated by our Umpire.

Many of my teammates removed their valuable watches for a mission but I always wore my stainless steel Rolex that I had purchased for $50 at the Base Exchange in Torrejon, Spain. I decided that I would never take it off my wrist while I participated over here. However, I realized that the hostile residents might get their hands on it if I was shot down. After closely observing the ground behavior of the aggressive Fans—there was no doubt in my mind that I would be killed if I had to eject during a day contest. I usually loaded my .38 pistol with five tracers and one hard nose bullet with my name on it—I vowed to fight to the end if recovery was impossible. Nonetheless, there was a slim chance that I could be rescued from Laos or Pack One during a night battle, if the Jolly Green Team could get to me at first light.

MARCH 26, 1966
ROLLING THUNDER MISSION #7

It started out as a routine Pack One contest until immediately after our wheels were in the well. The left side of my canopy suddenly sparkled with what looked like beads of red-hot liquid mercury running along the canopy. I was completely astonished! I had never witnessed this resplendent phenomenon in the cockpit and had no idea on how to react. I alerted Bill on the intercom to inquire if he was cognizant of this radiance of moving brilliance or if I was just hallucinating. Bill responded with an unconcerned comment that it was just St. Elmo's Fire, which I had read about, but never encountered. The brilliant colorful happening died away after a few minutes, which was disappointing. I thought that it was one of the most marvelous sights I had ever seen. I wished that I could have taken a picture of its magnificence but the fiery display would always remain as a glowing memory for me and maybe it was a righteous omen from God. I might need some assistance from the Big Boss to survive our deadly contests on hostile fields with murderous fans.

We continued on to the Pack One Park and recced the small dirty mole trail from Mu Gia Pass to Dong Hoi with no indication of movement. The North Vietnam ground crews maintained the roads in an outstanding manner—there was no evidence of even a pothole or a wrecked vehicle. It was difficult for me to believe there were any targets of importance on the Pack One fields and even the nasty stinkers ignored us tonight. We scattered our bombs and lead fired his rockets in the vicinity of the designated molehill but no secondary explosions were observed. I questioned why we continued to compete in solitary night contests in the Pack One Park when the Mole Team never appeared. Surely, the Target Master had to comprehend that there were no targets of consequence. We only encountered vicious skunks and aggressive Fans. I felt that we would be in for a long series of contests if we had to hunt shy moles that never emerged from their tunnels. Maybe the Thud Teams had detected targets in the Pack Six Park and possibly, the Navy had encountered something of worth along the coast. However, I had only discovered warlike skunk competitors that threw deadly fireballs and incensed Fans that wanted to shoot Owls.

Our flight recovered to a nice dry runway as the weather had been superb but I was convinced the rains would arrive before long. We signed in, debriefed, and then caught a ride to the OClub for a hot breakfast. I played a competitive game of darts with Bill and Crash at the Clubhouse to unwind after another useless mission.

Mission Results: 0 trucks. (1+35 night)

RTL Summary: 0 trucks.

-Mission Notes: St. Elmo's Fire was a spectacular glowing occurrence that might have been a good omen from God.

MARCH 27, 1966

Our Coach cancelled our exhibition contest in Laos, due to lousy weather, but rescheduled us for Rolling Thunder competition on the 29th. I hated these boring days when I was not on the flying schedule or pulling duties, but at least I could visit the cool library to read. Crash and I played bridge for most of the day and we managed to win eight dollars to split. We usually played a skillful game together with our own bidding system that actually worked. I noticed that very few of my teammates sat around talking about their missions or the war. Many Night Owls just wanted to fly the required 100 missions and then get their tails out of the Rolling Thunder League ASAP. It appeared that no one had destroyed any meaningful targets. It was obvious that we were not helping our teammates in South Vietnam. Crash thought we should take the bus to town to get a hot bath with a rub down. However, I declined his invitation because I never felt at ease in town.

I decided to attend the nightly movie in the small hot church, which turned out to be an old black and white flick. It was boring, one reel was out of focus, and the worn movie screen was not large enough. Nevertheless, there were some pluses as the hot fresh popcorn was tasty with plenty of butter. It proved to be another hot and sticky day, which made it more troublesome than ever to sleep under the uncomfortable netting. We had not been able to move into our new air-conditioned quarters due to electrical problems. Maybe the problem would be resolved before long since the electricity appeared to come from our military diesel generators. One of my teammates mentioned that a 433rd aircraft had been struck and downed in Pack One. I was pleased to learn that the crew was rescued. Our squadron had been lucky—we were not flying tough missions in highly defended areas during the day.

MARCH 28, 1966

I received an updated pay statement from base finance and it revealed that I was receiving $1,100 a month as a Captain with flight pay. I also received a big windfall because Congress allocated an extra sixty-five dollars a month for combat pay or about two dollars a day! I contemplated whether to write a letter to my Idaho congressmen thanking them for their generosity. It would be interesting to learn how much a civilian pilot would charge to fly night bombing missions in heavily defended areas. There would be no takers at any price for the missions near Hanoi that our Thud teammates flew every day. Congress had to be satisfied with highly trained and dedicated pilots that risked their lives for a few dollars.

I had never been interested in becoming rich, or I would have flown with the airlines, but I could remember when money had been very scarce. I recalled that I first started working when I was nine in a grocery store in California and was paid twenty-five cents an hour. I helped my father during the following two summers when he fished for catfish and received the profits from one fish trap. I used all my income to purchase a new Lionel electric train engine.

I was lucky to land a summer job after the seventh grade that paid fifty cents an hour to pick up sticks behind a bulldozer clearing land. I worked in a Texaco service station near our house for seventy-five cents an hour after completing the eighth grade. I labored the following summer for McLaughlin Motors, in St. Maries, cleaning the building and taking trash to the city dump for a dollar an hour.

I experienced an exciting summer after the tenth grade when I lived and worked on a ranch. I learned how to operate a tractor, branded cattle, erected fencing, and assisted with numerous chores. I really enjoyed the ranch life, and was able to save four hundred dollars to buy a 1941 Chevy coupe. I set pins at the local bowling alley during night league games to buy gas and insurance for my hard earned car. A summer job fishing for carp with my father and brother on Sprague Lake, Washington, after the 11th grade, was exhausting work with little pay. My first real job with worthwhile pay occurred when I worked in a mercantile store in Santa, Idaho, before entering college.

My mother helped me during my second semester at school by working in a small hamburger stand, when I had exhausted all my money on college expenses. I was finally old enough to work at the St. Maries Lumber Company Mill, after my initial year in college. I was earning about twelve dollars a day driving a forklift when my boss offered me a substitute job on the green chain for a month. The wet lumber from the mill came out on a long cable and was stacked on a designated pile—depending on size and type of wood. The green chain crew had worked out an agreement with the mill to do all the sorting and stacking with fewer workers for more pay. The company readily agreed with the workers as it benefited the lumber mill financially.

I had watched the crew slide and stack the lumber with ease and thought that I could handle the extra work. It was a chance to earn almost twice my daily pay that was desperately needed for college expenses. I readily accepted the offer and donned a large heavy leather apron along with hefty leather mittens for an eight-hour shift. I experienced a miserable laborious time trying to survive until the first 15-minute break! I was exhausted after stacking the heavy wet green lumber for only two hours. I was sure that I would not be able to stand up again after the one hour lunch break. However, I returned for the final four hours of torture because I never wanted to be looked upon as a college weenie and I needed the money. The other crewmembers took pity on me and accomplished a portion of my allotted work or I might not have been able to finish the shift. The leather mittens had not prevented me from receiving 10 blisters on each hand that I had to break open and then daub with Mercurochrome. I was weak from fatigue for most of the week before I finally learned how to maneuver the heavy wet lumber. I suffered for many painful days with my blistered hands, but they eventually healed and hardened. The extra pay for college was really appreciated but I had never labored so hard in my life. That unrelenting hard work convinced me I really needed to finish college. I had no desire to spend my life working at a job that required heavy manual labor.

MARCH 29, 1966
ROLLING THUNDER MISSION #8

I competed in another routine Pack One contest except for one problem. Our radio was lost for most of the flight, but Night Owls never needed to communicate, unless something unusual occurred. It was possible to key our mike in response to lead owl's instructions while the flight continued to hunt for moles in the night. Our bombs were scattered on the usual molehill after the lights went out. We eventually joined up with lead owl and flew on his wing back to Home Plate where he informed the tower that we had to land with no communications. Major Wilkins then dropped us off on final approach where he gave us a visual thumbs up signal to land.

I personally felt that our numerous ineffective contests in the Pack One Park appeared to be a waste of time. We had never discovered any targets of significance. It appeared to me that the Target Master was not interested in winning this league or he would have assigned the Buff Teams to obliterate the few targets of consequence in North Vietnam. My teammates agreed that we should be tasked to strike valid targets or we might as well leave the field. I was sad for the combatants in the jungles of South Vietnam—there were little that we could do to help by using pointless ground rules.

Mission Results: 0 trucks. (1+35 night)

RTL Summary: 0 trucks.

Mission Notes: Night Owls required very limited communications at night.

Bill was going to take a "time-out" from our competition for some rest and relaxation (R&R). I was sorry to see him depart. Now I had to fly with various other GIBs until he returned. I decided to drink free Kool-Aid at the OClub during the day to keep cool. However, sometimes it was nice to enjoy an ice-cold beer in the Clubhouse after a stressful night mission. It was inexplicable how someone could sit around and drink beer all day—it just filled me up and started tasting nasty. I noticed that only a few of my teammates spent time drinking booze from the multitude of expensive bottles lining the bar wall. It was obvious that we had stay on top of our game when competing at night on hostile fields. I preferred to spend my free time reading or playing cards and tried to avoid questioning why we were here. I missed our church service today because I was exhausted from the nightly contests and opted to sleep as long as possible. I was pleased that our ever-present rain helped cool the hootch.

8

MARCH 30, 1966
CLOSE TO DEATH
ROLLING THUNDER MISSION #9

We were fortunate, the weather cleared, and I blasted off with Lt. Wilson H. Parma in my rear cockpit. I missed Bill but Willie was a competent GIB. We recalled some of the good times we had experienced in the States. Some of the Zoomies from the Air Force Academy ruffled my feathers but Willie was a reliable teammate. I understood that he had been an excellent football player at the Academy, which explained why he was OK. I have discovered that most athletes proved to be good teammates, no matter where they attended school. I played football in high school because it was more or less expected of me, but it was not my favorite sport. I never had any fun playing football against Sand Point High School. I played across from Jerry Kramer who was about 30 pounds heavier and a lot faster. Jerry was now playing for the Green Bay Packers and doing very well against the big boys. I enjoyed playing basketball, but maybe I was meant to play baseball since I was bestowed with an excellent fastball when I turned 15. I called my fastball a "hummer"—a speeding object that was not always under control.

Our mission was directed to Dong Hoi where a previous flight started an extensive fire in the middle of the city that was very visible. Lead owl dropped their bombs on the target and then we were cleared to launch an attack on the burning fire with our six pods of rockets. I decided to make one pass heading west so we could recover heading toward Laos and on to home plate. I should have been aware that we were in a heavily defended area. I knew that our rockets would predict our flight path, when fired, and would illuminate our Night Owl for the Skunk Team. I was oblivious to the fact that we were in the middle of a great number of treacherous skunks that wanted to blast us off the Dong Hoi playing field.

Every sinister stinker in Dong Hoi must have been scanning the dark sky looking for an unsuspecting foolish Night Owl to show them a tail to spray. I obviously made their night when I presented them with an ideally illuminated bird when our rockets fired. The departing rockets also indicated our flight path. I only had to wait a few seconds, after pressing the red pickle button three times, before the dark earth suddenly came alive with sizzling red fireballs from all directions. The blackness below immediately switched into a beautiful display of crimson tracers that looked like a spectacular Fourth of July Celebration! I was dismayed that our little unsuspecting owl had become the star attraction of the night. We soon realized that there were more pissed off skunk dens than could be counted, and the little stinkers wanted to spray us with streams of deadly piss. The deadly red fireballs, rising from every vicious skunk den, were streaking directly for our defenseless bird! It was evident that the unfriendly opponents wanted to blast us out of the battle forever. I was dumbfounded when the AAA site, located directly under my nose, fired a constant stream of flak at our Phantom. This deadly accurate shooter really watered my eyes! His murderous tracers were actually tracking our bird's flight path! The lethal spray reached for our canopy and I tensed for a fatal bean ball. I desperately wanted to deflect the scalding fireballs as they flashed by our cockpit. I was sure we were about to be blasted from the sky.

Then my adrenaline kicked in and I yanked so hard on the control stick that I over "G'd" the aircraft! Nevertheless, I was not in the least bit concerned about over stressing our poor bird. I desperately wanted to get away from the blistering fireballs before we took a fatal shot to the head. It was now high PRF time as I anticipated that our poor bent "Hummer" would take a destructive hit during our "high G" dive recovery. I was anxious to complete our recovery and accelerate toward Laos in the eventuality we had to eject. I was not sure how we safely burst through a sky awash with uncounted tracers. We must have received some assistance from the Big Boss. Personally, I thanked God for riding shotgun and saving my life! I recalled that my life had not flashed before my eyes and maybe that was a good sign as we survived. Willie and I were completely speechless after our narrow escape with death! We never even uttered a single word during our "Hummer's" return to Home Plate. I recalled that I had never been scared during our frantic recovery, as trying to survive the murderous skunk spray required my full attention

I realized that the Big Boss's Score Keeper had given me a fielder's choice instead of an error that would have taken me out of the lineup. I knew that I would have to be more observant in the future. There was a short playing time for teammates who were not extremely careful and very vigilant. A complacent competitor could be blasted off the field with a fatal fireball and sent to the showers. I perceived that it was essential to pay closer attention to every play if I wanted to survive the nightly contests with destructive skunks.

I questioned why the Air Force had never warned us about firing rockets at night in heavily defended areas. There should have been a few fighter pilots in the military that had fired rockets during night combat operations in WWII or Korea. I found it troublesome to believe that we were the first fighter pilots to fire rockets at night in a heavily defended area. Regardless, maybe everyone who had attempted this ill-advised maneuver was now dead. I later voiced my concerns about firing rockets at night to Wing Intelligence but the non-rated participants were not interested in what I had learned the hard way. I believed that I would always be able to recall, with perfect detail, the hot crimson fireballs that flashed by my cockpit over Dong Hoi.

Mission Results: 0 trucks. (1+10 night & +10 weather)

RTL Summary: 0 trucks. (

Mission Notes: Never fire rockets at night in heavily defended areas.

Lt. George M. Hardwick (Mac) and I were scheduled to room together in our newly assigned air-conditioned sleeping quarters. I also learned that there was a possibility that we would move tomorrow. I checked the line up board, it indicated that I had an early briefing at 1500 hours for a day contest in the Pack One Park. Our squadron would start flying the later missions, from midnight until dawn, once we moved into our new four-star air-conditioned quarters. It seemed an extravagance to have two people to a unit. It was certainly a luxury to have a separate shower between rooms. However, I thought it was adequate compensation for competing in deadly night contests on dreadful fields.

I wandered over to the Clubhouse and talked Crash into playing bridge until the sun arose and we each won three dollars. I thought that we were becoming quite skillful at the game. I found it enjoyable to play cards since it allowed me to concentrate on a game with rules I could understand.

MARCH 31, 1966
ROLLING THUNDER MISSION #10

I had a smile on my face as we moved into our new air-conditioned quarters. I was gratified to see that each room even had a sink with running water. There was sufficient space in our room for two small cots with a footlocker at the end of each bed. We were very lucky Night Owls to have the use of a new small air conditioning unit that was located between the two cots. The unit emitted delightful icy cold air that could be controlled by a variable speed fan. Now it was possible to sleep twelve hours a day, if desired, as it helped us to avoid the miserable heat. We were possibly the only aircrews flying out of Thailand that had air conditioning. Regardless, I felt that it was justified because we were the only night contestants in the battle and needed to sleep during the hot days. Someone had started a rumor that the base swimming pool was supposed to open on Sunday.

I bought a used bike with worn thin tires from my new houseboy with the expectation that it might last until I completed my tour. I needed a bike, as our new quarters were farther from the squadron and the OClub. I recalled that I had never owned a new bike. I felt that I was lucky when I received my brother's old worn Road Master after I turned six. It was difficult for me to learn to ride a full sized bike, but I immediately pushed it to the top of the highest hill in our neighborhood when I was able to keep my balance. I had felt no fear as I flew down the steep hill pushing Mach I, but it was a tactical error when I tried to execute a 90-degree steep turn at the bottom of the hill. I was propelled through two residential lawns and then my "hummer" smashed into a wire fence where I was ejected from my seat. I had never been scared during my high-speed test run, but my father had to mend my numerous gashes and the damaged bike.

My new houseboy agreed to wash my flight suit and underwear on the rocks in the local stream if I provided the soap and increased his pay. I was gratified to discover that our Base Exchange had started to stock Tide—I quickly bought a box. Willie informed me that we had to attend a 1330 squadron meeting before briefing at 1600 hours for a Pack One contest. I promised Willie that I would pay more attention when competing on hostile fields. I would never fire rockets again at night in heavily defended territory.

Our flight of Night Owls flew from our roost on time to hunt for sly moles while trying to avoid stinkers. Our early mission allowed me the rare opportunity to view Pack One during the day. I was not pleased that we had to avoid numerous clouds along the route. We were in and out of the weather for the whole contest. Cloud cover made owls nervous! Wary birds needed to see the opposing threats at all times over hostile fields. It was critical to avoid devious stinkers that want to spray us with unsuspecting fireballs. We hunted moles on the well-traveled trail, but I was sure the wary creatures had heard or seen us coming because we never saw any movement. We failed to encounter any of the opposing Skunk or Mole Teams during the contest. Our flight was finally forced to scattered all the rockets and bombs on the designated molehill. I was not satisfied to know that I had now competed in ten contests without hitting a mole. I was beginning to get the big picture about how the Rolling Thunder League operated.

Our flight flew a weather penetration, followed by a ground-controlled approach (GCA), with a full stop landing in lousy weather. I thanked the Big Boss for the essential strobe lights! I needed them to locate our dark runway in the thick soup. I was sure that the weather was going to become worse in Thailand. I realized that I had better be extremely proficient at landing on a short wet runway during monsoon rains.

Mission Results: 0 trucks (+30 weather & +45 night)

RTL Summary: 0 trucks.

We returned in time to attend the 497th party at the Clubhouse that included free drinks for 1-½ hours with pizza and wine—who ever said that war was hell. Then I excused myself to attend the movie "Art for Love", but the flick almost put me to sleep. I loved my new quarters that allowed me to enjoy a cool deep sleep without the uncomfortable netting. I was not even upset when I had to adjust the air conditioner during the night because the room had gotten too cold.

I learned that our Umpire had scheduled the 497th TFS to start competing in late contests, from midnight until 0600 hours, starting the following Friday. I checked the lineup board and noticed that we were scheduled to compete in a non-counter exhibition contest on the Ho Chi Minh Trail in Laos. There was a slight possibility of being substituted into a League contest, since we were assigned to spare the Pack One event.

APRIL 1, 1966
BARREL ROLL MISSION #4

Our contest on the Ho Chi Minh Trail in Laos allowed us to team with a AC-47 Gunship (Spooky) that was equipped with three 7.62mm mini guns. The mini guns really emitted tremendous firepower, and our AC-47 teammates carried numerous flares. The old WWII converted cargo aircraft was capable of staying on station for hours. I thought that it might be possible for them to delay a limited number of trucks trying to drive down the road, but it would be unrealizable for them to cover the entire trail. I had never taken the field with a Gunship Team. It would be a new experience, and I looked forward to entering the contest.

We were fragged to carry six 500-pound bombs and a 20mm Gattling Gun that was capable of holding 1200 rounds. I was excited to have the opportunity to fire the SUU-16 six shooter in combat, as I had only fired it on the practice ranges in the States. I had always dreamed of strafing the enemy—like the WWII fighters I had viewed on the newsreels. We departed on time for our late night engagement that would not count towards the magic one hundred missions.

The Spooky Team had evidently surprised two moles on the trail. The dark trucks were motionless on the road under the night-lights when we arrived. I was excited to see a real target for a change, but it was not logical for wary moles to be out of the tall grass and just sitting on a trail. I was afraid that they were just decoys, but we rolled in for a high release dive bomb attack. I thought it was a good pass but my six bombs did not even come close to the trucks. I mused that the Umpire might as well transfer all the bombs to the Buff and Thud Teams—they appeared to be useless for hitting moles at night.

I then switched to the gattling gun for my next pass down the road. I was pleased with my attack and really nailed the solitary trucks with a long burst of 20-mike-mike. I was probably reckless during my aggressive attack. I flew very low and close to the trucks during our strafe run by staying on the trigger too long. Nevertheless, I had marvelous time shooting the gun! I could now direct my firepower to the target instead of dropping unguided ineffective bombs. I was lucky that there were no secretive skunks hiding in the grass to spray me, but that was probably because they were smartly lying low in their dens. The AC-47's mini guns would have taken the head off any varmint that poked his nose out of the grass to fling fireballs. We left the field with both trucks burning for my first winning contest since I had arrived at Ubon. I realized that we had only been successful because the Spooky Team had located the trucks, but I questioned why the vehicles were just sitting alone on the trail. I had a gut feeling that the competition had placed some old worn out equipment in the hot box to occupy us while the rest of their teammates were stealing to South Vietnam. Anyway, it was sporting of the Mole Team to field a few sitting ducks for us to practice on, even if they were just decoys. There was no doubt in my mind that the sizzling gattling gun was vastly superior to unguided iron bombs for hitting trucks at night. I informed Wing Intel that we had destroyed two trucks with our six shooter.

Mission Results: 2 trucks. (1+10 night)

Barrel-Roll Summary: 2 trucks.

Mission Notes:

-AC-47s were better equipped than F-4Cs for night contests in Laos.

-Truck decoys might be employed as a delaying tactic or for a flak trap.

-The SUU-16 gattling gun was effective for liquidating trucks at night.

I was pleased when my footlocker arrived safely from George AFB with some of my personal valuable possessions. The wooden locker contained my High School and College Annuals along with several other personal remembrances. The Annuals were important to me when I felt low and far from home. The old publications allowed me the opportunity to recall an uncomplicated life while I was growing up in God's country. I recalled that I had enjoyed my last two years in High School and all four years at the University of Idaho. Sometimes I missed that peaceful life when I was just a college student, playing baseball, with only a few tests of concern.

Mac helped me move a small white refrigerator into a shared area located between two sleeping rooms in our new complex. It was hard to believe that four of us actually had a fridge for our own use! We were really living high on the hog when you considered that we were at war a zillion miles from home. I walked to the base carpenter shop and talked our construction teammates into giving me a plywood board to fit my bed—my back was bothering me.

I rode my bike over to the Clubhouse for a tasty breakfast before I retired to my new quarters. I was delighted to see Bill, as he had just returned from Japan after a pleasing R & R. It was great to have him back in the lineup. We were a good team and certainly capable of getting a few hits in the future. I decided that I would try to sleep for the next 12 hours, in my dark cool room, after the delicious breakfast. Of course, I would want to eat my usual breakfast again after I arose to compete in the next night contest.

APRIL 2, 1966

I rode my bike to the library to read some newsmagazines, after I discovered that I was not in the lineup for flying or ground duties. I wanted to understand what our Nation's accomplished experts and experienced Senior Managers had to say about this unpleasant conflict, as I was in the dark. I could not understand why we were not allowed to fly within 10 miles of Haiphong, where Russian ships were outfitting North Vietnam with loads of equipment. I was gratified to read an article in the 28 March, U.S. News & World Report, that discussed shutting down Haiphong harbor by using mines. The writer went on to say that North Vietnam received 60 percent of its war material through Haiphong. I was flabbergasted and pissed off to read that the Russians were allowed to calmly unload weapons that would later shoot down our aircraft. The article indicated that the Joint Chiefs of Staff recommended bombing Haiphong but our Commander in Chief had ignored their advice. I questioned why our Wing Intelligence shop never briefed us on what our National Commanders were saying about this conflict.

U.S. News & World continued with another worthwhile article concerning the bombing of North Vietnam. The report implied that there were only a few important targets in Pack Six around Hanoi and Haiphong. It was interesting to learn that there were some important targets somewhere in North Vietnam. I had not seen any meaningful targets in Pack One or Five. The report indicated that it would be possible to quadruple the bombing in North Vietnam without any decisive effect on the ground war in the south, as the Viet Cong required few supplies to fight in this war. The enemy could find food in South Vietnam and were capable of carrying everything they needed on their backs. Maybe that is why we had only located a few trucks—the enemy only required ammo.

It was difficult for me to forget the solitary little North Vietnamese fisherman that I had seen face to face on the river. I recalled that my father was also a freshwater commercial fisherman who passed away in 1962 when I was stationed in Spain. My father had first been a truck gardener in southern Idaho, until WWII. He was elated when the State of Idaho opened their rivers and lakes to commercial fishermen to provide additional food for the war effort. Somehow, my father learned there were numerous catfish in the lakes around St. Maries. He decided that he was ready to start a new endeavor as a fisherman. My father left Rigby with my brother after school ended in 1942 to see if they could discover a way to trap the fish. They eventually constructed wire traps that would catch the fish in sufficient quantities to earn a living. It was possible to ship the freshly skinned and cleaned fish on a train traveling from Seattle to Chicago that stopped briefly in St. Maries for water.

My mother and I arrived in St. Maries during the summer of 1942; we lived in a small motel cabin with two bedrooms, a kitchen, and my first indoor plumbing. I was allowed to spend every day at a lake catching frogs, turtles, and playing with the animals on a nearby farm, while my father trapped fish. The nice farmer even gave me a little brown and white goat that my father allowed me to take to our cabin in the back of his old GMC pickup. I had two glorious days with my newly found pet that I tied up in an adjoining vacant lot, before the neighbors complained. It appeared that they thought the animal was not a city kid, and I reluctantly had to return my little goat to the country farm.

My father trapped catfish in Round Lake for the market all week and then took me pole fishing for trout on Sundays along the shadowy St. Joe River. I was surprised that he never seemed to tire of fishing. He also allowed me to spend special days in his rowboat, if I was quiet, while he emptied traps. My parents worked very late each night, as all the catfish had to be cleaned, boxed and iced for shipment on the midnight train to Chicago.

My father moved my mother and me to Bethel Island, California, after the war ended, since the commercial fishing was again closed in Idaho. It was necessary to use treated twine-fishing nets in the San Joaquin River Delta due to the salt water content in the rivers. He discovered that it was necessary to cover long distances on the local waterways to locate sufficient catfish to trap. I was allowed to accompany my father during the summer months when I was out of school. We had to leave at dawn and spend the entire day running numerous traps in order to catch enough fish to earn a living. My father also placed mink traps along the river to obtain additional income, as he could sell the fur for a good price. I loved to pull up a sprung mink trap from the dark cold water—it was exciting to see if we had caught a valuable pelt. I was thrilled when my father purchased a nice fishing pole and star drag reel for me to angle for striped bass when we were not running the traps.

My father and I spent a complete summer in 1954 seining carp in Sprague Lake, Washington, to sell to the State Fish and Game Department for fish food. I recalled that it had been exhausting work placing his large net far out in the lake and then pulling it to shore to trap the carp. Still, I soon discovered that it was much harder toting the fish from the lakeshore to our pickup in large buckets. I finally had my fill of burdensome fishing and decided that it was not the chosen career for me, but my father never tired of the wearisome work. I have found memories of his little handmade wooden rowboat that he commanded to take me fishing, whenever I could find time away from my baseball games and studies.

I wondered if the sight of the lone Vietnamese fisherman in his little wooden boat was an omen from God that I should not ignore. I had learned long ago that certain things would be revealed in God's own good time.

Bill and I were placed in the lineup for an easy league contest tomorrow night with a B-66 Team. Our Umpire ordered us to drop six 750-pound bombs while flying in close formation on the wing of a B-66 light bomber coming from Tah-kli. I had considerable doubts about the effectiveness of this new contest, but I was always willing to try a different sport. We had to remain on the bomber's wing until we received his signal tone that alerted us to release our bombs. Our bombers radar target was the Ho Chi Minh Trail that snaked through Mu Gia Pass. I questioned if any of the bombs would even come close to striking the road. Maybe the bomber was equipped with a super accurate radar bombing system! I only knew that it was difficult for me to position my bombs on a small road at night using flares. I believed it was a complete waste of time since the groundkeepers would probably repair the dirt trail quickly, if any bombs ever hit it. It was difficult to understand what the shrewd Senior Managers expected to accomplish by dropping a few "hummers"—speeding objects that may or may not be under control. I thought that our mission was pointless and concluded that the Target Master was off base for wanting us to bomb an empty pass. However, I had to remember that "mine was not to reason why".

APRIL 3, 1966
ROLLING THUNDER MISSION #11

Our flight joined with a B-66 Bomber Team over Thailand for an easy contest. We maneuvered into position and flew formation on their wing to Mu Gia Pass. It was an opportunity for Bill to get stick time, as we were high enough to safely avoid any 37/57mm fireballs. I relaxed and tried to contemplate on why we were flying on the wing of a light bomber to drop bombs on an empty pass. The B-66 teammates initiated a tone on their radio for us when we neared the target. We released our six 750-pound bombs, along with the bomber's ordnance, when the tone stopped. I questioned where the bombs had eventually hit but our squadron never received any damage photos—no one seemed to care. Maybe the Mu Gia Pass trail was one of the lines of communication that I had read about in the newsmagazines, but doubted that we had severed it.

The ground keepers, moles, and skunk competitors, had probably learned by now to run like hell when they heard us coming. It was obvious that our bombs could hit anywhere within miles of the trail. I speculated how long it would take before North Vietnam placed a SAM site in the Pass. Our straight and level flights would be a tempting target for a missile. We completed an easy contest and it even counted towards the magic 100, but I doubted that our work had contributed one iota to the war effort. We immediately departed the B-66 and returned to Home Plate for a TACAN approach, followed by a GCA full stop landing. I enlightened Wing Intel about scattering six bombs on a small deserted dirt road. We then departed to the Clubhouse for a game of darts.

Mission Results: 0 trucks. (1+30 night)

RTL Summary: 0 trucks.

Mission Notes:

-Playing with a B-66 Team proved to be a swift and simple contest with little risk.

-I theorized that dropping bombs on a barren mountain pass was a waste of effort and money.

APRIL 4, 1966
ROLLING THUNDER MISSION #12

Bill and I were lucky tonight as our practice event in Laos was canceled, due to crappy weather, but we were allowed to fly another high altitude mission over Mu Gia Pass. I still had a difficult time trying to comprehend why we participated with a B-66 Team to scatter bombs on an empty mountain trail. The Rolling Thunder League might last forever if the best we could do was to sprinkle bombs on a small dirt road winding through a mountain pass.

Our contest proved to be more demanding than I had figured. We were required to fly very close formation on our teammate's wing in heavy soup for most of the bombing run. The weather was violent with massive thunderstorms and blazing lightning everywhere.

I checked the scheduling board after returning to Home Plate and noticed that we were in the lineup to brief at 0030 for a contest in the Pack One Park tomorrow night. I felt disheartened for the POWs and troops in South Vietnam. It appeared that we were doing little if anything to end the war.

Mission Results: 0 trucks (+50 night & +25 weather)

RTL Summary: 0 trucks.

Mission Notes: Attacking an insignificant mountain trail contributes little to winning this war.

The squadron duty driver took us to the OClub for breakfast after we debriefed our pointless mission with Wing Intel. Crash and I played bridge until sunrise and my share of the winnings added up to $2.30. I used my earnings to pay for breakfast and a hot cherry pie topped with vanilla ice cream. I concluded that it was a grand extravagance to have the luxury of eating ice cream in a combat zone. It was obvious that our present surroundings were extremely accommodating when you considered what the troops in the jungles of South Vietnam were encountering.

APRIL 5, 1966
ROLLING THUNDER MISSION #13

It was a beautiful night for Night Owls. We were blessed with a moon so bright that we could see the ground distinctly and there was no requirement for flares. We soared back and forth across the trail during our recce run towards the Quang Khe Ferry crossing and enjoyed the clear night. It was very peaceful with nary a light on the fields below. We hunted for moles but there was no movement or unfriendly skunk activity. Lead Owl retained all his flares until we arrived at the ferry, since we were able to see the trail in the moonlight. The Umpire had ordered our flight to search for vehicles or ferries near the North Vietnam Navy Base at Quang Khe. We never detected any movement on the roads in the assigned area or even discovered a single wooden boat. It was difficult to give credence to the fact that this was the enemy base that had started a war by launching torpedo boats to attack our naval ships. In actuality, I could not even identify any facility under the flares that looked like a Navy Base.

We finally exhausted our flares and had to scatter our bombs on the usual molehill, as directed by our eagle-eyed target experts. Bill took control of our bird for the return to base (RTB). I used our flashlight to complete the standard hung ordnance inspection after we joined with lead. I enjoyed the opportunity to just relax and delight in the tranquil scenery while we followed a dark river westward toward Laos. It had not seemed like we were in a conflict tonight. We enjoyed a beautiful bright moon and the countryside had been peaceful. I wondered why the disagreeable stinkers were so quiet tonight, but maybe they were short of fire-balls. We executed a full stop landing, debriefed with the Intel player, and departed for the Clubhouse.

Mission Results: 0 trucks. (1+50 night)

RTL Summary: 0 trucks.

Mission Notes:

-Flares were not required for hunting trucks at night under a full moon.

-I had not observed any vessels along the coast.

I won $2.83 playing bridge all night with Crash, due to our excellent bidding. I enjoyed competing in a thought provoking rationale card game that passed hours of time and made life tolerable. Several of my teammates enjoyed drinking high quality booze, but I preferred to sip on a coke or drink hot coffee with breakfast.

APRIL 6, 1966

I remained out of the lineup for all ground duties, which was OK, but I thought that it was about time I started to participate in the mobile control position. The majority of the missions tonight were loaded with iron bombs as usual, which seemed such a waste. I was convinced that the unguided weapons were ineffective for destroying trucks at night. I preferred the six-shooter, when hunting for speedy elusive vehicles, so I could direct my attack.

I recalled that I had always treasured guns and played with cap pistols when I was a kid. I recalled committing my first crime by shoplifting a six-shooter cap gun from the local five and ten-cent store with my best friend when toys became available after WWII. We had no money and rationalized our theft by agreeing that we needed the gun more than the store. My short-lived criminal career came to halt when a clerk at the local drug store caught us shoplifting several comic books that we loved to read in our forest fort. We were taken to the rear of the store, where the angry owner chewed us out. I could still recall his comments and angry face. During his tirade, I turned and saw my mother and sister enter the store—my heart nearly stopped. For some reason, the irate owner never ratted on me to my mother and I was gratified that she never noticed me in the back room. We were finally paroled with a stern warning to never steal again. His lecture must have really gotten my attention because I never shoplifted anything again.

The Red Rider BB Gun was put into production after the WWII ended, and I desperately had to have that awesome rifle. I must have whined for a year before my parents bought me one for a combined Birthday and Christmas present in November 1948. I have since apologized to the Big Boss for wearing out two of the glorious weapons firing at every bird that ventured into my shooting range. After wearing out the second BB gun, I was finally permitted to shoot our Stevens 22-caliber semi-automatic rifle at selected targets, when my father emptied his catfish nets and ran his mink traps. I sat in the front of his boat and shot at mud hens while we slowly wound our way through the sloughs of the San Joaquin Delta. I have also apologized to God for firing at the poor distressed mud hens, but it sure facilitated my shooting skill. My father always carried his well-worn 12-gauge shotgun on his boat to shoot ring neck pheasant along the dikes. I was thrilled when he allowed me to fire his big weapon, at unsuspecting crows, after repeated begging sessions. Firing the shotgun was a spine tingling event! The recoil knocked me back and left a huge bruise on my shoulder.

I was granted the use of a Stevens's single shot sixteen-gauge shotgun to hunt after school and on weekends after I turned thirteen. I treasured the freedom of walking on dikes around large fields of grain while searching for ring neck pheasants and mallards. I was always thrilled to start my hunting season in the fall when the grouse season opened. I quickly ran home from school, grabbed my shotgun, and hunted for grouse in local mountains that were only minutes away. Later in the Fall, I would spend the weekends bundled up in a duck blind, waiting for dawn. I treasured the sight of that first mallard of the season coming down to my decoys. I was thrilled when my parents presented me with a new Remington Wingmaster 16-gauge shotgun for a combined 16th Birthday and Christmas. I will always keep that precious gun, as it provided fond memories of hunting in Idaho.

I earned my own money, working in a mercantile store, in order to buy a 30.06 Savage rifle for deer and elk hunting in the fall. I have never apologized to God for shooting game—our family needed the meat for our table. I recalled that I loved to spend stimulating days and nights in the beautiful Bitterroot Mountains of Idaho hunting deer and elk. It was possible to spend all day in the wilderness and never see another human. I was not concerned when I never caught sight of a deer or elk, as I treasured the splendor of the outdoors. Maybe the Big

Boss had been programming me to fire the gattling gun for a long time, but I questioned why here and now.

APRIL 7, 1966

Very few Night Owls were allowed to leave the roost as our Wing retained a very limited supply of ordnance to drop. Aircrews were instructed to bring their bombs and rockets back if no one spotted a vehicle or ferry. Our base was extremely low on all types of ordnance except for 20mm cannon shells. It was hard to comprehend why we had been expending our bombs on empty truck parks if the Managers were short of ordnance. Of course, I could have cared less if they ever found another bomb for my Phantom. I felt that a single gattling gun was superior to six iron bombs anytime. I was convinced in my own mind that I required a weapon that could be directed in order to hit a speeding truck. The rockets and CBU's were good for undefended areas but were not acceptable around heavy concentrations of AAA sites.

After much thought, I decided to account for my 100 missions by depositing a penny in an old coffee canister after I completed a Rolling Thunder mission. With any luck at all, and God willing, I would accumulate a dollars worth of coppers and fly away on the Freedom Bird for the States.

APRIL 8, 1966
ROLLING THUNDER MISSION #14

Our flight was initially scheduled to refuel with a KC-135 in north Thailand, near Udorn, for a mission in Pack Five. However, due to bad weather in the target area, we were tasked to strike poor old Mu Gia Pass again. The extra fuel from the tanker allowed us to remain in the pass, for a long time, searching for elusive trucks. I hoped that we could repeat our previous success of surprising a convoy in the pass by flying low across Laos, popping up, and pouncing on the trucks before they disappeared in the tall grass.

The SAC KC-135 Team was waiting for us in north Thailand and the weather was superb for night refueling. Our big tanker teammates appeared to be a good group. They were friendly towards Night Owls and always right on time. Nevertheless, it must be boring to fly long distances in order to pump fuel into a few little birds. The weather was clear, when our flight departed the tanker for Laos, but then it started to deteriorate with haze and clouds. However, Night Owls were good navigators, and we easily located the lofty mountain peaks next to the pass using our radar. I was disappointed that it was impossible to initiate a surprise attack due to the miserable haze.

Major Wilkins attempted to flare the pass but we were unable to clearly see the small trail under the flares due to the wretched haze. Lead Owl expended all his night-lights trying to catch sight of a dismal mole on the small dirt pathway, but never succeeded. We finally gave up the hunt and acknowledged that we had to return our ordnance to Home Plate due to poor planning by our leaders.

We recovered at Home Plate and learned that we were lucky as only four flights managed to get their wheels in the well. All the rest of our squadron's events were cancelled due to the lack of bombs or rockets. I questioned why the Umpire had not ordered a gattling gun for each bird. I thought that the six shooter was more effective for liquidating trucks at night, but "mine was not to reason why". Our astute Managers were in command of the contests and surely had a well thought out effective game plan for all the fighter teams to follow.

Mission Results: 0 trucks (1+15 night)

RTL Summary: 0 trucks.

I carefully rode my bike slowly from the squadron to the Clubhouse. I always searched for cobras on the road with my flashlight. The dark green loathsome snakes preferred to lie on the warm asphalt road at night. I always gave them more room than they could possibly desire. Watching for the detestable cobras at night was more stressful than playing night contests in Laos. It was always a relief when I finally arrived at the OClub without surprising one of the miserable reptiles. It would be more dangerous if they could strike as fast as a Texas rattlesnake.

I selected my usual bacon, eggs, and hash brown potatoes for breakfast before sitting down with an old friend, Captain Richard L. Penn (RL). He was one of the first pilots that I had became acquainted with when I checked into the 497th Tactical Fighter Interceptor Squadron at Torrejon, in November 1961. He had attended the first Air Force Academy Class, but he was not like the usual Bird U graduate who thought they were a cut above their ROTC teammates.

RL and I were probably the only fighter jocks that had ever been thrown out of North Africa, and by a SAC troop at that. I still had the Unauthorized Low Flying report dated 1 Mar 62, from Colonel Andrew J. Evans, Jr., Commander, 65 Air Division, in my file. We were chastised for low level flying in Morocco and restricted from cross-country navigation flights for a six-month period. I always attempted to blame the whole fiasco on RL. He was six months senior to me and had to be brilliant, since he attended the Air Force Academy.

It all started when our squadron allowed us to fly a two-seat version of the F-102, called "Fat Face", to Morocco for a refreshing weekend boondoggle. These very enjoyable cross-country flights were legal, as the Air Force required pilots to fly navigation flights each quarter. Our flights were restricted, to some extent, since we were only allowed to fly to approved bases that could service the Deuce. We figured that it would be great sport to fly to Morocco to ascertain the identity of camel herds, or flocks of sheep, up close and personal. We speculated that no one in the vast desert would be able to identify our unfamiliar TF-102. It was also a fact that there were few telephones in the remote areas for residents to report us, if they even knew whom to call.

Our first flight in old Fat Face led to an isolated B-47 Strategic Air Command (SAC) base, located at Benguerir, where the bombers were maintained on 15 minute Nuclear Alert. The Notices To Airmen (NOTAMS) warned us to watch for animals on the runway. The local residents stole fences and anything of value around the field. We wisely made a low pass over the runway to chase the goats away before pitching up into the landing pattern for a full stop landing. We then left our bird with the refueling crew and walked to Base Ops to plan for our next mission in the morning.

We considered ourselves highly skilled Deuce drivers that were capable of carefully planning a detailed low level mission. We ignored the fact that we were interceptor pilots who never flew these events. We decided that it was imperative to fly a very low-level mission over the desert, to the east of Benguerir, followed with a fly-by of the Moroccan Air Base at Meknes. We were hardly concerned that the air base was home to a squadron of Russian built fighters that were designated by the Air Force as MiG–15's. We were oblivious to the reality that the Moroccan pilots might become irate if an American fighter flew near their field. We also decided that it might be thrilling to continue our journey over the ocean to see how close we could fly to the waves. Then we would land and spend the night at Nouasser Air Base, where additional SAC B-47 nuclear-armed bombers were stationed.

The next day, RL and I were off and running in old Fat Face. We were excited when we blasted off at the break of dawn to play our game. We had the time of our lives chasing camels, goats, and anything that moved across the Moroccan desert. Then we decided to leave the desert to explore a range of mountains before heading north to Meknes. We were flying at treetop level, as we carefully followed a twisting highway through the mountains. It was a stirring challenge, due to the narrow pass, and we had to pay close attention to avoid hitting the mountains or the ground. We suddenly surprised an unaccompanied driver in a little red Triumph sports car when we banked around a sharp bend in the road. The motorist probably thought that his life had ended when he looked up and detected a large delta winged unidentified flying object coming directly at his head. The driver could not have heard or seen our aircraft until we were only yards away and the surprise on his face was something to behold. I hoped that he had not run off the road or had a heart attack from our sudden appearance, but we never returned to check on his fate. The astonished expression on the face of that poor driver was burned into my mind forever. I now realized that we should not have flown so low over a road, as we might have caused an accident to motorists.

Our navigation, we soon discovered, was not exactly on the mark when we departed the mountains and flew over a small ridge. We soon realized that we had badly miscalculated. It was obvious that we were extremely close to the MiG base that we had planned to skirt around. We tried to stay low and quickly depart the area but we could clearly detect the tower, which meant they could also identify us. At least we were lucky that all the MiGs were on the ground or we might have collided with one of their aircraft. However, we were not about to let a close encounter with a Moroccan airbase deter us from our duty and we continued on to the coast.

We turned south to parallel the beach after reaching the water. It had been exciting and pleasurable to fly over the sparkling blue ocean with its beautiful white capped waves. There were no ships along the coast to hinder our view of the beach as we streaked past Rabat and Casablanca at wave top level. The fuel gauge informed us that it was time to land at Nouasser Air Base where we had reservations for the night in the Bachelor Officers Quarters (BOQ). No one was waiting on the transit ramp to take us to custody; so we parked the Deuce and caught a ride to the BOQ. Later we located a local bus that provided transportation to Casablanca, where we explored the Casbah that I had seen pictured in a forgotten movie. We purchased camel saddles, inlaid wood, brass figures, and other souvenirs, that could be stuffed somewhere in our bird—with any luck at all.

We were airborne early and resumed our pursuit of the herds and flocks again the next day! I recalled that we had an enjoyable time watching the poor animals run in every direction. Our fun and games ended when a surly utterance on our radio ordered us to land our plane at Nouasser and contact the SAC Commander immediately. We tried to figure out what had transpired. Maybe the surprised sports car driver had reported our antics. We were not concerned about a desert herder's complaint—few rural residents were privy to a telephone.

We hoped that our unfavorable situation was not in any way related to our near miss with the MiG base at Meknes. It was soon evident that our slight error in navigation was the ominous problem and now we were in a dreadful predicament. An incensed SAC Colonel, who could not be reckoned with, met us on the flight ramp! He minced no words in telling us to fly our Deuce back to Spain at once and have our commander call him immediately. There was no doubt in my mind that he would have willingly thrown us into his brig, if we had been under his command. We learned that the MiG drivers had retaliated for our low pass on their base by returning the favor, which seemed reasonable to us since it was all in fun. Through his ranting curses, we learned that after we had flown over the Moroccan base, they had scrambled all their MiG-15 fighters. Then they repeatedly made low passes over his precious B-47's sitting on nuclear alert at Nouasser. The local air controllers had no problem finding us, as we were flying the only TF-102 in Africa. They were also aware that we had to land again before filing a flight plan for Torrejon.

The Nouasser base refueling truck quickly serviced our bird and it was evident the ground crews had gotten a kick out of seeing the Russian planes up close and personal. We immediately filed our flight plan for the Spanish Air Defense Identification Zone (ADIZ) en route to Torrejon. I conceive that we were in deep shit! I anticipated that my military flying days may become just be a memory in time. Looking back, it was inconsiderate of us to have chased the poor animals and scared the driver in the mountains. The passes on the SAC bombers had not seemed that harmful, as it was probably all in fun, but evidently bomber pilots just do not have a sense of humor. The SAC troops were always so serious about life and never seemed to have any fun, but they received rapid promotions for sitting on a bomb.

I retained a vivid memory of our squadron commander, Lt. Colonel George R. Halliwell, calling the SAC Colonel in our presence after we returned to Torrejon. The sight of him gently hanging up the telephone, as if it was a hot potato, after a one-sided conversation, was seared into my brain. It appeared that the Big Boss stepped in again to keep both RL's and my destiny on track because we never lost our wings. We were only restricted from cross-country flights for six months. I was sure the SAC colonel would have court marshaled us, since he thought we had placed nuclear-armed bombers in harms way. We were lucky that we had fighter pilot commanders who understood wayward Lieutenants.

9

APRIL 9, 1966
BOMB SHORTAGE

I wondered if our civilian and military leaders had a comprehensive game plan to win the series. It appeared that the McNamara had failed to buy sufficient equipment to compete in this deadly contest. We had a sufficient number of Fighter Teams, but ordnance was now in short supply. I was upset when our Umpire canceled all the contests tonight as the base was short of bombs. All my teammates were really pissed about the bomb shortage and the asinine ground rules. I questioned what the Target Master considered targets of importance in Pack One or Pack Five—I had never seen any. Maybe there were targets of significance around Hanoi or Haiphong, plus a few airfields, but I was not aware of any other meaningful targets in North Vietnam.

I speculated that we could have unlimited Fighter Teams, and still not stem the flow of supplies south. It was impossible to find trucks in the jungle with fast moving fighters. The enemy drivers could hear our loud jets or see our highly visible smoke trails and just hide in the jungle until we had to depart. An alert enemy would have placed observers on every mountaintop, of which there were a great many, to alert the truck drivers. The lookouts could see our smoke trails coming for over twenty miles in the daytime and could hear us coming for long distances at night. It was almost impossible to surprise the trucks, and even then, they could disappear into the jungle in seconds.

After questioning the Wing Intel Team, it appeared that the Thuds were fragged to constantly bomb areas that contained few targets of value. The enemy had transformed the area around Hanoi into an immense flak trap filled with hundreds of AAA sites blasting our aircraft out of the air daily. Maybe our Senior Managers thought fighters were simply expendable, as many unlucky aircrews had already been lost in North Vietnam. I decided to stop bitching and started playing a simple game of cards where I understood the ground rules. I was a lucky poker player, with a game plan, and won $15.00 before switching to bridge until sunrise. I felt sad when I realized that I had now competed in the Rolling Thunder League for over a month, with all my skill and cunning, without destroying a single truck in North Vietnam. However, I had earned an extra $65 for flying fourteen missions over North Vietnam and four over Laos. I pondered if there was something worthwhile at the Base Exchange to purchase with my new windfall, but I was lucky if they even had any writing paper.

APRIL 10, 1966

I was not pleased when all our missions were cancelled again. I joined the poker game with my old friends from Spain and lost $3.80, which made for a sorry night. I finally abandoned the poker table and wandered over to the old church to watch the nightly movie. I suffered through, "How to Stuff a Wild Bikini", it was a miserable flick, but it reminded me of the numerous beaches in Spain. I recalled that the military allowed us to fly on a SAC Rest and Recreation (R&R) flight that flew from Torrejon to Majorca each week in an old C-47. It was an opportunity to fly free to a splendid island with attractive European women on holiday. I rented a small under powered Vespa motor scooter and motored to a beautiful beach, with captivating scenery to enjoy the sun. I usually rented a small cabana near the water, for five dollars a day, where I could enjoy a bottle of the local wine while watching the sun slowly set in the Med. Sometimes I was lucky and encountered a charming English girl—they liked to fly from chilly Britain to enjoy Majorca. I recalled that I was fortunate when I met a friendly dentist's daughter from England who later drove me around London in her sports car after I flew our squadron's T-33 to her country. We had an outstanding time attending unrivalled stage performances in London. Ann gave me an English Crown after I explained that I had read about the coin but had never seen one. I also motored to many marvelous beaches in Southern Spain and flew to the Canary Islands for a delightful week. However, Majorca was the ideal island for single fighter pilots stationed in Spain.

The movie was bad, but the hot buttered popcorn and tasty coke had helped compensate for a lousy night. It seemed strange to always be flying at night and seldom see the sun, but I was beginning to welcome competing at night. However, I realized that I had to stay on the ball if I wanted to finish this series alive. It was necessary to dig in for all the deadly contests over hostile territory. I hoped the Target Master would not call for an Easter cease-fire, as it would take longer to complete a hundred missions if he kept delaying our contests. The pool was still not ready, but maybe someday it would open with any luck at all.

APRIL 11, 1966

Thanks to McNamara, we were still out of ordnance. I was upset when all our contests were cancelled for lack of proper equipment. I calculated that the Skunk Teams were arming to the teeth, and all the Mole Teams were stealing south while we warmed the bench. I had more free time to play poker and bridge, but I would rather have been trying to win a few battles. I played cards until dawn and ended up even after many hours of action. However, it was enjoyable to just play an organized simple game and not think about other convoluted contests that might last forever.

I received some good news tonight. Our flight was scheduled to fly air defense for the heavy hitting Bomber Teams! I was pleasantly surprised to learn that they would be dropping bombs on North Vietnam for the first time. It was hard to believe that the Buff's would be tossing a zillion tons of bombs on Mu Gia Pass after we had to cancel our contests due to a lack of ordnance. I speculated that it must cost a ton of money to fly B-52 Teams all the way from Anderson AFB on Guam to attack a small mole run. I had been to Mu Gia Pass many times this month and there was zilch to bomb except an insignificant dirt trail with lots of dense jungle on each side. I reckoned that thousands of groundkeepers would rapidly fill the craters.

10

APRIL 12, 1966
FIRST B-52 STRIKE ON NORTH VIETNAM
ROLLING THUNDER MISSION #15

We were fortunate to be the primary flight as that allowed us to compete in this new and interesting night contest with the heavy hitters. Bill and I were placed in the lineup with three other Night Owls to fly a "MiG CAP". We were ordered to protect the thirty B-52's, assigned to bomb Mu Gia Pass, from enemy aircraft. Wing Intel briefed that the dirt trail in the pass extended for approximately 21 miles which presented a large target to the Bomber Teams. Maybe a few of the 3240 bombs that the Buffs were capable of releasing would strike the enclosed trail. Our flight would refuel with a KC-135 tanker to allow ample flight time for us to protect our B-52 teammates. The Buff competitors might consider this a dangerous contest because Mu Gia Pass was located just over the Laos border into North Vietnam. This was the first time that the Bomber Team had ever competed on a NVL field.

Our Phantoms were each loaded with centerline and wing fuel tanks, four fuselage mounted Sparrow radar guided missiles, and two Sidewinder heat seeking missiles on each inboard pylon. There was enough firepower on each Phantom to destroy eight enemy aircraft. I would be surprised if the MiGs would compete against us tonight. They never seemed to fly at night and had very limited range.

Our flight conducted a detailed briefing on protecting the Buffs during their initial raid on North Vietnam. We had to crank up early—it would take longer than usual to taxi four aircraft and arm 32 missiles before departure. Each Sparrow had to be tuned in the arming area and the ordnance crew had to test each Sidewinder with a flashlight to see if it was tracking a heat source.

The maintenance and arming crews were superb! All of our birds passed the specified inspections, and we blasted off on time. We had ample time to contact the Tanker Team that was waiting for our flight. I was gratified to find that our weather was clear with no turbulence. We were all old Pros at the refueling game as we topped off our tanks, with no problems, and thanked the tanker participants for their assistance. I fell in trail with my flight commander, before our flight separated, and maneuvered into race tract patterns north of the Pass.

Our Phantoms established a protection zone between the Buffs and the MiG fields in North Vietnam, which placed us to the northeast of Mu Gia Pass. Each Owl flew a separate flight path so we could paint the bombers and observe our teammates on the radar of our aircraft. We would be able to intercept any MiG that tried to attack the bombers using our missiles. Of course, it would be difficult to detect the enemy if they attacked by flying on the deck before popping up to attack the bombers. However, that scenario was not realistic, as the MiG's had limited range and no air refueling capability.

The Buff Teams arrived at the Pack One Park exactly on time—SAC always competed using strict game rules. We listened to the Bomber Teams on our radio as the first flight of four started their bombing run to drop a zillion bombs on a dirt trail. We had been briefed by Intel that each Buff had the capability of dropping up to 108 five hundred-pound bombs. The bombers were using colors for call signs such as Red Flight, Green Flight, etc, as each flight made their attack. Suddenly our radio came to life with an excited call! Some of the B-52's declared they were under attack by opposing MiG contestants! All of our birds were in excellent position to cover every Buff, but none of us had any contacts on our radar, other than the bombers. I was frantically searching high and low for the attacking MiGs. Some of the Buffs were even firing their tail guns! I thought that maybe the MiGs had gotten by us by flying in at tree top level and were now attacking the bombers, but that was highly improbable.

I suddenly realized that our own airborne radar was painting the bombers and triggering their airborne radar warning system. We tried to radio the bombers that it was apparently just our radar painting them, but the Buff Teams never acknowledged any of our calls. I questioned if the bombers had even been briefed that we would be flying cover for them and operating our airborne radar. The Buffs continued to radio that they were under hostile MiG attack, until the last B-52 completed its bomb run. We finally ended our MiG CAP after the last bomber had left North Vietnam and was well on its way back to Guam. We never detected any of the aggressive MiG competitors that had supposedly entered the contest according to the Buffs.

I wished we could have been sitting in the Buff's debriefing room at Guam to hear the details on how they had been attacked by hostile fighters over North

Vietnam. I questioned why our Phantoms were not equipped with a similar radar-warning device to help protect us from the enemy. We also deserved to know when a AAA or SAM site was locked on and ready to fire, or if a MiG was ready to fire a missile up our tail. I was not pleased that our military leaders had not equipped our fighters with the same critical gear. However, fighter pilots might be considered expendable, as evidenced by the number of fighters shot down each day.

Mission Results: 0 trucks. (1.13 mission & 2+15 night)

RTL Summary: 0 trucks.

Mission Notes:

-Each B-52 was capable of bringing 108 five hundred-pound bombs to the contest.

-Each Phantom normally only carried six five hundred-pound bombs.

-Phantoms were not equipped with airborne warning devices.

I could not understand why the Target Master directed the heavy hitting Buff Team to drop thousands of bombs on an empty playing field. Nevertheless, it was an important sign to see that that the High Rollers were finally using heavy hitters against North Vietnam. It was obvious that the Buffs could quickly obliterate all significant targets in North Vietnam and maybe that would end the fighting in South Vietnam.

APRIL 13, 1966

I was disappointed that no one flew tonight. We all wanted to know the results of the monstrous Mu Gia Pass attack by the heavy hitters. I was convinced in my own mind that the road was already opened to truck traffic, since every ground-keeper in Pack One was probably working on the small dirt trail. Their ground maintenance crews had ample time to get the playing field ready for the next contest because we could not harass them due to the bad weather. It seemed logical that the trail would be opened in a few days, as North Vietnam appeared to have unlimited Fans to maintain roads.

I was anxious to inspect the trail the next time we were in the area, since I had bet my nightly combat pay of $2.17 that trucks were already speeding through the pass. The High Rollers must have spent an immense amount of cash to bomb the pass because the big spenders had to travel a long way to enter the contest. I questioned how the Rolling Thunder League could afford to compete in these expensive contests against the North Vietnam League. Maybe the Target Master was not aware that the road in Mu Gia Pass was only a small dirt trail and not a four lane super highway with a hard surface that could be destroyed. The bombs probably just blasted the earth up against the solid rock hillsides, and the ground crews simply leveled the dirt for immediate use in the next event. However, McNamara could claim that our forces had severed the enemy's "lines of communication" for a few days.

There was no one around the OClub that wanted to play bridge or poker, so I went to see "Ship of Fools" at the movie. I concluded that I might also be foolish for trying to hunt elusive moles at night with unguided bombs. I rode to the library to catch up on my reading and discovered an article in a recent 11 April 1966 U.S. News & World Report, that insinuated the war would become an endurance contest with slow and limited escalation. The report went on to say that thousands of bombs had been dropped on North Vietnam, but the attacks were not widespread enough to be decisive. The article appeared to be right on target. None of my bombs had been decisive, since they were usually scattered on a deserted patch of jungle called a truck park.

The writer also said that evidence showed the bombing had not greatly hurt the North Vietnamese war effort. That comment made perfect sense to me after watching our bombers scatter thousands of bombs on a deserted dirt trail. I was surprised to see that the magazine had published a picture showing a convoy of 50 enemy vehicles. For some reason, I had trouble finding even a single truck during 19 day and night low-level missions. I questioned why our Intel Shop never received any intelligence about where those big convoys were located. It would be nice to examine all the neat photos that were obviously available to the newsmagazines, to learn where the enemy trucks were hiding.

I was ticked off when I read another article, in the same magazine, indicating that Johnson and McNamara would not take advice from the Joint Chiefs of Staff regarding conduct of the war. I was disappointed that the Generals and Admirals could not get the attention of our civilian leaders. I was disappointed that our military leaders appeared to go along with the senseless game rules. It was evident to me that nothing was being accomplished on our playing fields. We needed to win some contests or this asinine competition might go on forever.

I noticed an American woman at the Officers Club, which was a rare event around here. She was the first American female that I had seen on base, because this sector was far away from any of the usual tourist routes. I recalled that I had my first crush on a girl in the first grade and had received my first kiss from cute Sally Donlan in the second grade and liked it. I remembered a birthday party from my childhood when I turned nine, and was allowed to invite girls. I only admired girls from afar until the eighth grade when a young girl allowed me to kiss her one evening when she was baby sitting. Another girl invited me to the

Junior Senior Prom, but we had very little to talk about, and I was not a praise-worthy dancer. I would always be grateful to Edna Thompson who took pity on me and helped me battle through the minefields of geometry.

I had decided to take easy courses in High School, since there was no money for college. My dream of becoming a fighter pilot had faded, and I had no idea what to do with my life. Maybe the Big Boss decided that I needed some assistance with my destiny after my junior year. My fortune changed one night at a country-dance when a tall blue eyed girl, whom I had never noticed before, indicated that she desired to go out with me. Lois Walker was the first attractive girl that ever expressed an interest in dating me, and I was immediately attracted to her too.

Lois was a year behind me in school and rode the school bus to St. Maries from a small village 14 miles from school where her parents owned the only store in town. Her parents were well off and allowed us to use the family lake house and a neat wooden Chris Craft speedboat for water skiing. They even granted us permission to drive their new Chrysler New Yorker for dating during the summer and my senior year. My life changed completely when her parents talked me into attending college. I was gratified when they gave me a job in their mercantile store to help make college a possibility. Their caring interest and generosity helped me attain my destiny to become a fighter pilot. I have always assumed that God had a hand in making sure that I attended college.

Lois and I had a few dates when she attended the University the following year, but evidently, we were not meant for each other. I thought that I was falling in love with a cute Pi Beta Phi, but she suddenly lost interest in me, which had always been a mystery to me. I dated a lovely girl for my last two years in college but felt I should complete my training as a fighter pilot before considering marriage. I had the opportunity to date lovely airline stewardesses, but a military career combined with an airline career resulted in "ships passing in the night". Sometimes, I felt as though the Big Boss controlled my love life as well as my destiny.

APRIL 14, 1966
BARREL ROLL MISSION #5

Our flight competed, without making an error, on the Laos fields for an hour, but we never scored during the long contest. Lead owl expended his flares over numerous sections of the Ho Chi Minh Trail, but we failed to notice any movement. I assumed the moles were smart enough to hide in the tall grass, as they could hear us coming long before the night-lights were illuminated. I requested lead to deploy his final flares on a straight section of the road for my final pass. I decided to release my CBU's while attacking very low and fast under the flares. I realized that it might be dangerous to fly for a long distance in the flare light, but I thought we would be OK. We had been fortunate that the resident skunks were not competing. I maneuvered down to treetop level, flew directly over the road, and precisely deployed the bomblets over the trail. Bill and I completed our attack without receiving a single hostile fireball, as we carefully placed our bomb-lets. We were satisfied when our leader radioed that he had noticed numerous secondary explosions all along the trail. It was evident that our ordnance had ignited something of consequence in the jungle during our attack.

I speculated that we might have hit some petrol storage areas positioned along the road or maybe a few parked trucks under the jungle canopy. There was no way of knowing what had exploded, but it may have been of some importance. I was gratified to think that we might have helped the troops in South Vietnam for a change! We returned to Home Plate knowing that we had scored a few hits dur-ing the contest, although we could not confirm any damage.

Mission Results: Numerous secondary explosions (1+35 night)

Barrel-Roll Summary: 2 trucks.

Mission Notes: CBU ordnance appeared to be an excellent weapon to use for mole contests.

I rode my trusty old bike to the OClub, after debriefing, for another breakfast as it was 0630 and the sun was rising. I located Crash in the game room and we talked two other teammates into playing bridge until ten AM. Then I pedaled back to the squadron and learned that our Coach had us on the schedule for a league contest in the Pack One Park tomorrow night. The swimming pool was still not open, but that was no surprise. I decided to see if I could sleep for at least eleven hours in my nice cool room with our luxurious air conditioner. I was well aware that I was fortunate to have the opportunity to enjoy tasty hot food and air-conditioned peace at night in a war zone.

APRIL 15, 1966
BARREL ROLL MISSION #6

I was very disappointed that our Pack One Park event was canceled due to a lack of ordnance. Nonetheless, we were then loaded with a single gattling gun and sent to Laos to compete in another practice contest. I glimpsed my first speeding mole on the Ho Chi Minh Trail tonight when we spied a little "hummer" before he disappeared into the tall grass. I selected my trusty six-shooter and played John Wayne by blasting both sides of the road with over a thousand rounds of 20mm cannon fire. I was optimistic of hitting the truck, but I was not sure of his position. The jungle all looked the same to me at night. It was probably all in vain, since there were no secondary explosions. I figured that the miserable mole had most likely escaped as usual. It was extremely difficult to hunt moles! They were tough sly creatures of the night and had a habit of disappearing quickly in the dense tall grass.

Mission Results: 0 trucks. (1+30 night)

Barrel-Roll Summary: 2 trucks.

Mission Notes: I preferred the gattling gun, instead of bombs, for trying to eradicate moles.

It was satisfying to shoot up the battlefield and reminded me of the time that I had met John Wayne when he visited the Officers Club at Torrejon, AB, Spain. He was not free to take me up on my offer to give him a ride in the Deuce, but he thought that fighter pilots were good patriotic jocks, and I got his autograph. I thought that the big guy would have enjoyed a ride in our squadron's TF-102. I recalled that he had made some movies about fighter pilots that were appropriate.

I walked down to the transit aircraft ramp, with some teammates, and inspected what was left of Dick Wade's poor bird after a missile scored a hit on it. The harassed bird was riddled with holes and I was impressed that Big Ugly was able to fly back to Home Plate. I was told that a MiG had lured them into a SAM Team's field of play, and then a devious competitor fired at the unsuspecting bird. Dick had immediately reversed course but the missile hit his bird in the tail before they could get out of harms way. The SAM exploded at the rear of the right engine and sent shrapnel through the right engine, wing, and tail section. The solid titanium stabilizer even had ugly jagged edged holes from the missile's 286-pound warhead that had a 200-foot kill pattern. It was astonishing to realize that their Night Owl had taken a direct hit and still kept flying for the home roost.

What was even more inconceivable, was that the shrapnel had cut the left engine's fire warning sensor—which triggered a fire warning light. Dick was then forced to shut that engine down, thinking it was on fire, and susceptible to a huge explosion. However, it was actually the reliable engine! The right engine's aft section and afterburner had been riddled with holes, but its fire sensor was not affected. Dick's gutsy bird made it home with its good engine shut down and the other operating with numerous holes everywhere. I knew that the Phantom was one rugged bird but this had to be one for the books. It appeared to me that the Big Boss was looking out for Dick and his GIB during their perilous contest.

Bert, our friendly telephone operator, offered to assist us if we ever had an emergency. We could call her at 114-6247840 in California. I thought that we were lucky to have at least one friendly American Fan on our side. She was doing this on her own accord and could get in trouble. I questioned why our Senior Managers never allowed us to call home, but at least we were permitted to write when paper was available.

APRIL 16, 1966
ROLLLING THUNDER MISSION #16

I competed in an uninspiring league contest with a B-66 Team against the Target Masters favorite target—Mu Gia Pass. I could not believe that we were ordered to scatter a few scarce bombs on the trail again. The heavy hitters had boasted four nights ago that they were going to close the pass forever, but they were obviously in error! I wanted to soar down to inspect the road and see what the Buffs had accomplished—it was probably nada. Nonetheless, I talked to my other teammates, who had recently competed in the Pass, and they indicated that it was already open to traffic. I had no problem participating in these unruffled league contests with the B-66 players, but we were not helping the war effort by wasting scarce ordnance. It was troublesome trying to understand how our few bombs could possibly be effective when thousands of B-52 bombs had not accomplished anything. I mused that if the moles over here were similar to ones I had battled in my yard—we would never pester them in a million years.

Maybe someday, the Target Master would realize that the groundkeepers could groom their mole trails faster than we could tear them up. The few bombs carried on an F-4C was nothing compared to a B-52, which begs the question of; "Why were we participating in contests that Buff Teams should be in charge of?" I was not comfortable flying missions that appeared to be ineffective and getting credit for it. The 497th was only averaging 10 league contests a month, for each man, and at that rate I would probably end up with 80 missions in 8 months. Nevertheless, I could then return to the States, as each 20 missions knocked a month off our obligatory 12-month tour.

Mission Results. 0 trucks. (1+10 night)

RTL Summary. 0 trucks.

Our Wing Commander, Colonel Joseph G. Wilson, joined us for breakfast and I was pleased to have a chance to talk with him. I recalled that I first met him after he had flown a Phantom to Maxwell AFB, with Captain Phil Offill, on a cross-country flight, while I was in Squadron Officers School. He had turned the bird over to Phil and me so we could use it over the weekend. I had the opportunity to fly the F-4 to Eglin AFB on Sunday, from the rear cockpit, to complete numerous radar approaches. I was gratified to get back in the cockpit, as I was rusty on the gauges. We then landed and refueled, before I assumed command of the Phantom for the return to Maxwell AFB. I decided to practice several landing patterns, since I had not landed the bird for many months. We were not aware that our landing patterns extended over the base golf course and would upset the golfers. I later learned that Lt. General Carpenter, the Air War College Comman-dant, golfed each Sunday. Our noisy aircraft was not appreciated when he was trying to score on the green.

I was pleased that Col. Wilson was interested in our comments and observa-tions about our nightly missions. He impressed me with his interpretations of the conflict. I thought that he was a conscientious Field Manager who grasped the meaning of this unproductive battle. Colonel Wilson appeared to care about pro-tecting his teammates from harm. He was also concerned about some of the deci-sions undertaken by the Senior Managers. It appeared that everyone was in the dark about why the Target Master was directing the heavy hitters to bomb an empty pass instead of airfields or ports. He indicated that he was flying to Saigon to see the Umpire in an attempt to grant us more credit for our night missions. We wished him luck, but it was doubtful that we would receive assistance or con-sideration from an Umpire's crew that never competed in any NVL night con-tests.

I was depressed today, as my life was passing by while I played in pointless games far from home. I appeared to be stranded on base with no way to reach home. I was frustrated in my attempts to make meaningful contributions to the RTL. I had competed in 16 league contests and six practice events, but had only scored a possible hit on two trucks in Laos. I finally decided to quit feeling sorry for myself and participated in a sporting game of basketball with my teammates. I soon regretted a decision that resulted in a stiff and sore back.

I recalled that my life would have been different if it had not been for sports and baseball in particular. I only possessed $450 dollars when I entered the Uni-versity of Idaho. It would have been impossible for me to continue my education if I had not received financial aid from the Athletic Department. I was a baseball walk-on my freshman year, but managed to be selected as one of the top two frosh pitchers. Our team was only allowed to play two games against Washington State College. I pitched the first contest, which I lost 5-3, but looked worthwhile to our coach. The Athletic Department came to my assistance and located a bus-boy position for me at Gault Hall starting my sophomore year. My new job paid for my room and board, which was a lifesaver, since those charges amounted to

75% of my school expenses. I appreciated the help from the University, because it would have been extremely difficult for me to continue in school without their assistance.

I recalled that I had pitched well during my sophomore year and won nine games. Coach Parberry took an interest my welfare and located summer employment for me in Sandpoint, Idaho, working for the Packriver Lumber Company. The lumber company sponsored an "All Star" baseball team and gave the players a job tearing down an old roller skating rink. We always received a days pay even if we had to miss work to play tournaments in Canada or depart early for night games in Spokane, Washington. It was exciting to play for a skilled team that made few errors! My team's exceptional support allowed me to register a 9-1 record. I was selected to pitch the final game that we won, for the Twilight League championship. I was thrilled when I was selected to the "All Star Team".

I returned to the University in the fall with greater confidence and improved pitching ability after a notable summer season. The Idaho Athletic Department finally endowed me with a quarter portion of a hundred dollar a month grant-in-aid given to athletes. I considered myself very lucky, since our team only had a few athletic scholarships to divide among the top players. I recalled that I had a memorable junior year at Idaho. I pitched our team to wins over the University of Oregon, Oregon State, and Washington State. I was very pleased to attain wins against the larger and wealthy schools in our conference, because most of their players were receiving full rides. I considered it noteworthy when I pitched our team to a win against Ray Washburn, who pitched for Whitworth College in Spokane, Washington. Ray later received a $50,000 bonus to play professional baseball.

I was offered an unprecedented opportunity to travel to Calgary, Canada, after my junior year, to pitch for an excellent semi-pro team in an exciting area. However, some unknown force convinced me that I was not meant to play high caliber baseball in a neat place. I was actually meant to attend the Air Force Summer Camp in Spokane to fulfill my destiny to become a fighter pilot. I pitched adequately my senior year in college but I would have been more proficient if I had played high level baseball in Canada. Baseball had to take a backseat to pilot training, but I always wondered what would have happened if I had not chosen fighters.

I was not able to play baseball again until I was assigned to Torrejon AB, Spain, where I pitched for the Base team. I was grateful to the 497th FIS for allowing me to fly one of our Deuces to other military bases in Spain to pitch on weekends. I was pleased to discover that my "hummer" and curve ball had improved since college days. I enjoyed the competition and helped pitch our team to the league championship. I was disappointed that I never competed at the European Championship Tournament, but I had a previous commitment to travel to Norway and Sweden with a good friend, Colin Nesbit. Maybe I was never meant to attend the games, since professional baseball scouts were there, and I could have chosen to depart the Air Force in a few years.

APRIL 17, 1966

I was no longer a Rookie Owl! My squadron finally authorized me to conduct ground duties. My team quickly placed me in the lineup to the squadron mobile controller's position in the tower. I spent the night recording routine takeoffs and landings and was required to lend a hand if an aircrew had an emergency. I had a taste of excitement when one of our "Hummers" blew a tire during the takeoff roll and aborted on the runway. There was no doubt in my mind that trying to stop a fully loaded Phantom on a short runway at night takes tremendous skill and cunning. The aircrew was in danger when the tire caught fire, but they were able to hastily scramble out of the wounded bird without a ladder. Then I had to divert all the airborne birds to Korat and cancel the remaining night contests. The base had to close the runway for the remainder of the night. At least, I was able to depart the tower early and adjourned to the Clubhouse for breakfast before organizing a card game.

I welcomed the opportunity to play bridge until sunrise as it took my mind off our ineffective nightly contests on empty fields, and I won $1.16 using 1/10 a cent scoring. It turned out to be a delightful warm beautiful day after the sun arose, so I decided to enjoy our tropical paradise. I borrowed a chair from the club, strolled across the street to the empty pool deck, and sat in the sun until I started to burn after a few hours. I pedaled back to the 497th and noticed that I was scheduled for a non-league practice contest in Laos with Major Hoyt leading the flight. Our Operations Officer informed me that the 433rd Squadron had lost a Phantom last night in Route Package One. It appeared that Major Sam R. Johnson and Lt. Chesley's Phantom had been shot down at dusk by ground fire. It was a reminder for me to never become complacent during twilight hours. You might think it was too dark for vicious skunks but they had exceptional eyes. The Jolly Green Team indicated that there was no evidence of them at first light. Their squadron teammates thought they had been captured during the night. I questioned if trying to find a few elusive moles hiding in the tall grass and protected by numerous venomous skunks was worth all this crap.

11

We witnessed an unusual experience tonight after we departed Home Plate for a routine contest in Laos. Our flight had just taken off, and we were departing to the east near a sinister thunderstorm that was boiling up close to the base. I had just cleaned up my gear, while closing on lead, when a large brilliant bolt of lightning discharged from the threatening storm and struck Major Hoyt's bird on its nose. The lightning charge that materialized from a dark cloud exploded every explosive charge on the pylons, ejector racks and tanks. It was very spectacular to watch all the rockets, flares, and tanks on his aircraft disengage at the same instant and hurl to the ground. I was impressed to see that his Phantom was still flying after taking the direct lightning strike that jettisoned all the external stores in the blink of an eye. I quickly joined up with our leader, so we could inspect their bird, as we circled around the base. We could see that the lightning had struck the F-4 in front of the canopy near the radar nose cone, but there was no serious damage to the bird. It was fortunate that the lightning strike had not set off their ejection seat charges, which would have left them swinging in the wind.

I speculated that their jettisoned equipment was now buried deep in some rice patty. I hoped it had not killed any Thai farmers when it hit the ground. It appeared that the rockets had not detonated, because we never noticed any explosions on the ground. It would be another tough job for the ordnance team—they would have to locate and extricate the buried equipment. Lead told us to continue alone to Laos to search for trucks before it was too dark to drop our bombs. Bill and I hustled over the border and hunted for moles on the trail towards Tchepone, but we could not even find a truck being used as a flak trap. It was always amazing to see how meticulous the groundkeepers kept the trail, which made you realize that trucks were probably rolling south each day. We decided to crater the trail instead of the designated molehill, to keep the groundkeepers busy for a few hours. I dropped our bombs in "singles mode" and spread them along the trail in hopes that we might just get lucky and hit a mole hiding in the tall grass.

Mission Results: 0 trucks. (+40 day & +30 night)

Barrel-Roll Summary: two trucks.

APRIL 19, 1966
BARREL ROLL MISSION #8

We had another no-show practice contest in Laos. Lead owl expended all his flares looking for moles, but they never accepted our invitation to compete. We finally released our ordnance on what might have been the designated truck park, although it was too dark to see anything. We finally gave up the hunt and flew home to roost. I was beginning to think that the Senior Managers were mistaken about the NV League owning any Mole Teams. I had not been able to locate any of the shy participants. Maybe most of the supplies were carried to South Vietnam by water buffalo, ox carts, or on the backs of a zillion NVL Fans. I had flown eight missions in Laos, and had only hit two burned trucks that were probably decoys. However, the groundkeepers maintained the mole runs in superb condition, so something was traveling south, but remained hidden in the tall grass from our prying eyes.

Mission Results: 0 trucks. (1+15 night)

Barrel-Roll Summary: 2 trucks.

Mission Notes: Maybe supplies were moving south, but not by trucks.

I had a variation in my appetizing cuisine at the Clubhouse tonight—I ordered fried chicken instead of my usual breakfast. The weather remained wretchedly wet and washed out some of our contests, but it was advertised to clear next month. However, the local weatherman informed me that extremely heavy rains would soon start in earnest as monsoon season was rapidly approaching. I joined a stimulating poker game with Braz, Dick, Crash, and Bill; I managed to lose $1.55, but welcomed the company of my teammates. No one talked about our ineffective contests, since few hits were scored, and we never seemed to win any battles. I had no idea on how we could compete more effectively to win a few engagements. It appeared that my teammates were also unable to offer any strategy on how to win a few games.

Several of my GIB teammates received orders to Europe, but had to remain in the back cockpit due to the needs of the military. They were aggravated and wanted to upgrade to the front seat as aircraft commanders, since they had served their country meritoriously. I certainly could not blame them, because they had been sitting in the back for two years. I thought that they certainly deserved some consideration from the Senior Managers. I imagined that they would depart the military to fly for the airlines at first opportunity, and I could understand why. The Air Force never appeared to give a rat's ass about losing experienced pilots because the Senior Managers just increased the number of students at the pilot training schools. The airlines certainly benefited—it allowed them to acquire highly trained pilots that would not cost them a cent since the taxpayers picked up the tab.

APRIL 20, 1966
ROLLING THUNDER MISSION #17

I participated in another uninspiring league contest—we strew six 750-pound bombs on Mu Gia Pass with our usual B-66 Bomber Team. Maybe some day the Target Master might realize the error of his ways and stop bombing an empty pass that even the B-52 Heavy Hitters could not close. I let Bill fly most of the mission. It had to be a bitch flying in the rear cockpit for an entire tour. I would certainly hate to be at the mercy of an aircraft commander who made all the decisions. We completed a routine landing and adjourned to the Clubhouse after debriefing our exhilarating mission. I played bridge until sunrise with Crash before making my usual inspection of the promised swimming pool that was still not available for fun and games.

Mission Results: 0 trucks. (1+15 night)

RTL Summary: 0 trucks.

I recalled that I had the freedom of choice to leave the Air Force after my initial tour and maybe I had made the wrong decision. I could now be flying for a large commercial airline like most of my classmates from pilot training class 61-E; or possibly playing professional baseball like a contemporary of mine. There was a very slim chance that I could have become a CPA and turned into a pencil pusher with a boring job for the rest of my life.

I could not explain my rationale for remaining in the military or participating in this war, but it appeared that I was just "meant to be" a fighter pilot. I speculated that I had decided to remain in the Air Force to help protect our country from the "Bad People" that wanted to destroy our way of life. I had not figured out how the little fisherman in his tiny wooden boat matched my definition of the "Bad People". I might not have remained in the Air Force if I had known that I would be attacking a small extremely poor country located half way around the world. It was not evident to me that they were threatening our way of life. Most of them had never enjoyed indoor plumbing or owned a motorized vehicle.

I realized that I would never be happy in a monotonous job like flying aluminum overcasts or sitting behind a desk for the rest of my life. I would rather live an exciting life and run the risk of being killed than be bored to death in a mundane job with only a yearly vacation to spice my existence. I had no idea what God might have in store for me, but it had been a great ride to date with no regrets if it ended tomorrow.

APRIL 21, 1966

Our Laos exhibition contest was canceled due to adverse weather—I spent the rest of the night in the tower pulling mobile control duty. I was aware that rain had now been coming down in torrents for over 24 hours and the whole base was saturated. I was disappointed that we were not on the schedule for tomorrow night—it made for a long day when we did not compete in a league contest. I was so bored that I even considered dusting off my civilian duds and going to town with Crash. I decided that going to Ubon was a hassle, and we still had to attend a squadron Intel briefing. I decided to join some teammates at the Clubhouse for a meal and then take in the evening movie although it was an unknown ancient black and white flick. I completed my daily inspection of our promised swimming pool in my damp and moldy flight suit. The pool was still not open, but maybe it would be ready for action before my final contest in this league.

I rode my bike to the Wing briefing room for the late night intelligence briefing that accounted for all aircraft lost during the daylight missions and learned that seven Air Force and Navy fighters had been lost. It was my opinion that fighter pilots were like teenagers and considered themselves invincible with nothing ever happening to them. Thus, all the losses were disregarded. They always happened to other unfortunate combatants. Intel instructed us to listen for emergency beepers and note their locations. I questioned why downed teammates would leave their beepers on, as that would allow unfriendly Fans to locate them. I decided that I would never be taken alive if I were shot down. I could not live in captivity and be tortured. I had grown up in a small town in North Idaho where I could roam by myself in the mountains hunting elk and seldom saw another human. I had always been a free spirit and would not last long jailed in a tiny cell. Thus, I always loaded my sidearm with five tracer rounds and one bullet with my name on it if rescue was not possible.

APRIL 22, 1966

Bill and I were not flying tonight, so I peddled over to the library to check out another novel and read the newsmagazines—It was always interesting to read what the perceptive journalists and politicians were saying about the war. TIME magazine had a picture of Thuds releasing bombs, but they were flying straight and level, which seemed odd, unless they were also bombing Mu Gia Pass. The article also stated that the Navy was conducting bombing missions North of Hanoi with 750 and 3000-pound bombs. I questioned what they were dropping 3000-pound bombs on! I had not spotted any targets that required a bomb of that magnitude. The largest bombs that we were loaded with for our battles only weighed 1000 pounds.

I made a major blunder by sitting through a bad movie that was possibly one of the first films ever made. It was called "Irish Eyes Are Smiling" and had probably been stashed in a military warehouse for the last thirty years. The military might have been saving it to show to some captive contestants involved in an inexplicable conflict with asinine ground rules.

I was depressed as we were not winning our contests against hostile teams and even the food was starting to lose some of its taste. Thank God for Bert, our friendly telephone operator in California, who made an appearance and patched some of us through to the States. It was remarkable that she jeopardized her job by connecting us to our home telephones. I felt that our resourceful Senior Managers should allow us to telephone our home country if we paid for the call. I thought that it should be permissible to call home once a month or at least on special occasions, like completing 100 missions. We were all fortunate that a lone American Fan, who cared about our teams, would patch us through to the States at her own risk. Each of us should try to find her when we returned to the states and treat her to a nice dinner with champagne. Sometimes I questioned if the High Rollers and Senior Managers were concerned about their teams.

APRIL 23, 1966
BARREL ROLL MISSION #9

Bill and I competed in another humdrum exhibition contest in Laos tonight without ever seeing a single skunk or mole participant. We took turns flying our bird while searching miles of empty mole trails and finally squandered our bombs on an Umpire's truck park that appeared to be just generic jungle. I questioned if our Senior Managers would ever comprehend that Night Owls could not find and destroy trucks near jungle cover.

I wondered if the Spooky Teams were contributing more to the war effort and knocking out trucks. I had noticed our teammates old C-47 prop job on the base, but never talked with any of the team. I certainly had no desire to fly ancient WWII cargo aircraft at night with no ejection seats for any teammates on the bird. They really had big balls to compete in night battles with vicious skunks lurking in the tall grass waiting to hurl blistering fireballs at them. Our Spooky teammates were probably more effective than Night Owls in Laos but they would be in trouble if they competed against the dangerous 37/57mm skunk dens in the Pack One Park. In any event, my hat was off to these gutsy Spooky Teams flying ancient birds.

Mission Results: 0 trucks. (1+05 night)

Barrel-Roll Summary: two trucks.

APRIL 24, 1966
ROLLING THUNDER MISSION #18

I realized that we might be a couple of lucky owls. We were assigned to fly another easy bomber mission, high and sheltered, in the sky over Mu Gia Pass. I should be embarrassed to scatter bombs on an empty road that might be repaired before we landed, but what the hell, each mission counted towards the magic 100. Sometimes I felt a pang of guilt when Intel told us the number of Thuds that were lost attacking targets protected by the world's largest concentration of harmful skunk dens. I was perturbed with the Target Master's game plan, but the pointy nosed contestants, with a bomb bay were entitled to be infuriated! They were losing many teammates every day! The Thuds were apparently ordered to bomb the same targets every day, and they were surrounded by a zillion skunk dens!

The Mu Gia Pass bomber mission was a short ineffective league contest, but it still contributed towards the magic 100, and allowed me to place another old copper penny in my little tin can. I had flown 18 missions over North Vietnam without destroying a single truck. That might be an inauspicious record, but I was really trying to help the troops in South Vietnam. It appeared to me that the Master Bean Counter's Team had no idea what was going on over here. I questioned if anyone ever analyzed our reports or they would notice that our missions were usually ineffective.

Mission Results: 0 trucks (1+15 night)

RTL Summary: 0 trucks.

APRIL 25, 1966

I was assigned mobile duty tonight and had time to read the "Listener" by Taylor Caldwell, while monitoring the takeoffs and landings. I enjoyed a tasty treat from Idaho as my Mother had sent my favorite coconut fudge—but the chocolate chip cookies were smashed beyond recognition. Nevertheless, I still ate every crumb as I relished my delicious treat from home. I noticed that our base usually received mail every other day. I figured that was acceptable since we were in the middle of nowhere.

I played a fair-to-middling bridge game with Crash as I won a dollar but we played with a couple of players that smoked up a storm. I felt very fortunate that my mother had stopped my secret smoking habit when I was eleven. I recalled that my best friend and I had been at liberty to walk along the highway and retrieve cigarette butts that we stripped of tobacco and then rolled into cigarettes. We also had another source of cancer sticks, as Johnny's parents operated a service station that sold cigarettes. He would borrow a pack for us every so often. I recalled that I always wanted him to pilfer Wings because they were the only king size cigarettes the store carried.

One day we were having a grand time constructing model airplanes and smoking in my family's chicken coop when my mother walked in with a newly cut switch. Johnny was ordered home with some choice words, and now, I was free to be swatted all the way to the house, which was a long way. The thrashing mainly hurt my feelings, but I was sure that the future sting of my father's razor strap would be a different story. I was pleased when my mother promised not to tell my father if I would never smoke again—I readily agreed and I seldom polluted the air again except for an occasional cigar when studying for tests in college. I also tried a pipe once, but could never keep the damn thing lit, and decided that it was a complete waste of time anyway.

I visited the library, after eating breakfast, and located an interesting article in TIME about our unprecedented B-52 raid on Mu Gia Pass. The article indicated that the heavy hitters had dropped 630 tons of bombs! It was one of the largest raids since WWII. I questioned the writer's informatory sources that insinuated the bombs had sent huge avalanches cascading into the pass and blocked the vital artery. We all knew that the road opened after a few days, but it was a little wider thanks to the American taxpayers. I also disputed the information reporting that there were stalled convoys waiting to drive through the pass and 42 trucks had been destroyed. I could not believe that trucks were parked in the middle of the road waiting to be bombed. They could have disappeared into the nearby jungle in seconds. I found it ridiculous that any trucks could have been destroyed because no one could fly for a few days after the raid due to adverse weather. I could not hypothesize where all this favorable information had originated for the report, as it was incredulous to me.

I was pleased to see another TIME article with a General asserting that fighters could not carry sufficient bombs to do the job and that B-52s should strike North Vietnam whenever needed. It was only logical to throw the heavy hitters into the contest to take out the targets that were killing the Thud Teams. Maybe I was wrong about the Senior Managers—they might be serious about ending this war if they started using the B-52s over North Vietnam.

APRIL 26, 1966
BARREL ROLL MISSION #10

Bill and I participated in another lonely night exhibition contest in Laos hunting for crafty moles that never emerged from the tall grass. Maybe the High Rollers had it all wrong and there were very few mole contestants around to compete against owls. I decided to scatter my bombs on the well-groomed mole run, instead of the designated molehill—it just might piss off the groundkeepers hiding in their dugouts.

I had to admit that we were not helping the troops in the South with our ineffective contests on deserted practice fields. I was convinced, in my own mind, that it was impossible to discover moles when there was dense tall grass nearby for cover. I was very frustrated! I was striving to win an event, but it was impossible to score a hit in these irrational contests. The Target Master should designate vital targets in North Vietnam that would be worthy of our time and effort. We returned to Home Plate and logged the usual 1.3 practice contest. Then we completed a quick debriefing with the Intel participants before heading to the Clubhouse for food and cards.

Mission Results: 0 trucks. (1+35 night)

Barrel-Roll Summary: 2 trucks. (10 missions) (Average .200)

APRIL 27, 1966
BARREL ROLL MISSION #11

At last, we caught a glimpse of two speeding trucks on the trail tonight before they disappeared into the jungle. We were lucky and caught them on a winding portion of the road without a turnout. There was one devious skunk den, hiding in the tall grass, that tried to hose us but the stinker could not direct his spray accurately. I noticed that there were very few experienced and battle tested 37/ 57mm AAA sites along the Ho Chi Minh Trail, but their numbers and accuracy would probably increase. The only harmful skunk den that had gotten my attention in Laos was the deadly fireball hurler over at Tchepone—he was an extremely accurate stinker. I noticed that many of our teammates never seemed to get the word about the murderous Tchepone skunk den. The "aircraft loss" board at Wing Intel was continuously adding more losses in that area.

We ignored the light skunk spray as I strafed the area where the trucks had disappeared and was pleased to notice a few secondary explosions. It was always gratifying to fire the gattling gun as it generated a distinctive reverberation when the six barrels spit out lead. I realized that the enemy might salvage the thousands of expelled 20mm brass casings and eventually return them with vengeance. I recalled how the scavengers in the California desert had sneaked on the range at night to steal the brass—it was a good cash crop.

I informed the Wing Score Keeper that we might have tagged two trucks, but it was impossible to call them out of the contest. I was not concerned that we were only toting the six shooter on our Phantom due to the ordnance shortage. I considered bombs unsatisfactory for attacking trucks.

Mission Results: 0 trucks. (1+25 night)

Barrel-Roll Summary: 2 trucks.

APRIL 28, 1966
ROLLING THUNDER MISSION #19

Bill and I enjoyed flying with our leader tonight, as all the fields in the Pack One Park were calm and peaceful. The shy moles remained off the trails, and the nasty skunks must have been sleeping in their dens. I felt that on some nights the enemy could care less that we were flying over their land and eventually scattering a few bombs on a suspected truck park. It was logical to assume that the moles were aware that night owls were hunting for them. It was also rational to assume that they were not going to run on the trails while we were in the air. In was my opinion that we were in a mole and owl contest, with the skunks as a wild card. However, this owl appeared to be losing the game, because I never seemed to be able to get a single hit.

We illuminated the fields near the Quang Khe Ferry crossing to search for moles but never spotted the dark critters. We had to return our bombs to home plate as the Wing was running out of ordnance. Nonetheless, I was pleased to have finally competed in a RTL contest, although it was ineffective, as I was fed up with the practice events in Laos.

Mission Results: 0 trucks. (1+15 night)
RTL Summary: 0 trucks.

APRIL 29, 1966

I was down in the dumps today because I had not seen one significant target to attack in the Pack One or Pack Five Parks. I theorized that all the consequential targets were up in the Pack Six Park, but it looked as though this country was very poor, with few industries, and no vehicles. Maybe we should be assisting this country to help it out of the Stone Age instead of destroying what little they owned. Someday it might be turned into a nice tourist attraction with its beautiful mountains, rivers, and seemingly worthwhile beaches. I recalled that Germany recovered nicely after WWII. I never noticed any war damage as I traveled around their country.

However, the beaches in Libya were beautiful with their spectacular Roman ruins on the Ocean, but it had not yet become a tourist Mecca. I remembered a time when we flew from Spain to Wheelus, AB, in Libya once a year to fire the F-102's radar missiles. I always found time to visit the exquisite beaches. Several of us would drive to the well-preserved Roman ruins at Leptis Magna that had a magnificent amphitheater on the beach with a spectacular view of the Med. I was disturbed when the resident children would throw rocks at us unless we gave them money. It appeared to me that none of the inhabitants in Libya liked Americans. It would be interesting to see if Libya initiated a tourist trade in the future.

I had the night off from all duties, so I headed to the cool library to read the latest news. I read an interesting article in the 25 April, U.S. News & World Report, quoting General's MacArthur, Bradley, Eisenhower, and Taylor. The Generals were in thoughtful accord that our country should not be involved in a land war in Asia, but our High Rollers were obviously more informed than any military general. I read that Senator Dirksen was optimistic that the heavy bombing of VC supply routes might "take some of the steam" out of the enemy. It appeared that our Senior Managers had not notified the Senator that we were unable to even detect, much less stop the trucks or troops.

I was really pissed when I read where McNamara denied that there was a bomb shortage and said, "It just isn't true,—there is not any such shortage of bombs". I hated to disagree with the Edsel Kid, but we canceled all our sorties from the 9th to 12th, and then, just flew with a gattling gun for many missions. I was also pissed to read that President Johnson described McNamara as a "great Secretary of Defense." It was deplorable that our National Command Authorities never listened to our military leaders and were misrepresented the facts to the tax-payers.

APRIL 30, 1966
ROLLING THUNDER MISSION #20

Our flight hunted for sly moles on all the usual mole runs in the Pack One Park, with our six-shooter, but we never spotted any movement. We returned to Home Plate without scoring a hit and I logged it as another ineffective contest in the North Vietnam series. I was embarrassed to acknowledge that I had struck out for the 20th time in a row and maybe I should be traded for a better hitter. I knew that my eyes were trustworthy, and I had good athletic reflexes but I could not seem to get into this contest. I was certainly open to suggestions from our coaches. I have always been a team player but I was at a loss on how to get a hit. My batting average was 0 for 20 or .000 for our NVL contests, but none of my teammates appeared to be averaging any higher in this frustrating series.

Maybe the High Rollers should negotiate with the enemy and pay them a million dollars to destroy each truck! I figured that it had to be less expensive than following their current game plan. I questioned if our Senior Managers were even concerned that we seldom discovered any moles at night, unless we encountered one that was deaf and dumb. I was always amazed at how fast a mole could disappear into the tall grass. I speculated that they must have tunnels all along the Ho Chi Minh Trail!

Mission Results: 0 trucks. (1+30 night)

RTL Summary: 0 trucks. (Playing average is 0% for 20 RTL missions)

MAY 1, 1966
BARREL ROLL MISSION #12

We had bad luck tonight as our mission in Pack One was cancelled, due to weather, but we regrouped and blasted off for a practice contest in Laos. We searched for many miles but found no evidence of vehicles, oxen, bikes, or hand carts along the red dirt trails. I strafed the jungle beside the road, hoping there might be an unsuspecting mole sleeping in the tall grass, but neither Bill nor I noticed any secondary explosions. We failed to entice a single stinker to toss a hot fireball our way during our multiple strafing attacks. It proved an unrewarding night as we never exterminated a single mole or assisted our troops in the South. We returned to Home Plate and signed the score book, showing another ineffective practice contest.

Mission Results: 0 trucks. (1+20 night)

Barrel-Roll Summary: 2 trucks.

I rode my bike to the OClub for my usual breakfast. Then I played poker with friends until dawn. I was lucky and won seven dollars which would more than pay for my monthly club dues. I later decided to lie in the sun for a few hours but terminated this ill advised maneuver when it reached 103 degrees. I investigated the Base Exchange each day to see if they had something of value in stock, which was usually fruitless, because I had trouble just finding writing paper. Maybe the Edsel Kid and his teammates were also in charge of buying writing paper for our Teams, because we were still short of ordnance. I was pleased when I checked the lineup and discovered that our Coach had scheduled us for a league contest tomorrow night in the Pack One Park.

12

MAY 2, 1966
CLOSE CALL IN MU GIA PASS
ROLLING THUNDER MISSION #21

It proved to be a perplexing and dangerous mission tonight! Bill and I had an extremely close call during our battle. We were very fortunate that we had not been blasted from the sky with our own bomb shrapnel in Mu Gia Pass! It had started out as a routine mission as we departed on time and refueled with a KC-135 Team, near Udorn in northern Thailand. We were ordered to search for trucks in the Red River Valley, before going to Mu Gia Pass. It was a beautiful day for our flight over Laos, and I was pleased that the disagreeable skunks were dormant. Nonetheless, we were aware of the numerous destructive skunk dens situated around Thud Ridge. We knew that the Skunk Teams in that area were very experienced. We were cautious owls and changed our altitude and flight direction every few seconds. We wanted to play another day.

We never spotted any movement on the roads in Pack Five. There was simply too much tall grass available for the timid moles to use for cover. It was obvious that bashful moles were very wary creatures. I speculated that they could hear us coming from a great distance, or see our two jets spewing black smoke during the day. We finally departed the Red River fields, without spying a truck, and headed for Mu Gia Pass.

It was dark by the time we reached Mu Gia Pass and our leader expended all his flares searching for moles that might have been hiding in the tall grass or tunnels in the hillsides. There was no evidence of even a single destroyed vehicle. The trail appeared to be in perfect condition as usual. I decided that the TIME article claiming 42 destroyed vehicles around Mu Gia Pass was a bunch of bull. Bill and I still had six scarce 750-pound bombs that we had to drop due to insufficient fuel for recovery to Home Plate. We radioed lead that we would execute a blacked-out attack, towards the south, on the road going through the pass. I intended to complete our attack by maneuvering for a roll-in from the west to place our bird in a steep dive heading directly south through the pass. I asked Bill for an extra high release call. The mountains were very high around the pass, and we needed to recover well above the highest peak. I confirmed that our bombs were armed, and climbed to position for our dive, which had to be flown on instruments. It was now very dark, but I could vaguely see the valley and the mountain peaks.

I maneuvered our soaring Night Owl for an attack down the valley. I reached my desired altitude, lowered our birds nose, and dove into the darkness. I rolled our wings level while placing the gunsight's pipper into the darkest section of the valley and waited for Bill's call to release. The Big Boss might have come to our assistance! I suddenly felt uncomfortable and concluded that we had been in the dive too long. I had already started dropping our bombs before our preplanned pickle altitude when suddenly the altimeter cut loose. Bill immediately yelled "pickle and pull"! The altimeter had malfunctioned and was unwinding way beyond normal. It appeared that the instrument had stuck, which placed us way below our desired altitude. I could tell by Bill's voice that I had better pull immediately with force.

I had no sooner gotten the nose up, using excessive G's, when the bombs started exploding under us and illuminating the valley. I will never forget the fearful spectacle of seeing dark mountain walls on each side of our bird! I was dismayed to discover that we were near the bottom of the valley! Our best-laid plans had gone to shit, as we had not safely recovered above the highest peak. I speculated that the Big Boss might have been looking out for us—we would have been dead if I had released a few seconds later, or if our heading had not taken us straight down the valley. The vision of our bombs exploding, under our bird, to highlight the menacing mountain walls was burned into my brain forever—maybe God had saved my tail again! I was stupefied and could not even utter a word during our return flight to Home Plate. It was obvious that we had only been a few seconds, or degrees, away from becoming a solitary flaming spot on the canyon floor. I speculated that the military would have scored our disappearance as just another aircrew lost in combat from unknown enemy actions.

Mission Results: 0 trucks. (1+10 night & +40 day)

RTL Summary: 0 trucks.

Mission Notes: "Hummer" altimeters could malfunction without warning.

MAY 3, 1966
BARREL ROLL MISSION #13

I was awarded my first Air Medal at Wing Headquarters. Lt. General Bowman decorated a few selected aircrews for completing 10 Rolling Thunder missions. A few of the old Pros complained about having to arise in the middle of the day for this meeting with Senior Management—they were exhausted. I had to smile when I heard a decorated pilot's comment that "two-bits and an Air Medal might buy you a cup of coffee back in the States". I recalled reading somewhere that The Target Master had received a Silver Star Medal when he was a passenger on a plane back in WWII. The Thud drivers should be receiving the Silver Star for many of their missions up in the "Valley of Death". I speculated that most civilians had no idea what it took to be awarded an Air Medal and probably could care less. It was possible that I would end up with ten Air Medals, with any luck at all, as the Air Force awarded one for each ten missions over North Vietnam. Receiving the Air Medal would permit me a to wear a ribbon on my uniform or a miniature medal on my Mess Dress attire. However, fighter pilots normally lived in a flight suit and never wore a uniform unless it was a special occasion.

We blasted off for Laos on time for our routine mission on the Ho Chi Minh Trail hunting trucks. Our bird was loaded with two canisters of scarce and expensive cluster bombs. I recalled that we had obtained numerous secondary explosions the last time I expended CBUs on a seemingly empty trail in Laos. I contemplated that if we never saw any trucks, I would go down low, under the flares, and drop the bomblets directly on the road. I was convinced in my own mind that there might be trucks hidden close to the road, in turnouts, along with fuel storage depots. We would be taking a chance by attacking under the flares at a very low altitude but it was necessary in order to keep all the bomblets directly on the road. The bomblets were not capable of penetrating through the jungle canopy and striking the trucks or fuel storage areas.

As usual, we never spotted any trucks during our long hunt. Lead radioed that he could only make one final flare release. I realized that it was time to execute our final attack under the flares to deliver the cluster bomb units. Lead selected a long straight portion of the road and released his flares over the trail for our low altitude run. We may have surprised the resident stinkers, because they never even threw a fireball at us, while we flew at a very low altitude for a long distance. It appeared to be an effective attack. We observed numerous secondary explosions, but there was no way of telling if any trucks or fuel depots had ignited. I concluded that we might have gotten the enemies attention! Now they would have to reposition trucks and fuel farther from the road. I was reasonably sure that we could compete competitively under the lights at night if we were equipped with CBU Dispensers for every contest, but that would be very expensive.

I was convinced that the 497th Old Pros were in error about not flying below the flares, and I would continue to attack targets under them. The low altitude assault had not appeared to be overly hazardous. It enabled me to place my ordnance directly on a target instead of losing it in the dense jungle. I speculated that the skunk dens had insufficient time to acquire a speeding owl flying under the flares, much less have an opportunity to pull lead. Nonetheless, we would have to be extremely careful when dropping iron bombs. The bomb fragments would blast us out of the sky if we released too close to the ground.

Mission Results: Numerous secondary explosions. (1+15 night)

Barrel-Roll Summary: 2 trucks.

Mission Notes:

-CBU dispensers were excellent for night contests away from heavily defended areas.

-Flying low under the flares was required to complete precise attacks.

-AAA sites seldom fired when we attacked under the flares.

-Enemy gunners would be hard pressed to pull lead on a speeding bird flying through the flares.

MAY 4, 1966

The wretched weather forced our Coach to cancel all our contests tonight—so I used my free time to attend a newly released movie that are seldom distributed to Ubon. "Thunderball" was playing, but it was necessary to wait for the 0100 showing because the movie theater was completely packed a full hour before it started. It was obvious that everyone was excited that the base had gotten a current flick to watch. I was gratified that we had the opportunity to see movies during a war. I assumed that many of the troops in South Vietnam might not be so fortunate.

The library had some new magazines, and there was a bang-up picture of Defense Secretary McNamara buying bombs at a surplus store. The TIME article also stated that the Secretary refuted Gerald Ford, Republican Leader of the House, when he stated that "we were running short of bombs, despite billions spent on the war". The April 25th U.S. News & World Report had an appalling report titled "Did the Whiz Kids flunk their Arms Test?" Secretary McNamara stated "It just isn't true. There isn't any such shortage of bombs". He told reporters that American planes had dropped 50,000 tons of bombs in March from a total U.S. inventory of 331,000 tons. He failed to mention that most of them were dropped on empty dirt trails or deserted truck parks. It was also interesting to learn that it costs $400 for each 750-pound bomb that we scatter around the jungle.

McNamara failed to explain that many missions were ineffective, and that it was impossible to hit trucks with unguided iron bombs. It was stupid to brag about a great number of missions and tons of bombs dropped, when they were just scattered on a pseudo truck park. I was not concerned about the bomb short-age, as the gattling gun was better for trucks, but I was shocked to read about McNamara deceiving Congress. The article went on to say that High-ranking military men have voiced skepticism about Mr. McNamara's use of statistics. I personally thought that the bomb shortage was not a determinant, since the Tar-get Master never assigned any worthwhile targets to attack.

I was shocked to read that the President Johnson was one of the strongest backers of McNamara and described him as a "Great Secretary of Defense." I was bewildered when I read that President Johnson had also experienced a critical supply problem. He stated that he had run out of lead pencils during the night and had to find one all by himself. I marveled about our National Command Authorities ability to direct a war when they never listened to our military leaders and lied to the people. It was finally coming to me that my life would forever be changed because the Target Master had gotten pissed at a small country, with very limited indoor plumbing and fewer vehicles. He managed to sell congress on a war that only two of our elected officials voted against. It was hard to compre-hend that any knowledgeable elected representative would believe that a country without a navy or air force would attack the most powerful naval force in the world.

I had flown 22 missions over a small agrarian country and had yet to perceive a threat to our nation. I could not fathom how a country with no navy, airforce, or vehicles, could be bent on destroying our American values. However, it was true that every resident appeared to own an automatic weapon and defensive AAA sites were rapidly increasing.

MAY 5, 1966
ROLLING THUNDER MISSION #22

We competed in another lonesome contest on the fields of Pack One, as none of the home team contestants attended the event. All our night-lights were eventu-ally doused so we decided to crater the trail with our $400 bombs, instead of the designated truck park. I recalled that I had always been interested in blowing up something. My first experience with explosives started when I was a teenager while working on a ranch. One of my best friends in high school helped me acquired a job on his uncle's ranch, where they farmed and raised cattle. It was a big opportunity to earn a dollar an hour driving tractor, branding calves, bailing hay, and erecting fence. I was very excited to have a summer job, since I needed money to buy my first car. I was fifteen years old, with a license that authorized me to drive during the day. I was looking forward to my sixteenth birthday, so I could drive at night.

It was a great experience to live and work on a farm in the country. It became rousing when we discovered a case of dynamite in a storeroom on the ranch. Ron convinced his uncle that we desperately required the blasting powder to help us unearth fence pole holes in a rocky area. We explained that there was a steep region in the forest where it was extremely rocky, and the site had thwarted our post hole diggers. We were very convincing, as we won our case after a long discussion about explosives. The owner provided fuses and blasting caps to insert into the dynamite. We were excited when we loaded our jeep with the blasting equipment to create holes in the rocky ground and maybe find other uses for the dynamite. It was my first experience with using dynamite, and we were lucky that we never killed ourselves when we blasted holes everywhere on the ranch. Maybe a few fish, that might have survived the explosions, were now appreciating the fishponds that we created in several creeks on the ranch. We were invincible teenagers, so we carried the blasting caps around in our shirts

Mission Results: 0 trucks. (1+15 night)

RTL Summary: 0 trucks.

MAY 6, 1966

It was very difficult for me to forget about the little fisherman. I wondered if he was an omen from God that should be taken into account. I consciously never associated human life with trucks. I considered the vehicles to be inanimate objects that we were ordered to destroy. I endeavored to blank the existence of any drivers out of my mind, and just concentrated on striking a metal truck. I never wanted to consider that it might be a young kid or even a girl driving a truck to help their country. Maybe the drivers were just doing as directed, like the rest of us, and were not the "Bad People".

I have always felt that God provided omens for me, but I never seemed to be able to interpret them. I recalled a time in Idaho, when I was 12, and hunting grouse with a 16 gauge Stevens shot gun. I suddenly encountered an enormous bear along a small timbered trail not far from town. It was the largest bear that I had ever seen in Idaho! It was certainly not one of the black bears that populated our mountains. The beast was only about 50 feet in front of me when I first noticed its presence to the side of the trail. I immediately froze in my tracks, as the bear looked dangerous. I was surprised when the large animal completely ignored me, and stared down the valley toward town. I realized that I would only have one shot if the brute charged, and it had to be a close shot to the head. However, the massive bear never looked in my direction. It simply turned away and silently disappeared into the forest. I inspected the area where I had seen the animal, but I could not even find any paw prints. I never saw the bear again, or another one like it, in all the years that I hunted in that area. I contemplated that it might have been an omen from the Big Boss.

Maybe the little fisherman was an omen from God, but I had no idea as to what it meant. I tried to thank the Big Boss every night for all that I had been given in this life. I also apologized for killing all those poor defenseless birds with my BB gun. I hoped that God would not give up on me. I needed considerable support during our many tough contests on these fields.

MAY 7, 1966

The nightly battles were called off due to violent stormy weather. I had never seen it rain so hard in my life! The powerful thunderstorms in Texas had gotten my attention, but they could not compete with the torrents of rain in Thailand! I thought that I was standing under a cascading waterfall that was spreading and inundating every inch of our small base with a covering of water. Our squadron Supervisor of Flying was finally compelled to cancel all contests due to excessive water on the runway. Now I had an understanding of what a monsoon rain was all about. It was obviously a force that had to be taken into account. I failed to see how the natives could live in this kind of weather. I also questioned how Night Owls could survive in this wet madness. I thanked my lucky stars for having a nice warm room with an individual shower that had gallons of hot water to command.

I sloshed over to the library and discovered a good interview in the May 2 U.S. News & World Report with Senator Russell, who was having second thoughts about the war. I thought that he was right on target when he indicated that we should go in and win or get out. I was pleased with his comment where he said "It's not good manners to stay in a man's house against his wishes'," and that he had never bought the so-called "domino theory". The Senator's comments about how our present methods would take eight or ten years to win the war seemed appropriate and tragic. I agreed with his logic when he said that we should not be enforcing peace in the world unless U.S. interests were directly involved. I hoped that President Johnson would listen to an expert on military affairs, who was also chairman of the Armed Services Committee. However, I assumed that the Target Master thought he was more gifted than any military or civilian expert. I was downhearted for our POWs and more convinced that I would never be taken alive, if shot down. I was greatly troubled by what I had read and believed that this contest was evolving into a deep tar pit.

I checked out "Night of the Generals", after reading all the current news articles. I noticed that the pool was still not open but I could care less. I seldom saw the sun anymore. I learned that many of our aircraft commanders had received orders directing them back to George AFB to become instructors, although they had not requested this assignment. As always, it was the needs of the Air Force, so it was ridiculous to expect any consideration, even if you had completed 100 perilous missions. It appeared that many of my teammates would be departing the Air Force for the airlines ASAP.

MAY 8, 1966

All the contests were canceled again due to the torrential downpour that put Home Plate under water. I might need to stop by the Base Exchange to see if they sold hip boots, because I could not keep my feet dry. I had to give up riding my bike, as it kept stalling out in the newly formed ponds and streams of dirty water. I decided to wade over to the library to see if they had received any new magazines. However, I had no idea on how the war experts obtained their information. I had never seen or heard of a Senior Manager competing in our events or even watching a contest. The High Rollers might be talking to many 'yes' men on their staff, who had never experienced a battle, or ever observed our events. It would be beneficial if the Senior Managers would at least talk to their teams now and then; a word of encouragement would help. Friendly American Fans never visited Ubon, and only one Senior Manager had flown in for a very short period. Maybe someday, the American taxpayers might grow tired of bankrolling the RTL. It was obvious that we were winning few battles.

I focused all my skill and cunning on the poker table for a nightlong session with the Torrejon Five and won $14. I was required to forecast for a new assignment, but had not decided on what I wanted to do or where to go. The Air Force would require another year of military service, after I returned to the States, before I could apply for the airlines. I also wondered if the Big Boss would allow me to change my destiny.

MAY 9, 1966

A large portion of the base and runway were still under the miserable, ever-present water, and all the night battles were cancelled again. I headed for the Clubhouse to join a poker game with the Torrejon Five. I was very lucky and managed to win twenty dollars for a personal record. I decided to quit a winner and sloshed over to the library feeling that it was my lucky day. I had lots of time to read the latest TIME along with several other papers and periodicals in the library. I was gratified to read an article where the House Armed Service Subcommittee had gotten on McNamara about his conduct of the war. It was entertaining to read that Leslie Arends perceived that McNamara seldom asked for advise and listened only when he wanted information. The report also indicated that B-52s had unloaded 300 tons on Mu Gia Pass, and the Navy had sunk 248 junks moving men and arms south. I questioned how the magazines received their figures. I had never seen a single Junk along the coast, and B-52s had not bombed Mu Gia Pass since 12 April. All the misinformation in the news was really getting to me. I wondered who was behind all this crap.

The constant rain made it possible for me to read one novel a day along with playing cards for hours at the Clubhouse. I thought about attending the 0100 movie, King Rat, but I was reading the same book and the title reminded me of someone.

MAY 10, 1966
ROLLING THUNDER MISSION #23

Bill and I were very fortunate tonight. We blasted our poor soaked bird off a very wet runway to compete in another easy night contest with the B-66 Team. It boggled my mind to keep bombing Mu Gia Pass, but it counted towards the 100-mission obligation. I speculated that our mission would probably contribute to some deceptive statistical presentations. Nonetheless, we agreed that it was more valuable to participate with the B-66 Team than flipping cards, but it seemed like we were spitting in the wind. Nonetheless, I was pleased for the opportunity to renew our contests, and split the flying time with Bill. The NV League never seemed to care that we were bombing their ballpark, or they might have fielded some SAM Teams in an attempt to catch us off base. However, the opposing Managers were probably happy to have us bombing an empty pass so any important targets could remain untouched. None of us had a single hypothesis concerning the Target Master's game plan! I speculated that North Vietnam was probably very pleased with our pointless action, because we never scored a hit or won a contest.

Mission Result: 0 trucks. (1+35 night)

RTL Summary: 0 trucks.

Mission Notes: I questioned the probability of hitting the trail with bombs dropped from 20,000 feet.

All the miserable rain was finally getting to me. I decided to avoid the two-bit booze at the Clubhouse, and return to my tiny room. I wanted to review my 1955 Lumberjack High School Annual tonight. My old yearbook had some great pictures of "God's" country" that showed the rivers, lakes, and mountains that I longed to visit again. I recalled that my original commitment to the Air Force was completed last year, and I could have returned to the Northwest, instead of battling here. I speculated that many of my high school friends would never leave St. Maries, and I could understand their rationale. I thought that it was one of the best regions in the world. Sometimes I pondered why I was "meant to be" fighting against a small dirt-poor country. It seemed ridiculous to hunt for trucks that could hide in the jungle all the way from China to South Vietnam. I had wanted to become a fighter pilot to protect my country from the "Bad People", but there was nothing here except venomous skunks and warlike Fans with automatic weapons. It was obvious that I was scaring the children and had become the "Bad People" to them. I would rather be hunting evasive elk on small mountain trails in the beautiful Bitterroots than elusive moles on red dirt roads. Maybe someday, God would allow me to return to the Northwest, but I would not hold my breath. I knew that I had no control over my destiny.

MAY 11, 1966

All of the night contests were canceled again due to wretched weather on all the fields. It was raining so hard on the theater's tin roof that I could not hear the lousy old black and white movie. However, I understood that the monsoon season would not start for three more weeks. This was just an unusual storm. I finally yielded to nature, finished my popcorn, and headed to the Clubhouse to play a game of darts with Crash. We had a friendly discussion about life. He wanted to know why I had remained in the Air Force, because he had to make that decision in the future. I told him that I had always thought that it was my destiny to fly fighters and to protect our country, but now, I had second thoughts. I told Crash that I had completed an application to fly for American Airlines, and still carried it in my footlocker. I had the option to resign from the military a year after returning to the States and had not decided what I would do.

I told Crash that I was distressed that the High Rollers had no qualms about losing highly qualified teammates during our daily ineffective battles. Our teammates were killed every day, while trying to fight against numerous deadly skunks. It appeared to me that our Senior Managers were not concerned about the losses. Maybe none of the Generals were concerned, since the Air Training Command was cranking out three thousand new pilots a year.

I informed Crash that it was troublesome for me to fathom why fighter pilots remained in the service. There were only a few Lt. Colonel and Colonel slots available for fighter pilot command positions. Non-rated personnel appeared to have a much better chance of making Colonel. The Air Force seemed to need more supply, maintenance, and numerous staff officers at the Pentagon. Fighter pilots were seldom, if ever given additional benefits or spot promotions like bomber pilots, and non-rated officers received the same retirement pay and benefits. It appeared to me that it was best to become a staff officer and go to the Pentagon if you wanted to be promoted quickly.

MAY 12, 1966
ROLLING THUNDER MISSION #25

We actually competed in a worthy contest tonight, and we observed several missiles explode to the north of our park. The Sam Teams were probably firing at some Navy birds up in Route Package Two, as they were the only ones that normally flew in that area. We were operating on the coast between Ron Ferry and Quang Khe Naval Base when we surprised three trucks that appeared to be waiting for the ferry at Quang Khe. I was immediately suspicious, because the vehicles were not moving and they were heading north. Nevertheless, they might have been valid targets, since there was no tall grass to use for cover.

I was concerned because our astute Umpire had equipped us with risky rockets, and we were competing in a well-defended area against multiple deadly stinkers. Rockets provided a large damage footprint but they also illuminated our bird for every harmful skunk den to respond with sizzling fireballs when I fired. I had learned the hard way to always fire rockets in the ripple mode and instantly initiate a 5-6 G pullout. In addition, I always made my attacks toward the water, when operating along the coast, in case we took a hit and had to eject. Bill had no heartburn about attacking under the flares—it provided a better possibility of annihilating the vehicles. We accomplished our attack by firing low under the flares, and were rewarded with commendable battle damage. Two of the trucks were burning when we departed the area. The stinkers might have been surprised by our low pass, or blinded by the flares. I was surprised when we only received short ineffective bursts of red fireballs from three dens. We completed our high G pullout towards the east and were soon safely over the ocean.

I was gratified to have finally hit two trucks after 25 missions over North Vietnam, but at that rate, I would only destroy eight trucks after 100 missions. I questioned if the Master Bean Counter had computed what it costs the American taxpayers to destroy one truck in this never-ending struggle.

We departed to the Clubhouse for a beer after telling a surprised Intelligence player that I had finally destroyed two trucks after 25 strikeouts. However, I speculated that the Mole Team might have positioned useless empty trucks by the ferry for every flight that operated in that area to attack. It would be interesting to identify how many trucks had also been destroyed at that same location during the day missions. Numerous flights may have struck those identical trucks a dozen different times, but at least McNamara's statistics would look good for the reporters.

Mission Results: two trucks. (1+20 night)

RTL Summary: 2 trucks. (25 missions) (playing average=8%)

It had been 30 days since the heavy hitters bombed Mu Gia Pass, and there was no indication that the Buffs were ever going to rejoin our contests. It was distressing and not logical to continue employing Fighter Teams to compete in events that conformed to B-52 Teams. Maybe the High Rollers were saving the Buffs for an important engagement on the Pack Six fields in the near future.

MAY 13, 1966
ROLLING THUNDER MISSION #26

I wanted to leap out of the pad early and enjoy the sun, but the cool dark room was too enjoyable. I decided to lay low and never arose until it was almost time to brief at 1500. I realized that I had slept for almost 12 peaceful hours. I really appreciated the rest, as the frustrating missions tended to make me tired, and my back had been bothering me. I realized that I had to become accustomed to a schedule of 12 hours on and 12 off for the next series of engagements. I noticed that I always knew the date, but seldom knew the day of the week. We were scheduled for a mission every day with no regard for weekends or holidays.

We finally had a chance to compete in a day contest in the Pack One Park. I was pleased to see that it was a nice sunny day when we lifted off 45 minutes before sunset. We searched for trucks along the well-groomed trail to the Quang Khe ferry crossing and then to Dong Hoi, but we never even noticed a damaged vehicle or bomb crater. The resident Skunk Teams could not be drawn into tossing a few fireballs our way. I assumed that there were no moles to protect. I was disappointed that we never discovered any trucks, barges, or ferries on our tour of the fields and roads. I speculated that any rolling stock was well hidden, and the ferry crossings might be located below the water.

We had a scare during our mission when it appeared that a MiG had suddenly attacked us along the coast. I glimpsed an aircraft descending towards our bird from high in the sky when we were flying along fat, dumb, and happy, south of Dong Hoi. We finally determined that the boogie was an F-105 diving through our formation, to release his bombs, but neither Bill nor I could see a target below us. There was no indication that the Thud even knew we were in the area, or maybe he was just trying to give us a shock, which he accomplished. I had to admit that the Thud teammate watered my eyes, because he materialized right on top of our bird before we noticed his ground attack. If it had been a MiG, we could have been shot down before we had time to react. We were essentially defenseless! We were only carrying iron bombs and two radar guided missiles that were undeniably worthless.

Mid-air collisions between friendly aircraft could be avoided if the Umpire in Saigon would inform the contestants when different teams were scheduled for same ballpark. Sometimes I had to wonder if the Senior Managers that were in command of the Rolling Thunder League had the slightest idea of what was unfolding on the battlefields. We never found any trucks or ferries and finally bombed the well-maintained trail north of Dong Hoi.

Mission Results: 0 trucks. (+45 day & +35 night)

RTL Summary: 2 trucks.

MAY 14, 1966
ROLLING THUNDER MISSION #27

Our flight hunted the mole runs in Pack One looking for spoor between Quang Khe and Dong Hoi on the coast, but finally had to scatter our bombs on the usual molehill. Then we soared along a scenic river to enjoy the landscape on the way back to Home Plate. I was very comfortable, as Night Owls were able to see quite well in the moonlight. Maybe all the nasty skunks had retired to their dens for the night, because no one shot at us. It was deathly still with nary a light on the ground, as we flew over little villages with small dark huts.

Maybe there were little children huddled together in the tiny shelters waiting for the sound of the bogeyman to go away, and I could certainly relate to that feeling. I recalled a night when I was four in Rigby, Idaho, after the Japanese had bombed Pearl Harbor. Following the enemy attack, all the residents in our small town were instructed by the authorities to blacken their homes at night. I still had a vivid memory of my mother lowering the blinds that night and darkening the windows to make sure no light emanated from our house. I had just turn four but I still recalled my mother's words stating that it was necessary because the "Bad People" might want to hurt us. I was too young to understand why anyone would want to hurt our family. We only had a small residence with an outhouse in the back. Now it was possible that I had become the "Bad People" to these children, and maybe, they were asking their mothers why someone would want to bomb their small homes. It was always my intention to defend my country and not to scare innocent children, who could not understand why the bogeyman had come for them. All I could do was to make sure that I never destroyed their tiny homes.

Mission Results: 0 trucks. (1+20 night)

RTL Summary: 2 trucks.

I rode my bike to the Clubhouse for my usual breakfast and received some bad news. Two of our dedicated teammates in the 433rd TFS were taken out of the battle in Pack One! Captain Don L. King and Lt. Frank D. Ralston III were shot down last night, after we had landed. I was surprised to hear the news, because we were flying in the same area, and the fields had been peaceful with no harmful skunks shooting fireballs at us. I was sadden by the loss of good friends that I had known for years.

13

MAY 15, 1966
UNIDENTIFIED FLYING OBJECT

I joined my Flight Commander, Major Wilkins, for dinner and listened to an interesting tale about a strange green light that he, his pilot, and wingman, had perceived during their mission a few nights ago. They had watched a large green light levitate from the ground and stabilize near their flight, before suddenly disappearing into the dark. They all agreed that it might have been an unidentified flying object (UFO). I decided that this was a good time to tell about my breathtaking struggle with a bright flaming object that was not of this world.

My narrative took place when I was flying F-102 Delta Dagger Fighter Interceptors at Torrejon AB, Spain, after I was assigned to the squadron in November 1961. Our primary mission was to provide high altitude day and night air defense for Spain. Our squadron was required to have two aircraft on 5-minute alert, with two more on 15-minute alert. The five-minute alert aircraft were positioned at the end of the runway in a large hangar, along with two Spanish F-86 aircraft that were on duty for day low altitude missions.

Two of us were scrambled one night from five-minute status—about 45 minutes before daybreak. It was an ego thing to see how quickly you could become airborne, because you never wanted to be ribbed about taking your time. I recalled that I had forgotten to attach my parachute one night when I blasted off in a great rush with a high PRF. The first pilot reaching the runway assumed the lead position, and the wingman would then join on the runway for a rolling wing takeoff. The tower always cleared us for immediate takeoff, with a hand-off to the local Ground Control Intercept (GCI) facility south of Madrid, called Matador.

That night, the GCI site vectored us east to the Mediterranean Ocean to run an intercept on two aircraft coming out of North Africa. I speculated that it was a couple of French Mirage fighters returning to France, which occurred often, from their outpost in Africa. Matador then handed us off to another GCI site (Siesta), located South of Valencia on the southern coast of Spain. The US Air Force also maintained GCI sites on the coast in Northern Spain and on the Island of Majorca in the Med.

We had a reciprocal deal arranged with the GCI sites in Spain. The Government allowed the pilots and controllers to cross train every six months at taxpayer expense. We would drive to a coastal site, or fly to Majorca, to visit their site for a few hours, before spending the rest of the temporary duty (TDY) time on the beautiful Spanish beaches. The controllers would travel to Torrejon AB to visit our squadron for a few hours before heading to Madrid to enjoy the excellent restaurants and entertaining nightclubs. Everyone enjoyed these paid for weekend vacations and even learned something now and then.

On that night, Siesta vectored our flight far out over the Mediterranean to identify an unknown radar contact that had emanated from Africa. We always completed our intercepts by closing from the rear, and the unsuspecting travelers would never know that we were just a few yards behind their tail. We were instructed to identify the type of aircraft and airline before silently departing to the rear. However, I had a great longing to ease up on the wing of an airliner and light the afterburner while sharply turning away. It would have been entertaining to hear the passenger's comments regarding a bright fiery light that suddenly materialized close to their window. I had to restrain my inner desires, since it might have ended my military flying career.

On this night we maneuvered into the low six o'clock position of the unidentified radar targets and identified the aircraft as two French Mirages, who were oblivious to our presence. I questioned why they had not filed a flight plan but maybe they were anxious to depart northern Africa and get to some hot spots in Paris. We then broke away from the targets, so Siesta could separate us for practice intercepts over the Med. Siesta vectored me to the east and my controller instructed me to maintain an altitude of 20,000 feet. I noticed a very small extremely bright light directly over the nose of my Deuce shortly after rolling out 090 degrees. The Med. was completely black with no lights to be seen anywhere, which made the tiny brilliant light very noticeable.

I immediately radioed my controller to inquire if he was painting a contact off my nose, but received a negative response. He indicated that there were no radar returns on his scope in that direction. I was now becoming very concerned! The blazing light was rapidly becoming larger and brighter, which indicated to me that we were closing on each other. I again informed my controller that there was definitely a bogie in front of me, but he maintained that there was nothing on his scope. It was now getting to be high PRF crunch time! I needed to maneuver away from the looming bogie, and I was starting to think it might be a UFO. The eerie dazzling object now appeared so close that I initiated a steep climb in an attempt to fly over the manifestation, because it was huge and appeared right on me. I finally selected maximum power with my afterburner. I was rapidly running out of airspeed and ideas. I finally reached the conclusion that it was definitely a UFO, because the phenomenon was taking the shape of a saucer. However, Siesta continued to assure me that there was nothing in the sky, but I was convinced that it was an alien UFO. It appeared that I was going to be destroyed by this flying entity, and there was nothing that I could do about it.

My poor deuce was now falling out of the sky, and I waited for my demise from this supernatural monster. Suddenly I discovered that my deathly UFO was merely the brilliant sun slowly rising out of the black ocean! The tiny blazing light was the first tip of the sun as it emanated from the pitch-black darkness and became larger as it emerged. Siesta was also excited and eagerly awaiting my report about the mysterious bogie that I had insisted was out there, though it was not on his scope. I finally responded in a casual matter of fact voice that I was wrong, as my bogie was just an early morning star—I was now ready to resume our intercept training. I seldom discussed my extraordinary duel with a blazing star. I decided that it was only another inexplicable omen from God.

I visited the cool library again—I had not been placed on the flying or duty schedule. The 9 May U.S. News & World Report had an interesting article about the air war that illustrated the increased use of MiG fighters by North Vietnam. Maybe someday, I would get the opportunity to engage a MiG, but Night Owls seldom flew day missions. The article indicated that more than 200 U.S. jets had been destroyed over North Vietnam, but none of our Generals or Admirals seemed to be concerned about that huge number. The Senior Managers appeared worried about MiGs, but B-52s could quickly demolish the fields, and the problem would be eliminated. The Air Force Generals wanted to bomb the important targets, but our civilian leaders had their own game strategy that was still a mystery to me.

I was not exhilarated when I read another U.S. News & World Report article that summarized an interview with the Air Force Chief of Staff. General McConnell implied that air power was effectively interdicting supplies heading South. I wondered who was accomplishing this interdiction, as our Wing was interdicting nada. He never suggested that B-52s should bomb North Vietnam and appeared to think that fighters, carrying a few bombs, could do the job. He never pretended to be concerned about losing 200 aircraft over the North and insinuated that it had been worse during WWII. The General indicated that it was acceptable for the enemy to have SAM sites, unless they interfered with a mission. I speculated that he was one of the astute Generals that never allowed us to perform dissimilar air-to-air training missions in the States and ordered us to war with no warning equipment or internal gun. The Air Force Chief of Staff also liked to quote statistics—he stated the Air Force flew more than 4500 sorties in April. However, he never indicated that the majority of the missions were not effective, because there were few if any meaningful targets to attack. I theorized that General McConnell and our National Command Authorities must have a strategy for winning this war, but they were keeping it a secret.

MAY 16, 1966
ROLLING THUNDER MISSION #28

We competed in a nasty contest along the coast. It appeared that the resident Skunk Teams were becoming more proficient, and had attained an "experienced" level. We were on the receiving end of numerous sizzling fireballs! I noticed that the stinkers aim was becoming more effective. It was my sincere desire to be long gone from here before they attained the deadly accuracy of the dangerous skunk den at Tchepone. It appeared to me that there were additional 37/57mm Skunk Teams competing around the ferry crossings and along the coastal roads. Some of the blistering fireballs had really gotten my attention. I realized that I had better pay closer attention, or I might be thrown out of the contest like Don and Frank. Our best combative efforts resulted in zero battle damage to the elusive moles. Our leader finally decided to strew our bombs on what he called a suspected skunk den. It was a miserable night with too many close encounters from scorching fireballs. Mission Results: 0 trucks. (1+20 night)

RTL Summary: 2 trucks.

I rode my bike to the Club for breakfast and then headed home for 12 hours of restful sleep in air-conditioned splendor. I was getting tired as the contests were starting to wear me down, and we seldom won an event no matter how hard we battled. I questioned how the Thud Teams kept going to the Pack Six Park to bomb the same old targets without losing their minds. I decided that I needed a break and requested a few weeks leave in June. I had survived 28 counters with an additional 13 freebies. There was a tad bit of good news at Home Plate. The base swimming pool was finally opened for action.

MAY 17, 1966
ROLLING THUNDER MISSION #29

It was impossible to work on my tan today—it was cloudy with thunderstorms over and all around the base. Our Coach canceled our primary engagement at Mug Gia Pass, due to crappy weather, but we lucked out and competed in an alternate contest on the coast near Dong Hoi. It proved to be a difficult mission with lousy weather. We were in and out of the clouds, while we hunted trucks along the road heading east to the coast. We never spotted any movement, and I questioned if we were really in a war. There was never any evidence of damaged vehicles or road craters during our missions. Lead flared the route north of Dong Hoi leading to Quang Khe after the sun set, but there were no targets in sight. I never noticed any enemy activity until we reached the coast. The stinkers finally fired a smattering of inaccurate fireballs from several skunk dens that I could not locate on the ground. I had to admit that the Skunk Teams were experts in the art of protective coloration, because I could never find their camouflaged dens. We blasted some holes in the road leading into Dong Hoi from Quang Khe after reaching our minimum fuel level.

Mission Results: 0 trucks. (+35 day, +25 night & +25 night weather)

RTL Summary: 2 trucks.

I learned that there was a chance of competing against a rare MiG Team soon—it appeared that something big was going to happen! I had always wanted to take the field against a MiG Team and throw some sizzling "hummers" at their aircraft. I wondered if the High Rollers were actually going to put the B-52 Heavy Hitters into the lineup to attack the North Vietnamese airfields, along with Haiphong Harbor. It was about time that the Buffs entered the NVL! We needed some home runs from the heavy hitters, because too many of our teammates were being placed on the injured or unavailable list.

I had not been able to play poker or bridge due to our early schedule, which fouled up my routine. I switched to darts and really took Crash to the cleaners, but he voiced the opinion that it was because I had pitched a baseball once upon a time. Ed Collins told me that he only needed two more missions for his hundred. Then he would upgrade to the front seat and fly with another squadron until December. He would get what he wanted, and the Air Force saved money by not requiring another aircraft commander for a few months. It seemed as though most of the old Pros were receiving assignments to George AFB or Davis Monthan, Arizona. However, many of my teammates had requested to get out of the Tactical Air Command (TAC) and never wanted an assignment to another

TAC base. Many indicated that they were going to leave the Air Force to fly with the airlines. It appeared that few of my teammates enjoyed competing in these ineffective contests. Our attitude might improve if we were assigned to compete on some decent fields, where we could get some hits.

14

MAY 18, 1966
NOT PREPARED TO FIGHT

It was a good day to lay in the sun, but I only lasted an hour—it was too hot to stay any longer. I tried to watch the movie "Once a Thief", but the downpour of rain drowned out the sound in the old church. I would never understand how it was possible for such an immense amount of water to come out of the heavens at one time. Most of the missions were cancelled due to the rain, but they were just exhibition engagements, so no one was too unhappy. We were told that our squadron would compete in distant contests up north of Hanoi in the near future, which received our undivided attention! I hoped that our fearless Target Master would finally assign worthy targets for us to strike if we had to fly into the "Valley of Death". I was going to be infuriated if we had to fight a zillion bad-tempered skunks and offensive SAMs at night, in order to search for a few trucks north of Hanoi. There was a rumor in the squadron that we might have an opportunity to battle around Hanoi during the day, which would give us an opening to compete against a MiG Team.

I was convinced that the Air Force had not prepared us to fight against MiGs in the F-4C. We had only practiced air-to-air maneuvers against other F-4s in the States, which was asinine to say the least. To my knowledge, North Vietnam was not flying Phantoms and they never appeared to be in the market for any. The Tactical Air Command (TAC) believed that it was dangerous to fly against dissimilar aircraft! It appeared that the Generals had not wanted to experience any accidents, because it might affect the Tactical Air Command's safety record. Now it was OK to fly against MiGs, although they were dissimilar, because any losses could be attributed to the war. I realized that it might be hazardous to fly against a Russian aircraft due to our lack of training. I was not pleased with the dim-witted planners who designed the training program for air-to-air combat in the States. It was troublesome to believe that a fighter pilot might have been responsible for a senseless training program that never prepared us to go into combat with enemy aircraft. It also boggled my mind to conclude that our astute military leaders never even equipped the Phantom with an internal gun!

I hypothesized that we had practiced maneuvers, at George AFB, that might be disastrous if employed against a proficient MiG driver. I had flown 731 hours in the F-102 and was well aware of how well a delta wing aircraft like the Russian MiG-21 could turn. I loved the deuce, as it turned like a rattlesnake, and the nose could be position even when falling straight down with little airspeed. It was under powered, but the latest delta wing aircraft, designated the F-106, took care of that problem. We should have been practicing air-to-air maneuvers against a delta wing aircraft in the States, but apparently, our sagacious Generals thought that it was too dangerous. It appeared that it was better to practice all the wrong maneuvers that might get us killed over here so TAC could keep the accident rate low during our training.

Big Ugly was a huge aircraft, which was good, since the beast had to carry ordnance, missiles, guns, and fuel tanks to fight far from home. It was approximately twice the size of a Russian delta wing MiG 21 fighter. It was obvious that the MiG was extremely maneuverable and not constrained with excessive external garbage to slow it down. It was obvious that the enemy would see our bird first. A good MiG driver could possibly out maneuver us if we had to go canopy-to-canopy. I assumed that it would be difficult to win a close engagement. The MiG competitors could just follow our highly visible smoke trail; it would lead directly to our bird. I was not pleased that our engines were always spewing out black smoke unless the afterburners were operating.

I wondered if the engine designers, obviously not fighter pilots, were aware the aircraft might actually have to be used in combat some day against an enemy that could fight back. It would be interesting to learn if any of the future operators of this aircraft were ever approached for their input. I assumed that recommendations from fighter pilots were probably never requested or wanted. Maybe the astute engineers decided on their own that, every fighter pilot desired an aircraft that could accelerate to Mach II for a few minutes if it was squeaky clean. The planners were not concerned that there was no internal gun or that external heat seeking missiles would slow the bird. Engineer sense would indicate that a fighter pilot would not have to turn and fight head on if he could outrun the enemy, after firing a radar guided missile that was designed for destroying non-maneuvering bombers.

I had to give the designers some credit. It was true that the F-4C could haul a lot of ordnance and went like hell in a straight line. The Phantom really would accelerate to Mach II—I had eyeballed a 1500 true airspeed indication at 35,000 feet. Nonetheless, it was a challenge to attain Mach II, unless you followed an engineer designed high-speed profile, and the aircraft had to be clean—no missiles or gun. The Phantom was required to climb to around 38,000 feet and then accelerated straight and level to 1.5 Mach, while checking to see if the J-79 engine ramps were programming correctly. Then you had to slowly descend to reach Mach II, while making sure the canopy overheat warning light never illuminated. The Phantom was truly a Mach II aircraft, but I doubted if I would be attacking at that speed in a clean bird while hassling with a MiG. I wanted a fighter that could rotate on a dime, with good acceleration in the turns, and an internal gun with a lead-computing sight.

The "Hummer" had very limited endurance at high speed, which greatly reduced fighting time over enemy territory. A clean bird only held 1260 gallons of internal fuel, and the fuel guzzling jets were sucking up about a 1,000 pounds of JP-4 each minute at Mach II. It appeared to me that the F-4 was designed to fire a sparrow missile at a bomber from long range, and then disengage at high speed. This strategy might work well for the Navy, while defending the fleet over the ocean with a carrier below, but it had many limitations over land. The F-4C was not designed for canopy-to-canopy combat with a delta wing fighter. I was very disappointed that it was not equipped with an internal gun.

The APQ-120 fire control system (Hughes) was a more advanced state of the art system than in the F-102 (also Hughes), but it still had difficulty painting small targets when looking down over land. It appeared to be designed for use over the ocean against large non-maneuvering targets that seldom shot back. MiGs were small highly maneuverable targets that returned fire with two 23mm nose cannons in the MiG 17. The MiG 21 was equipped with an internal 23mm cannon along with heat seeking missiles.

I was disappointed when I discovered the hard way that Big Ugly could not turn worth a damn and might flip over if I pulled too hard. Not all was bad, since the uncompromising bird signaled its intentions early. I learned that it aggressively shook its wings before departing. A "Hummer" required ten thousand feet to recover from a deep nose down attitude, which was a critical concern during low altitude combat maneuvers. I truly missed an aircraft that could turn without throwing you for a loop and was easy to fly, even if it could not accelerate to Mach II.

The only aircraft that I had ever been able to out turn in the F-4 was an F-105 that was sporting enough to hassle with me, even though it was illegal for both of us. I always attempted to bounce another type aircraft for experience, although the Managers could have taken my wings away, if I was caught trying to prepare myself for war. I learned that even out maneuvering the Thud was iffy, because I lost all my airspeed after a few turns at high G's. Fortunately, I was able to fly against Spanish F-86's in the deuce when I was stationed at Torrejon Air Base in Spain. The air-to-air contests with the Spanish were not authorized, but they gave me a feel for how a MiG 15/17 could maneuver, since the F-86 had similar turning capabilities. I was convinced in my own mind that if I attempted to turn with any competent MiG driver that I would be in a world of hurt. I decided that my air-to-air training in the F-4 had been of little or no value to me, and might even be detrimental to inexperienced fighter pilots.

I decided that I never wanted to be caught in the hot box with a competent MiG driver over his playing field. I would try to make a high speed pass against a MiG, if I ever saw one, and then haul ass, because I had a gut feeling that he would eat my lunch if I turned with him. Maybe I was just paranoid to feel that incorrect air-to-air training had been provided for going to war against MiG air-craft. Surely, our astute leaders must be right, they told us that we were the best-trained pilots in the world. I just hoped the word was getting out to the enemy! I assumed that our Air Force Managers had extensive experience and would never commit Fighter Pilot Teams to distant contests in unfriendly stadiums with hostile Fans, if we were not ready to take the field.

MAY 19, 1966

We arose at 0500 to be briefed for a Big Strike, but it was cancelled due to weather. The Umpire would not divulge what or where the contest was to be conducted, but maybe Owl Teams were poor security risks. I speculated that it would be a big B-52 strike on North Vietnam airfields, Hanoi, Haiphong, and maybe the railroads coming out of China. The Target Master surely had better targets other than unoccupied roads or deserted mountain passes for the Home Run Hitters attention. We had protected the Buff Teams that had bombed Mu Gia Pass, and not one Skunk or SAM Team had even thrown an errant fireball or missile at them. I could not understand why the Buffs were not participating in our battles, but maybe, they were more critical to the Air Force than Fighter Teams.

I adjourned to the Clubhouse and sat down with Crash and Ed to discuss the Big Strike. I expressed my opinion that it was only logical for the Managers to make use of the heavy hitters that had struck Mu Gia Pass and order them to attack important targets in North Vietnam. I thought that our Phantoms should enter this big battle equipped with a centerline tank, sidewinders on the inboard pylons, and CBU's on the outboard stations. The 497th had sufficient Fighters to silence all the SAMs, Skunks, and MiGs, with CBU dispensers. It appeared to be the perfect weapon for competing against those teams. We could attack at first light, so we could see the offensive Sam sites, and the devious Skunks would not have a good shot at us. Then we could escort the Buffs to any valuable targets and shoot down the MiGs that were stupid enough to show their tails in this contest. I sure hoped that this was the game plan and that the High Rollers were finally getting serious about winning the war. I had a sneaking suspicion that the NVL thought we were a bunch of pansies! The enemy was probably bewildered, but pleased, when we just scattered our bombs on empty mountain passes and on vacant jungle sites. We had to get serious about this conflict or it could go on for-ever, because our current missions were ineffective. Lt. Robert D. Jeffrey had been shot down last December and it was possible that Johnson, Chesley, King, and Ralston could be POWs—they could use our assistance.

Some teammates had taken 'GO' pills for the important contest, but I was glad that I had refrained. I always had plenty of "Go" Juice in me, and now I could go back to sleep. I arose later and played poker with the Spain Five, I lost twelve dollars, but it was good entertainment. The local residents said that this was the wettest May since they had been keeping records. I doubted if the rice farmers really cared—this whole place always looked like a swamp to me. I attended the movie "Lord Jim" and was surprised to see that the base had made some theater improvements. I was pleased to see that we now had a shiny new projector and a larger movie screen.

I rode back to my tiny abode to sleep after the movie, since we had another 0500 briefing for the Big Contest. My squadron indicated that I was scheduled to participate in a three-ship flight. I could not reckon how or what we might be attacking. I had never competed in a contest with three teammates. I really needed to take some leave next month, because this contest was starting to wear me down. After much deliberation, I made a command decision to depart the Air Force if my leave request was denied. Nevertheless, I had to survive this conflict and then serve a year in the States, before I could fly for the airlines. It was obvi-ous that I needed some assistance from the Big Boss, or I was ending my fighter pilot destiny.

MAY 20, 1966

I felt like spitting today—all the critical NVL contests were rained out again. Still, I was pleased to see that I had remained on the schedule for the big battle tomorrow. Only four Captains, three Majors, and one Lt. Colonel were participating in the major strike, which gave me a warm fuzzy feeling about being selected. I could not conceive why we were never briefed on the important mission, but there were few targets of value other than the airfields and Haiphong. Nevertheless, I assumed that the Target Master had selected the targets. I was really going to be pissed if the Buff Teams were not in the lineup, as they could each carry 108 five hundred-pound bombs. The 30 Heavy Hitters that dropped on Mu Gia Pass could have taken out every major target in North Vietnam in just a few missions. I decided not to hit the sack, since briefing time was only five hours away at 0500 and my "Go" Juice was boiling. I attended a movie titled "Walk on the Wild Side" to take my mind off the mission—it was the best flick that I had seen lately.

I decided to review the recommended SAM defensive maneuvers, after the movie, because I might have to spar against the missile teams. The old pros recommended placing the missile 60 to 70 degrees off your nose, if it was attacking you, and then start a gentle 2-G pushover. The missile would then adjust and correct down to track your bird when it accelerated to Mach 3. Then it was necessary to execute a high G pull on the stick when the missile neared your bird. The experts voiced the opinion that it would require at least 5-6 G's to defeat the attacking missile, or so you were led to believe. An Owl could be blasted out of any battle quickly when flying above overcast, since it was impossible to see the missile coming up through the clouds. There had been no advice from the ingenious Pentagon experts on how to defend against a SAM at night. I decided to try to defeat the missile by flying so close to the ground that the proximity fuse of the missile would explode. I realized that there was a good chance I might strike the ground before I defeated the missile.

MAY 21, 1966

It was another miserable day! No Owls were able to lift off in the worse weather that I had ever seen in my life. A number of Phantoms flew in from Da Nang because they feared their base would be hit by a menacing typhoon. I sure appreciated our isolated location in Thailand. I knew that the Da Nang Teams operated in a tough neighborhood with unfriendly neighbors. Though, the visitors had one advantage—they never had to fly at night.

I arose at 0430 for the 0500 brief, but it was all a waste of time and effort, since all missions were cancelled again. There was a new rumor that the 497th would start participating in additional battles over North Vietnam. It appeared the resourceful Air Force Generals had concluded that we were behind the Navy, in total events, and had to catch up or look bad. No one seemed to care that we would be attacking targets with reduced ordnance. We had a limited supply of bombs and rockets thanks to the Secretary of Defense. Yet, there was an ample supply of 20mm ammo for the gun, but we had trouble finding a target to hit. I speculated that our ingenious Generals might be satisfied if we just blasted off on any type of a mission with only a solitary gun. McNamara would be able to statistically point out that the Air Force had completed X number of missions without mentioning if any were effective. Our Senior Managers never mentioned that many contests were no hitters, and their teammates were blasted out of the lineup each day. The Pentagon Managers never came out of the dugout to watch the fireballs, and missiles, thrown by the enemy teams.

Bill was departing to attend water survival school for a week, which seemed to be a little late in the game, but it allowed him to steal away from Home Plate. I was not looking forward to flying with a new GIB. I relied on Bill to help me compete in demanding contests on unfriendly fields. The Wing had scheduled me to fly on my flight commander's wing for this important strike, but tomorrow he was flying to Clark in the Philippines. I speculated that I would probably lose my starting position in this significant engagement, since I was a junior competitor.

All the waiting around and bitching about everything was taking a toll. It was troublesome to constantly battle on the road against nasty teams, and you were benched, for good, if you made an error. It was even more difficult to compete for Managers and Umpires that allowed unfair ground rules and never appeared to care if a player was ejected. I could not understand why the Heavy Hitters had not been allowed to participate—a few home runs might win this war. I questioned why the High Rollers never provided a convincing game plan, so we could at least win a few contests. It was obvious that our current game plan was not effective and could last forever with many fatalities.

I was disheartened when the Umpires delayed the Big Strike again, and I was scratched off the starting lineup. Nonetheless, my Coach scheduled me for a new contest on the distant Pack Five fields with a 0600 briefing. I decided to return to my nice air-conditioned quarters to sleep for a few hours, before proceeding to the runway tower to assume my mobile controller duties.

MAY 22, 1966
ROLLING THUNDER MISSION #30

I was really pissed today! Not one team flew up North for the important contest, and it was evident that the Heavy Hitters had never been scheduled to participate. It was a vast mystery why the High Rollers had not scheduled the Buff

Teams! I theorized that our bomber teammates really wanted to participate in our contests over North Vietnam. The High Rollers absurd strategy was a mystery to all of us, but we were captive teammates with no prerequisite to receive an explanation of the tactics.

We lifted off on time for the Pack Five Park, and I shared the flying time with my new GIB as we flew north to meet the Tanker Team. We completed our refueling without any problems and thanked our tanker teammates for the petrol. We were well into Laos, on our way to the Red River Valley, when our Guard frequency radioed an alert. We learned that a Thud had been struck with well-aimed destructive fireballs! The pilot had to eject in the dense jungle of Pack Five. We attempted to assist our downed Thud teammate, but we could not discover where he had landed—there was no sign of a chute. We searched the area until our fuel gauge indicated that we had to return to Home Plate. I was sad to leave because the rescue chopper had not arrived. We sure hoped the Jolly Green Team would rescue him before darkness. We never communicated with our Thud teammates during our engagements because the F-105s operated on different radio frequencies. Nonetheless, all our aircraft could transmit and receive on guard channel. (243.0)

We returned our bombs to Home Plate, because our Wing was still short of ordnance. I was gratified to learn that we received credit for a completed NV League contest, since we were operating over hostile fields in the Pack Five Park.

Mission Results: 0 trucks. (+50 day &+40 night)

RTL Summary: 2 trucks. (30 missions for a 6.67 % playing average)

The Marines had been flying into Ubon all day, due to all the severe weather around Da Nang. It was getting crowded on the parking ramp, and our temporary teammates from South Vietnam had filled the Officers Club. Many of my teammates had been drinking free booze. The unsuspecting Marines were caught wearing their caps when they entered the bar. The Wing had not responded to my leave request, which would determine if I should continue my fighter pilot destiny, or fly for the airlines.

MAY 23, 1966

It was another crappy flying day for the Night Owl Team. All the engagements were washed out again. It appeared that the Big Boss wanted me to remain in the Air Force—the Wing approved my leave request for two weeks in June. Sometimes I questioned why God wanted me to remain a fighter pilot, but I figured that it was just "meant to be". Notwithstanding, I would never understand why I had to compete in deadly contests against vicious skunks in an insignificant country with deserted dirt roads and little industry. It was extremely difficult for me to comprehend why this country was a dire threat to our way of life.

I attempted to stay unflappable and resolute about competing in the Rolling Thunder League, but I was really pissed today. Wing Intel indicated that the Buffs were still not conducting missions over North Vietnam! It appeared that our leaders were not concerned that we were losing numerous aircraft to a zillion AAA and missile sites. I could not ascertain any rationale for our ineffective deadly battles that were constrained by absurd ground rules.

15

MAY 24, 1966
FORWARD AIR CONTROLLER MISSION
BARREL ROLL MISSION #14

Our flight diverted to the fields of Laos for a day engagement after our NV League game in the Pack One Park was canceled due to Weather. We were directed to participate in a day clash with a Forward Air Controller (FAC) who controlled the mission. The FAC commanded a small Cessna 0-1 that operated at less than the speed of light—115-125 Knots. The FAC's call sign was 'Bird Dog" and he located targets by firing 2.75" marking rockets with white phosphorous warheads called "willy peat" on or near the target.

I recalled that my friend from basic training days, Lt. Uwe-Thorsten Scoble was thrown out of the contest by a Cambodian T-28 aircraft while he was a FAC flying out of South Vietnam. We had sipped a few beers together at the McGuire Officers Club just before he departed for his FAC tour, and he was looking forward to the battle. It was unfortunate that he had to be scratched from the line-up—he was an exemplary teammate with movie star looks.

Bird Dog discovered a large dark truck that initially gave the appearance of having stalled in the water while it was fording a stream. However, crafty owls knew how to spot a flak trap surrounded by sinister skunk dens hidden in the nearby jungle. Our FAC was also controlling a Thud Team and had cleared them in for high altitude releases on the truck, because they were running low on fuel and needed to RTB. Our Thud teammates each made a pass on the truck but never came close to the target with their six bombs. Then the FAC cleared our Team to attack, since there were no other targets available in Laos.

Our flight established a pattern similar to the ones we had practiced at George AFB in an attempt to nail a desired 30 degree dive and place the pipper exactly on the truck. We decided to drop one bomb on each pass as we had sufficient fuel for bombing practice. Nonetheless, not one of our 12 bombs even splashed mud on the truck! The winds were unknown, and it was infeasible to repeat the same attack heading, because it was impossible to locate visual markers in the dense green jungle. I was not surprised, as I was convinced that dive-bombing trucks was difficult, if not impossible, using high release parameters. I thought that it was asking too much for a contestant to hit a small target with unknown release winds and unguided ordnance. The only way to insure success with bombs, napalm, rockets, cluster bombs, and the gun, was to attack low and close to the target. However, low altitude attacks presented very high risks, when around numerous offensive and deadly skunk dens.

But, It was a fun practice contest, and I felt that I validated my theory that most fighter pilots could not hit a truck with a bomb when using high releases—unless they were just flat lucky. The event was scored as an exhibition contest in Laos that we thoroughly enjoyed playing, but we never helped our teammates in the South.

Mission Results: 0 trucks (+35 day & +35 night)

Barrel Roll Summary: 2 Trucks (14 missions for a 14.3% playing average)

Participating with the FAC brought back memories of when RL and I attended the Combat Operations Special Course, for Forward Air Controllers, at Eglin Air Force Base, Florida, that lasted for three weeks in November 1964. I had learned that it was very difficult to direct fast moving aircraft in the open woods of Florida. I assumed that it had to be a great deal more demanding trying to control aircraft from the jungle. I had no desire to be a ground FAC, and I certainly never wanted to tool around in a high speed O-1.

The momentous mission was rescheduled for tomorrow, but I was not in the lineup, since Major Wilkins was not available to let me fly on his wing. Yet, not all was lost, I was on the roster to compete in a night/day contest in the Pack One Park with a 0400 briefing. The late night departure would permit a rare day landing when I returned to base after sunrise.

MAY 25, 1966
ROLLING THUNDER MISSION #31

It was fortunate that I was deleted from the strategic mission, since it was rained out again. I was surprised when our flight of owls received clearance to compete in the Pack One Park. It was stimulating to watch the dawn break and reminded me of a shimmering morning when I was back in Idaho. I recalled a time when I was enthusiastically hunkering low in a duck blind on Round Lake awaiting a rising sun that signaled opening shooting time. I was not concerned if any ducks ever visited our decoys that morning. It was great to be alive with the opportunity to live in God's Country.

The countryside on the Pack One fields looked green and lush, with a clear river flowing to the ocean. Nonetheless, I never noticed any resident fishermen or ducks on the tranquil river this morning. I imagined that any sensible duck had flown away long ago to escape the turmoil and madness of our conflict. I surmised that all the Fans in North Vietnam were happy about the recent rains and enjoyed their peace and quiet while we were grounded. Our flight never eyeballed even one elusive mole on the miles of trails we hunted, but I speculated there were shy critters well hidden in the tall grass.

The beaches between Dong Hoi and Quang Khe reminded me of my carefree days in Spain, when I enjoyed the pleasurable sandy beaches in Southern Spain. I wanted to buy a sea side parcel of land near Benedorm, but the Spanish Government never permitted a foreign buyer to purchase land. I wondered if the local residents would construct high-rise hotels for visiting tourists someday when this conflict was finished. It would be interesting to return someday, after the unfortunate battles were over, and see if the beaches were as nice as they looked from the air. We eventually shattered the peacefulness when I released our destructive iron bombs on a designated truck park. We flew along the river, and enjoyed the quiet fields in Pack One during our return to Home Plate.

Mission Results: 0 trucks. (+45 day & +45 night)

RTL Summary: 2 trucks.

I adjourned to the Clubhouse for breakfast with Ed Collins and learned that he had been approved to remain in Thailand for additional missions over North Vietnam in the front seat. I thought that he was a glutton for punishment, but I acknowledged that he was a dedicated fighter pilot who wanted to protect his country. I had a lucky session at our poker table and won fifteen dollars, before pedaling back to the squadron to check the schedule. I was pleased that our Operations Coach had placed us in the lineup for a fiercely desired mission—we were selected to fly MiG CAP for the Thud Teams attacking near Hanoi. It was not the big important mission, but, it would be my first match against a MiG Team, and I was eager for a hit.

16

The meaningful mission was weathered out again and may never go. Some of my teammates indicated that the High Rollers had arranged extensive TV and Press coverage for the big show to demonstrate how we were winning the war. I thought that the limited number of bombs and rockets, carried by fighters, never accomplish squat. Only the B-52 Teams carried enough ordnance to complete the task. I was gratified that we were on the schedule for a distant contest in the Pack Five Park to provide air support to Thuds bombing near Hanoi. I had no idea what the Thuds were attacking, but it had to be very important to the Target Master—they returned every day with heavy losses. I would never understand the logic that required small fighters to repeatedly bomb targets that B-52's could completely obliterate in a few missions.

Today would be my first real chance to shoot down a MiG! We were on the schedule to provide air defense for the F-105s attacking at dawn near Hanoi. Bill and I were number four in a flight of Owls that would be orbiting to the west of Hanoi and prepared to come to the aid of any Thud attacked by the MiGs. We were scheduled to refuel at night with a KC-135 that would be waiting for us near Udorn, before we turned north for Laos and then to Pack Five.

We had a profusion of deadly equipment for our contest. Each Phantom carried four sidewinders and four sparrows to throw against the opposing MiG Team, but no guns. The Umpire instructed our flight to punch off the centerline tank, after it had become empty, before we started our contest, which was a new experience for me. I had some misgivings about releasing the tanks. I felt that it was possible for the crafty moles to use the discarded tanks for fuel storage along the Ho Chi Minh Trail.

Our flight took the field and established a racetrack pattern that allowed each aircraft to cover another teammates. We used our radar to clear our players and to paint any MiG competitor that might try to enter the contest. The Thuds entered the conflict by flying low level routes from Thailand, but we never caught sight of them during their attack. Nonetheless, we observed occasional bright flashes and heightened smoke to the east near Hanoi. I questioned why the Target Master never permitted fighters to strike the MiG's home fields that we could see in the distance. This stupid ground rule was very damaging to our side, since the enemy fields could be quickly neutralized. This irrational rule allowed the MiG Teams to stay in the confrontation and use bean balls against our teammates competing in the NVL.

I decided it was unlikely that any MiG competitor would cede his home field advantage and travel east to contest us today. It was obvious that the Thuds were already operating near their home turf and an easier target. Nonetheless, we were ready willing and able to enter the battle, but our teammates never called for our assistance. The MiG Team never took the field and remained safely in their dugout. Maybe someday, they would enter the contests, but I assumed that they would only compete when they had an advantage.

The Thuds were lucky today, not a single aircraft was hit, they safely returned to their bases in Thailand. We departed our adjoining field and flew home after our Thud teammates had departed Pack Six.

Mission Results: 0 MiGs & 0 trucks. (1+40 day & 1+35 night)

RTL Summary: 2 trucks.

Mission Notes:

-MiG Teams appeared reluctant to participate against Night Owls.

-Fighter Teams were never allowed to attack MiG fields.

The 497th was scheduled to return to all night missions in a few days and I would miss flying some of the day missions. Sometimes it was enjoyable to see the NVL fields in the sun when the stinkers were silent. I was pleased that we were in the lineup to brief at 1730 for another contest on the Pack One fields.

MAY 27, 1966

All the missions of the Wing were canceled—the weather was still too wretched for Owls to fly. I decided to use my free time for fun and games. I played poker all night with the Spain Five, but was not lucky, I lost fifteen dollars. It was getting difficult to locate bridge players, because Crash and I had become very adept with our bidding expertise. I left my poker game and rode over to the library to read what the civilian experts had written about the war before heading home.

TIME quoted McNamara as saying that the destruction of communist communication and supply lines had produced "a noticeably adverse effect on Viet Cong morale and expectations of victory". I had no conception of what communication and supply lines had been destroyed because the roads were always in perfect shape. It was obvious that the McNamara had no concept of what was going on in our war! I wondered if someone was feeding him this ridiculous information or if he was just making it up.

Another TIME article indicated that U.S. jets had been sinking Sampans, junks and other vessels at record rates of up to a thousand in the past month alone! Those statistics were incredulous! I had never even discovered one vessel along the coast during day and night operations. I had never heard a single teammate declare that he had sunk a boat. I could not believe that North Vietnam even had a thousand little wooden fishing rowboats. I felt that the Master Bean Counter was not providing accurate intelligence to our citizens about the war over the North. The news failed to mention that every resident in North Vietnam had an automatic weapon handy to fire at our aircraft, and eagerly squeezed off a clip at every opportunity.

I noticed that every time I glanced at the ground during a daytime mission, it was twinkling like a thousand fiery sparklers on the Fourth of July. It was doubtful that the eager shooters would ever hit our bird. I assumed they were most likely firing at our cockpit and not pulling lead. It reminded me of a time when I was duck hunting in Idaho and a flock of speeding mallards came whistling over our duck blind. I snapped off a shot at the lead duck's green head, but hit poor old "tail end Charlie" in his black rear feathers. It was a lesson for me—I had no idea that you had to shoot that far in front of a fast moving target to score a hit. I guessed that it would be necessary for the resident gunslingers to lead me by hundreds of yards to come close. Maybe it just made the Fans feel honorable when they blasted away at the "Bad People". They could also tell their children that they had scared the enemy away from their rice patties and shelters. I pondered if I might be helping to create a crop of angry young Fans that would throw deadly fireballs at us for a long time to come.

I decided that I would no longer shoot defenseless ducks in the future—I had a new outlook on what they experienced in life. It seemed a shame to destroy birds that were so beautiful and spectacular when they formed their wings in a dramatic curve while descending for a splash down. Participating in these deadly contests had given me a heighten awareness of living and dying. I might never shoot another animal again.

I shared dinner with Captain Roger Jaquith, who was an old friend from the good old days in Spain. I recalled that Jake and I had flown our squadron's T-33 to Rome on November 22, 1963, to celebrate my birthday. We toured the historical ancient city and later joined several TWA flight attendants for dinner at a cheery restaurant. We were enjoying their company when we received word that JFK had been assassinated! We spent the rest of the evening cussing and drinking!

I speculated that this miserable tar pit would not have occurred if JFK were alive. Nonetheless, I recalled that McNamara had also worked for him. JFK had handled the Cuban situation well, and I recalled that we had flown fighter escort for the Buffs when the bombers were flying nuclear alert off the coast of Spain. I surmised that JFK had known what war was all about, since he had experienced combat during WWII. I theorized that he was too smart to have committed us to participate in lethal contests against a third world country in Asia.

17

MAY 28, 1966
SPECIAL MISSION

I awoke and rode to the Clubhouse for breakfast, and learned about an unbeliev-able mission that was in progress. I was told that Rags and Ned Herrold were fragged to fly in a special mission directed against the Thanh Hoa Railroad and Highway Bridge. It spanned the Song Ma River located three miles north of Thanh Hoa and the Vietnamese called it the Dragon's Jaw Bridge. They would be part of a flight of two Night Owls that would participate in a diversionary attack near the heavily defended bridge located between Vinh and Hanoi. Mean-while, a C-130 Team flying from Da Nang was going to attack the bridge by dropping five 5,000-pound mines, with a magnetic fuse, upstream in the river. The huge C-130 would have to fly below 500 feet during a long route that would expose them to ground fire for over 15 minutes. I was stunned by this incredu-lous news! I could not imagine that a mammoth noisy C-130 would attack a heavily defended target—it would be a sitting duck for innumerable vicious skunks.

I wonder who was responsible for developing a game plan that directed some mines to float down the river and explode directly under the bridge. It was diffi-cult for me to grasp how a cunning engineer could program a mine to float to a predetermined location! It was also perplexing to believe that the C-130 Team, with eight players, were experts in the art of laying mines in a river. It was obvi-ous that some fearless planners were not concerned about the numerous offensive skunk dens located around the bridge. I thought that the brilliant planners who had dreamed up this theoretical event should be required to push the mines out the rear door of the C-130.

I knew that this would be a very difficult and treacherous high PRF night bat-tle. The bridge was one of best-defended areas in the North Vietnam, and no one had been able to destroy the elevated structure. The Umpire should have a rule that Managers could not insert their teammates into absurd games, unless they had played in similar contests and understood the ground rules. I mulled over who had conceived this fantastic mission! It appeared to be unrealistic and very dangerous.

I knew that the C-130 Team really had big balls to fly low over a heavily defended river while dropping mines our their rear door. I questioned how the resourceful planners had ever trained a mine to float down to a protected bridge and blow up. Every Night Owl was aware that bridge was defended by a huge number of venomous skunks that could spray deadly fireballs at any aircraft flying down the Song Ma River. The brave competitors could only hope that the Skunk Teams would be sleeping in their dens, but I knew that they were nocturnal varmints and not easily surprised.

I was gratified that I had not been selected to participate in this preposterous battle. Nevertheless, I was anxious about Rag's involvement, since he only had a few more missions to complete before leaving Ubon. We had been good friends since our time in Spain, when we both lived in the BOQ, and I enjoyed listening to his war experiences. He was the only black pilot in the 497th, and the first black fighter pilot to shoot down a MiG in Korea. Rags had a great attitude and fun loving personality, with countless entertaining stories that made you laugh. He really loved his freedom, especially since he had to give it up when he was a POW in Korea for six hundred days. It was evident to me that Rags would never give up his freedom again if he were shot down with no chance of recovery. I had the same mindset in that I would rather die than give up my independence. We both kept the last bullet in our pistol for ourselves.

I had a discussion with RL, who knew Rags very well from our days in Spain, and he was concerned about this mission. He said that Rags had become very anxious and eager to leave Ubon after he received his orders to Davis Monthan, Arizona. He was ready to depart Home Plate, and had shipped his personal gear. Rags had also told RL of his experiences in the Korean POW camp and indicated that they were not something he could ever live through again. I could not conceive why he had been placed in the lineup for this dangerous event. Rags only required a few more missions to complete his tour.

May 29, 1966
ROLLING THUNDER MISSION #33

Everyone in the 497th was elated to see that all the Night Owls and the C-130 Team had safely returned from the hazardous mine laying expedition to the Dragon's Jaw Bridge. Captain Bob Frasier was also participating in this treacherous contest with Rags. He indicated that the mines had been dropped. Their flight had been ordered to make a diversionary strike on a SAM site, ten miles east of the bridge, and had just descended to 300 feet for their attack when the mission ended. I was gratified that this dangerous contest was over and no one was killed

Our flight was tasked to recce Mu Gia Pass to hunt for trucks, but the odds of finding a vehicle were slim to none, due to the dense jungle in the area. We approached the Pass at tree top level, after our flight over Laos, in hopes of surprising a convoy. However, the enemy had probably improved their mountain lookout posts, because we never encountered any moles lurking in the pass. Lead Owl expended flares both north and south of the Pass, but nary a mole would come out of the tall grass—they detested lights. It was formidable searching for timid moles at night. They never liked to show their black tails on the trail. Maybe there would come a time when the High Rollers realized that Night Owls could not easily find moles at night.

Mission Results: 0 trucks. (+45 day & +40 night)

RTL Summary: 2 trucks.

I learned to my dismay that Rags and Bob were ordered to participate in a duplicate engagement on the Dragon's Jaw Bridge tonight with the same time on target, which seemed absurd. It appeared that the trained mines had not performed their amazing trick. Nevertheless, the fearless planners were not about to cancel this contest. I surmised that the deadly AAA sites would not be surprised this time. I assumed that they would relocate additional guns along the river and around the bridge! It was going to be a long dangerous night for the C-130 Team! Their bird presented a very large and loud target for vicious skunks to fireball. The C-130 competitors really had gigantic balls to keep battling in this fight, but I recognized that they were captive combatants and had to take the field. I could only imagine what was going through their heads at this time, but I might be writing my final letter to give to someone. I concluded that the fighters would be able to fly out over the ocean, if they took a hit, and could make use of their ejection seats. However, the C-130 crew only had a few precious seconds to jump out the rear door of a mortally wounded bird.

I hoped that our Night Owls could distract all the bad-tempered skunks in the area while the C-130 made its attack, but I had my doubts. At least the C-130 would be flying down the river toward the ocean in case their bird took a hit. Bob indicated that their Phantoms would be carrying cluster bomb units for their attack on the SAM site, which meant they could not maneuver once the bomblets were being released.

MAY 30, 1966
ROLLING THUNDER MISSION #34

Our flight squandered a perfectly lovely evening searching for trucks and ferries on the coast of Pack One. The elusive transit moles remained in the tall grass or tunnels, and the disgusting resident stinkers hid in their dark dens. I pondered that there might not be any trucks to be found. Maybe all the supplies were going south on handcarts and bicycles. I was definitely aware that every Fan had a gun with plenty of bullets to shoot at low flying owls, and probably would not mind carrying ammo south. We finally scattered our bombs on the designated truck park, before returning to Home Plate, for another ineffective mission.

Mission Results: 0 trucks. (1+10 night)

RTL Summary: 2 trucks. (34 missions for a 5.88% playing average)

Mission Notes: My game average was certainly embarrassing but I was striving hard to compete in every contest.

We received a severe shock and were nauseated early this morning! We learned that Rags and Ned were lost on their high PRF mission last night, along with the entire C-130 crew. Bob Frasier informed us that Rags was leading the Night Owl attack, and the destructive skunks were expecting them. Bob said that Rags radioed that "he was off the target but having trouble with" when his transmission was cut off and his Phantom exploded. He was not certain whether Rags and Ned had been hit or flown into the ground, but was positive the explosion and the final radio transmission were simultaneous. Bob immediately terminated their attack and initiated rescue operations on Guard channel. He said that he could see inland where the C-130 Team was attacking and witnessed the biggest explosion that he had ever seen. He related that the C-130 and the gigantic mines had blown up with a tremendous blast.

I realized that the C-130 crew needed more than mere luck to complete this very disturbing and dangerous contest. Nevertheless, I thought that our fighters could have escaped and ejected over the water if they had received a damaging blow from the AAA sites.

MAY 31, 1966

I was still infuriated today about the loss of Rags, Ned, and the conduct of this war. I would never be able to understand the rationale to fly a huge C-130 into a heavily defended area and order it to fly down a river protected by a zillion skunks. I speculated that the news of this mission might never be released. Still, I would read the newspapers and magazines in Hawaii for any reports.

I was fortunate and found an empty seat on a C-47 departing Ubon for Bangkok. I was satisfied to be on my way and hoped to catch a Charter flight to the States after I arrived in Bangkok. I relaxed in my jump seat and tried to perceive why God desired my participation in deadly contests. I thought that we were accomplishing very little, since the opponent's trucks could easily disappear into the jungle in seconds. I had never discovered any targets of significance in North Vietnam during my 48 day and night missions. Maybe that was because there were few targets worth hitting except for several airfields and the port at Haiphong. It looked as though I was just scaring kids and providing live target practice for numerous bad-tempered skunks. It appeared to me that we were creating a miserable climate for the residents, and they would want to head to South Vietnam to kill American troops. I questioned if it was possible for fighter aircraft to halt the flow of supplies to South Vietnam.

JUNE 1, 1966

I learned that a hostile 37/57mm AAA site had shot down Captain Armand Myers and Lt. J.R. Borling's Phantom. They were teammates from the 433rd squadron, and had been blasted out of the air during a night battle. They had been participating in a distant contest in the "Valley of Death" north of Hanoi. The Target Master had ordered them to attack the northeast railroad in Pack Six, that runs from China to Hanoi, and protected by a zillion destructive skunks. It was now apparent that the 497th would also be participating in these deadly distant battles each night. I realized that I would be getting my fair share when I returned from leave. The new high PRF missions would be flown to Route Package Six A—they had to be the worst possible night contest for us. It was impossible for the Jolly Green Team to operate in that area. I knew that it would be my death if shot down, because I would not be taken alive.

I learned that Myers and Borling ejected over hoards of pissed off skunks and thousands of hostile Fans. There was no possibility of escaping from that part of North Vietnam, and they were now presumed dead or captured. I could not understand why the Target Master failed to use the Buffs; it might end this series, and get our teammates out of prison. I had trouble trying to comprehend why our Senior Managers had not appeared to be contributing to the game plan. They must realize that our little fighters could not carry sufficient bombs to inflict adequate damage to major targets. It was obvious that we could not find trucks in the daytime or at night. Our Generals rarely came to Ubon, and appeared to have no impact on how the High Rollers ran the Rolling Thunder League. I felt dejected for our teammates fighting in South Vietnam and the POWs. I surmised we were in a conflict that could never be won by using the current ground rules. I caught a Continental Airlines charter flight out of Bangkok for Travis AFB, California—they always had seats available heading in that direction. My squadron commander was also on the plane, so we sat next to each other for the long flight. There were many empty seats on our 707 aircraft because many passengers were coming to the war, but only a few were leaving. I was aware that many troops had to be returned in body bags, and some of my teammates would remain as guests of Ho Chi Minh.

It appeared to me that our leaders lived in another time and place far distant from the world that I saw every day. I speculated about the reports coming from our military leaders. I had only seen one General on base for a short period. I had flown 34 missions over North Vietnam, 14 over Laos, and only destroyed four trucks, which was ludicrous. Moreover, it was possible that the claimed trucks were only worn-out decoys used for flak traps. It should now be apparent to all concerned that it might not be possible to win this war by using fighters. I surmised that it would be imperative to use the B-52s, if our leaders really wanted to get serious about ending this war. I questioned if any of the Generals, who read our mission reports ever told the Target Master that we could not win the war by scattering a few bombs on deserted truck parks. It was evident to me that our squadron was not accomplishing squat. It might be cheaper to pay the enemy a million dollars for each truck they trashed.

I was pleased that it had only taken a few hours to catch a flight from Travis back to Hawaii for rest and relaxation. I was going to read the local newspapers to see if Rags, Ned, and the C-130 crew, had gotten recognition for their heroics—they should be honored as heroes. I wondered if anyone cared how many aircraft were lost each day, since the losses received little publicity in the news. Rags should get major recognition, as he was one of the best black fighter pilots in our war, and possibly the world. I had met another notable black pilot, Colonel Chappie James, but he was not currently flying in this conflict. Our leaders should tell everyone what Rags and Ned had done for their country. They had attempted to protect the C-130 crew from being gunned down in one of the biggest flak traps ever conceived. They could withhold the fact that they were ordered to fly the exact same attack twice. I thought that Rags should not have been flying in North Vietnam, since he had been a POW in Korea, but that was obviously never considered. It was not appropriate to order Rags to fly a dangerous mission when he only had a few more to remaining. I would search the papers and magazines for articles, but I had a gut feeling that my search would be in vain.

18

I enjoyed the grass, near the beach in Hawaii, and thought about the training that we had received at George AFB before leaving for combat. It was apparent to me that our air-to-ground training was fun to fly in peacetime, but had not prepared us for deadly combat in heavily defended areas, such as in North Vietnam. I had derived immense pleasure from our practice games on the George AFB gunnery range, and never thought about the possibility of a deadly war during these events. We initiated our routine events by flying a low level training flight to the Cuttyback gunnery range just north of George AFB. It was exciting to fly the route through Death Valley. I enjoyed the challenge of inducing the altimeter to read less than zero feet altitude. I flew my Phantom so close to the floor of the valley that I could clearly see the black rocks flashing by. It now seems strange to have practiced low level routes that were the ideal height for the enemies 12.7mm machine guns.

Then our flight joined for a nice controlled echelon entry to a range complex that we could easily recognize on the desert floor. The range officer cleared the flight onto the expanse and relayed the current winds. Now we could compute the exact pipper offset, and adjust the mil setting, which depressed our fixed gun sight for the range release. I never thought to ask if precise current winds would be relayed to us from the enemy. It would be difficult to get satisfactory results without the latest wind data.

Our flight then took spacing in order to established a nice race track pattern at a predetermined altitude and ground speed. Maybe our experienced leaders had forgotten to mention that this pattern would be ideal for enemy 37/57mm AAA gun crews. These canned patterns enabled each pilot to use familiar ground references on the desert floor to place his plane in the perfect position for the attack. Conceivably, some of our eagle-eyed leaders should have whispered that it was impossible to locate distinct ground references when flying over a jungle. It was easy to obtain the correct dive angle and release airspeed with canned patterns, but we were never informed that this would be impossible in defended areas. I never practiced night attack patterns while I was at George AFB, but maybe they were too dangerous for peacetime operations.

I wondered why we had never practiced any missions with unknown winds and shallow dive angles. It is now obvious that we should have been performing missions that simulated war conditions. Surely, our perceptive military planners were not using our unrealistic range averages as an indication of what could be accomplished in a war—or did they.

I recalled that I had never thought about what might happen in a war—I just had fun on a peaceful range dropping practice bombs from a dispenser that held six little blue bombs. The bombs were dropped using a thirty or forty five-degree dive angle against a clearly visible target with range rings to help you nail the aim point. The range officer radioed each pilot his score measured in feet from the center of the circle—a perfect hit on the middle pylon was called a "shack". No one ever thought to ask our experienced leaders if there would be range circles during a war and immediate information on where the ordnance had struck.

Each F-4C also carried a rocket pod on an inboard triple-ejector-rack (TER) loaded with three 2.75" folding fin rockets that were separately fired using a thirty-degree dive angle. We also practiced low level passes that simulated high drag ordnance or napalm with a release close to the pylon. Not one "Old Pro" bothered to tell us that we could never use these attacks in a heavily defended area—we would be duck soup for any automatic weapon. However, these precisely controlled patterns and attacks sure looked impressive for our guests at last year's military fire demonstration in New Mexico

I recalled that we all loved to fire the six barreled SUU-16 20mm gattling gun, located on the Phantom's centerline position, that made a nice roar as it blasted away. The cannon could be loaded with up to 1200 rounds that could be fired at a maximum rate of 6,000 rounds a minute. However, it also ejected all the brass casing over the ground for crafty desert scavengers, or the enemy, to salvage. We were only allowed to fire from one to two hundred rounds on a training mission—we had to be quick on the trigger during three passes. A large white panel with a bull's eye was used for strafing. Our passes were flown at a low altitude of less than 500 feet. The initial burst was triggered around 2000 feet and we had to observe a foul line of 1200 feet. The practice attacks were great sport. It was a thrill to fire the weapon in an attempt to obtain the best score in the flight. I never envisioned what the enemy's response would be if we tried to fly this type of attack near one of their rapid-fire cannons. Common sense should have told me that the enemy was allowed to shoot back with multiple weapons. I now realize that it was foolish to employ attacks that placed us so close to a target that the enemy could hit us with a well-aimed rock. The range officer had his crew count the strafe hits for each pilot after we had cleared the range. We would later obtain the ordnance results, at our squadron, for debriefing and collecting bets.

I recalled that the Wing Intelligence shop at George AFB presented aircrews with detailed briefings on all the AAA sites and missiles used by North Vietnam. However, none of our shrewd leaders bothered to point out that our practice gunnery patterns would be at just the right altitude for maximum exposure to enemy AAA. Not one experienced teammate had bothered to explain that the low release altitude we had been practicing for dive-bombing and rocket passes would place our Phantom at the ideal range for the multiple barreled 23mm guns. Some adept old fighter pilots should have mentioned that the 12.7 machine gun crews would love our low angle strafe and napalm passes. I might have missed something but it appeared to me that I had been practicing ass backward at George AFB before we went into combat.

JUNE 15, 1966

The beaches in Hawaii were just what the doctor ordered and now I felt ready to complete my hundred missions—I needed 66 more sorties over North Vietnam. I was very disappointed that I had never discovered any articles in newspapers about Rags, Ned, and the C-130 Team, that were shot down. I was convinced in my own mind that the Senior Managers wanted to keep it a secret from our Fans.

JUNE 16, 1966 CLARK AFB, PHILIPPINES

I was pleased when I was assigned a seat aboard a Continental charter flight to the Philippines and later found a room at the Clark AFB, BOQ, when we arrived. I walked over to the Officers Club for dinner where I was invited to join our Wing Commander and my Squadron Commander for dinner. I had no luck in trying to grasp what they thought about the war. I was thankful for the luxury of a delicious dinner with wine before leaving for Bangkok and then on to Ubon. I wondered how the war had been unfolding, but doubted if it had changed much in the last few weeks. I hoped I was wrong and that we were accomplishing more to assist our troops in South Vietnam, but I would not hold my breath in anticipation.

JUNE 17, 1966

I almost felt elated when I returned to Home Plate. I could start competing in my last 66 league contests and get the hell off the field. The Night Owls had been flying every night, and I was sorry to see that I had missed numerous battles. Bill competed in 12 major battles while I was gone and had now completed 70 valid missions. Some of my 497th teammates had almost completed their hundred missions. Many of my longtime friends would soon be departing for the States. The ground rules required our squadron to take a teammate off the roster as soon as he finished 100 missions. The lucky combatants were very fortunate to be leaving the hostile battlefields and departing on the Freedom Bird for the States. I anticipated that the reduced number of teammates meant that I should be in the lineup every night. I found my old bike and rode to the squadron to check the scheduling board. I was pleased to see that I was already on the roster for a Pack One contest.

JUNE 18, 1966

I was thrilled to be back in the lineup for a league contest, but my mission was canceled due to rain. I was pissed—it seemed like the lousy weather had been waiting for me to return from Hawaii. I shrugged off the bad luck and spent the night at the Clubhouse where I won $16 playing poker with the Torrejon Five. The hot sticky humid weather settled in, as usual, once the sun arose. I decided to spend a few hours lying around the pool, so I could add to the tan that I had gotten in Hawaii.

JUNE 19, 1966
ROLLING THUNDER MISSION #35

Our flight of Night Owls lifted off on time for a dark contest on the coastal fields in Pack One. We were lucky and spotted two stationary moles, facing north on a road void of tall grass near Dong Hoi. I was extremely leery of tranquil moles lying motionless on a dirt trail—it was not their way of operating. I speculated that they might be decoys, used to lure us down under the flares, for conniving skunks to fireball. Nevertheless, I decided to play their game and attacked with my six 750-pound bombs that missed as usual. I was apprehensive about the sitting moles and kept waiting for the nasty skunks to stink up the place.

The home team Fans were probably entertained by our flight's inability to hit dormant moles in the middle of a road due to the high winds. Even the secretive stinkers never made an appearance. It was a good indication that the trucks were not important. All the residents probably realized by now to stay at least a mile or more away from all trucks. There was no telling where our bombs would hit. A clever Mole Team might plant worthless trucks, for wasting our ordnance, so they could get loaded trucks on the road after we departed. However, it was a good warm-up contest. It gave me an opportunity to toss some "hummers". I needed to get back in the groove after my relaxing vacation.

Mission Results: 0 trucks (1+30 night)

RTL Summary: 2 trucks.

JUNE 20, 1966
ROLLING THUNDER MISSION #36

Our routine contest to the Pack One playing fields was uneventful and tedious. There were no shy moles on the dirt trails or any waiting for a ferry by the river at Quang Khe. Our flight finally scattered our bombs and rockets on a designated truck park for another ineffective mission. I gave the Phantom's controls to Bill for our ordnance check during our return to Home Plate

I checked our squadron's schedule after our debriefing. I was surprised to see that I was tasked to lead my first flight tomorrow night. Our Coach was upgrading me to lead missions because all the old Pros would soon be returning to the States. Many of our experienced Owls were very close to completing their final mission and would be overjoyed to provide 100 free drinks at the Clubhouse.

Mission Results: 0 trucks (1+10 night)

RTL Summary: 2 trucks.

I learned that the 497th had to start flying four high pulse rate frequency (PRF) sorties each night to strike the distant northeast railroad in Pack Six between Hanoi and China. Our fearless High Rollers made it even more difficult by delineating a 25-mile buffer zone extending from the Chinese border. We were also ordered to remain 30 miles away from Hanoi and 10 miles from Haiphong. The Target Master's fettered ground rules only allowed us to strike a 25-mile stretch of the railroad between Hanoi and China. We were even further constrained because we could not strike targets of opportunity during our run from the coast to the railroad. Every Night Owl was also aware that the enemy had positioned a zillion skunk dens along the railroad. I had a queasy feeling that I might be flying into one of the biggest flak traps ever known to mankind.

We were probably not getting any sympathy from the Thud Teams—they competed in battles up there every day. However, we allowed every evil stinker the opportunity to concentrate their spray on a small flight of two birds. We had the dubious honor of receiving the full attention of every aggressive Skunk and

SAM Team when we battled at night. I speculated that every bad-tempered stinker in North Vietnam would eagerly scan the sky for crazy Night Owls.

To make matters worse, we had to fly through numerous deadly missile sites extending from the coast to the railroad. The copious malicious skunk dens could spray us with blistering fireballs in the "Valley of Death", if we survived the SAMs. I remembered that Myers and Borling were sprayed by harmful skunks while attacking this railroad on June 1 and had to eject. I pondered if the hostile Fans had killed our unlucky teammates, as we had never received any news of their fate.

I had no reservations about flying to Pack Six to compete in high PRF contests, but doubted if there would even be one caboose on the railroad track. The enemy had 10 ½ minutes from the time we departed their coastline, until we reached the railroad, to move any rolling stock off the tracks. The Target Master ordered us to ignore any lucrative targets during our flight to the railroad, which seemed asinine to me. Maybe our calculating leaders wanted us to fly all the way to the railroad solely for harassment. I was not pleased that the Air Force had the adverse fortune to be assigned Pack Six A—it was as far away from safety as you could get.

There was absolutely no possibility of recovery if an aircrew was shot down in the "Valley of Death", as our Jolly Green teammates could not survive in that region. I considered myself scratched from the lineup for good if we had to eject—I would never be captured alive. I felt that it was impossible for an independent kid from the hills of Idaho, who had always been a free spirit, to endure years of captivity and torture. I just hoped that it was not my fortune to die in North Vietnam, but I had no control over my destiny. I was not going to lose any sleep over these high PRF missions—I felt my fate had already been written.

JUNE 21, 1966
ROLLING THUNDER MISSION #37

I was pleased to be placed on the scheduled to lead a flight. I had finally battled long enough to be designated a skilled combatant. I also out-ranked most of the new Rookie Owls who were being assigned to our squadron. I noticed that many were very inexperienced young lieutenants. Our team schedule had been reduced from twenty to sixteen events nightly, which made it more difficult to obtain playing time in the NVL.

Our flight finally blasted off with the usual unproductive bombs, at 0400, with Bill and I leading. I was pleased to be in command, so I could control my two-player game plan. I decided to attack under the flares when we were equipped with ordnance that could be released close to the deck. I was convinced that high altitude releases were ineffective for trying to hit a small target. We hunted high and low for conniving moles, but we never even found an immobile decoy in the middle of the well-groomed trail. I briefed my flight that I thought the enemy was using worn out trucks for flak traps—we had to be very cautious. The new pilots needed to be extremely vigilant if they were going to live through wild night contests with crafty skunks and hostile Fans. I used my last flares to release our 12 bombs on the well-maintained ferry crossing at Quang Khe.

Mission Results: 0 trucks. (1+15 night)

RTL Summary: 2 trucks.

I quickly pedaled to the OClub for breakfast, while watching for menacing cobras. I was lucky and won seventeen dollars playing poker with several of the new Rookie Owls. The free booze was flowing at the Clubhouse after several of my Torrejon teammates had completed their 100 missions. The mail was coming in every other day and someday it might arrive daily if the war lasted long enough.

JUNE 22, 1966
ROLLING THUNDER MISSION #38

It appeared that I would get my wish to be on the schedule for a mission each night. but it was not as I had hoped. I was now considered an experienced squadron teammate and given the dubious honor of competing in distant contests on the northeast railroad. I recalled an old saying about "be careful of what you wish for"—now I understood with perfect comprehension. I was scheduled to team with Major Paul Blease, who would be leading the risky mission to the distant Pack Six Park. I was pleased to be flying with Paul. He was an excellent team player and I liked participating with him. I hoped that our intrepid Target Master had assigned a meaningful target that justified flying a vast distance through numerous detestable SAM Teams. Then we had to compete against aggressive skunk dens with thousands of antagonistic Fans on the sidelines ready to kill us if we made an error.

I was pleased that we had a short mission to the Pack One Park. I led our flight along the dirt road leading to the coast to hunt for evasive moles, but we never noticed any activity on the well-manicured trails. I finally made a command decision to scatter our bombs on what I considered a suspected ferry at Quang Khe instead of blasting the designated truck park. I pondered why I had never spied a single destroyed vehicle or any craters in the roads during my recce runs. I had to give the North Vietnamese ground maintenance crews credit for keeping their trails cleared and in superb condition.

Mission Results: 0 trucks (1+30 night)

RTL Summary: 2 trucks.

19

Paul briefed our distant mission to the dangerous Pack Six Park. We agreed that we could be shot down if the numerous AAA sites along the railroad caught sight of our birds. We were not pleased knowing that we might have to avoid deadly missiles, while flying through numerous hostile SAM rings before engaging the sinister skunks. I recalled General McConnell's distasteful comments about not destroying the enemy's missiles unless they interfered with operations. Our heroic Senior Manager apparently assumed that it was easy for fighter pilots to evade missiles during the day. However, our eagle-eyed leader had never offered a solution on how to escape from the deadly missiles at night.

I told Paul that I would only make one low angle attack on the railroad, after his flares deployed, as radar-tracking guns might shoot me down if I climbed. I would complete my high-speed attack, break for the coast, and try to avoid any hurtful skunk spray or damaging missiles. Paul indicated that we would return to the KC-135 tanker on our own, before proceeding to Home Plate. We concluded our briefing and headed to our bird for a risky long distance contest in the "Valley of Death".

It was a hectic night! We had to hustle around like crazy to locate a spare aircraft after we aborted our first bird. Nonetheless, we managed to join Paul in the arming area and blasted off on time for the Gulf of Tonkin to join with a KC-135 Team traveling from the Philippines. We were refueling with our tanker teammates when we received information that our mission was canceled due to inclement weather in the target area. I was gratified to learn that someone was watching the weather—it would be suicide to fly through numerous hostile SAM sites at night in the clouds.

I questioned why our Senior Managers had not equipped our Phantoms with warning gear to detect if a SAM site was tracking us, or if a missile had been fired. I recalled that the Buffs bombing Mu Gia Pass had all sorts of exotic warning gear, but for some reason, we were never authorized to have this critical equipment.

Paul diverted our flight into Pack One to hunt for trucks along the coast. We eventually scattered our bombs on a deserted mole trail north of Dong Hoi before returning to Home Plate. I was still in the dark about flying into the "Valley of Death", but I had a gut feeling that the Target Master would keep sending us north as long as there was a Night Owl available.

Mission Results: 0 trucks. (1+45 night)

RTL Summary: 2 trucks.

We learned after landing that the 497th would curtail our schedule. We would only compete in 16 NVL contests each night.

JUNE 24, 1966
ROLLING THUNDER MISSION #40

I spent four boring hours in the tower and then I had to wait four more hours before our team briefing. I learned that Bill and I had been rescheduled for a league contest on the Pack One fields. Our original engagement in the distant Pack Five Park, which required an air refueling, was canceled due to weather. I was satisfied with the shorter mission—there was nothing to bomb in Pack Five.

We received profuse skunk spray tonight, which usually indicated that there were well-hidden shy moles in the tall grass. I caught a glimpse of a speeding truck on the trail but it was impossible for me to hit a fast vehicle with a dumb bomb—they were all unguided "hummers". I wondered if anyone ever read my Intel debriefing reports that stated it was virtually impossible to hit trucks with bombs. I also mentioned that rockets would most likely get you killed in heavily defended areas. I kept recounting that it was infeasible to locate trucks at night, unless you were very lucky and surprised a driver with no foliage for cover.

Mission Results: 0 trucks. (1+10 night)

RTL Summary: 2 trucks.

I spent some time at the Clubhouse tonight congratulating my teammates for completing 100 missions. I even sipped a whiskey sour for an hour. The departing Night Owls realized that they were leaving at the ideal time. They would never have to battle in the "Valley of Death" at night.

JUNE 25, 1966
ROLLING THUNDER MISSION #41

Bill and I were fortunate tonight. We completed an easy league contest in the Pack One Park and only received light skunk spray along the coast. I was surprised that the Umpire had somehow located a new truck park for us to find in the dark. We eventually scattered our bombs on the new pseudo truck park and returned to Home Plate for another ineffective mission.

Mission Results: 0 trucks. (1+05 night & +10 night weather)

RTL Summary: 2 trucks. (41 missions for a 5% game average)

I was displeased with my terrible game average! I knew that I had to dig in deeper and look even harder for shifty moles on the Ho Chi Minh Trail. I enjoyed a late breakfast, before walking to the library to read the latest news. I enjoyed an article in TIME that gave me a chuckle, until I realized that some people might actually believe the lies. The article indicated that the Air Force had destroyed more than 300 bridges and damaged 800 more, along with cutting the highway system in more than 2000 places.

I speculated that the writer had never been to North Vietnam, or he would have known that there were no highways. I had only seen small dirt trails in Pack One and Five. The article failed to mention that the "highways" were always in immaculate condition for vehicles that we could never locate. I wondered where the 300 bridges were located—I had only spotted a few. It appeared to me that the enemy never really required bridges. They could use hidden ferries for any trucks that had to cross the water.

The article also stated that U.S. fliers had interdicted and harassed lines further to the south. This action had caused trucks to roll by day and provided fat targets for fighters. This observation was laughable! I had never noticed a single significant interdiction or discovered any fat targets during 41 missions over North Vietnam, plus 14 over Laos. The writer also stated that nearly 10% of Hanoi's truck fleet of 15,000 had been destroyed since the first of the year. This was an absurd statement! I had only seen a few destroyed trucks during day and night missions, and they were probably decoys.

Maybe the Thud Teams were destroying trucks like crazy during day missions, but I had never noticed even one of their kills. I had only gotten two of the alleged 1,500 destroyed trucks. I knew that my teammates were not doing any better. This article appeared to be completely off base, with incorrect information disseminated to the American people.

JUNE 26, 1966
ROLLING THUNDER MISSION #42

My flight blasted off on time to attack the Quang Khe Ferry crossing in the Pack One Park. I had just released our first flares when it appeared that an enemy AAA site had targeted us. We were suddenly blinded by a long series of white flashes that appeared to be exploding near our left wing. I was convinced that a radar-tracking gun had locked on to our bird and was firing 85mm shells at us. My first reaction was to jink desperately away from the flashes! I thought the enemy had positioned a radar-tracking site to protect the ferry crossing. I immediately broke hard towards the water in the event we were hit by one of the brilliant white fireballs and had to eject. I finally realized that the long series of dazzling flashes were coming from one of our own reconnaissance birds flying north at the speed of light.

It was obvious that we had nearly collided with one of our F-101 aircraft! I speculated that the unarmed snapshot grabbing teammate never even knew we were competing in the same ballpark. The Umpire should have required Fighter and Recce teammates to communicate with each other to avoid spectacular night collisions on the same playing field.

It was obvious that our reconnaissance teammates were taking pictures of North Vietnam. I assumed they were for Senior Managers far from the battlefields. I was pissed that we were seldom shown any new photos that could identify enemy defenses. We spent the next few innings bitching about our half-witted Umpires lack of consideration. We continued to search for fleeting dark moles, but I finally had to scatter our bombs on the ferry landing after our flares were expended.

Mission Results: 0 trucks. (1+25 night)
RTL Summary: 2 trucks.

JUNE 27, 1966
ROLLING THUNDER MISSION #43

I led our flight directly to the coast to search for apprehensive moles at the ferry crossing and roads between Dong Hoi and Quang Khe. We never spotted any evasive moles on the trails or encountered any stinkers along the coast. The ominous skunk dens were not interested in participating and completely ignored our nightly invitation to battle. Maybe they were just conducting some ground training, or more likely, there were no skittish moles in the open to protect.

We were surprised when the unusually strong winds from the west blew our flares from over the coast road to the seashore where we distinguished some suspicious round areas on the beach. I speculated that our resourceful opponents might be concealing supplies under the strange coverings. We could not tell what the accumulations might be, but it was possible the enemy was sending equipment down the coast at night in small boats and storing it on the sandy beach. It was conceivable to use small inconspicuous craft to ferry supplies along the coast because we seldom dropped flares over the water. The small wooden vessels and sailboats would not require precious fuel and would be extremely difficult to see at night.

The Umpire had not cleared us to strike the beach but I should have ignored his call and scattered our bombs on the suspected storage sites instead of on a deserted truck park. I related my observations to the Intel players at our debriefing but wondered if anyone ever read my reports.

Mission Results: 0 trucks. (1+20 night)

RTL Summary: 2 trucks.

We hustled to the Clubhouse to watch the advertised USO show, but it had been rained out. Nonetheless, there were still a few American women in the Clubhouse—they reminded me of another stimulating world of long ago. I longed for my speedy bronze Jag that I loved to drive at high speed on the High Desert roads. I also missed dancing at the Manhattan Beach nightclubs in Los Angeles. I recalled that I had always loved to dance, but I could only maneuver around the floor when a slow song played during high school. I wanted to learn how to dance the fast numbers but I was too shy to ask anyone to teach me. I was pleased when I finally met a cute little Kappa Alpha Theta during my sophomore year in college who taught me how to jitterbug. We had fun dancing in a small room on the top floor of the Student Union Building called The Dipper. I recalled that we could play three songs for a quarter on the jukebox—I really looked forward to our dance sessions. I would always be beholden to Ann Redford for teaching me how to dance during an unruffled time long ago.

My dancing days had to take a break during pilot training and never resumed until I joined the 497th in Spain. Several of us enjoyed the exciting Casa Blanca nightclub in downtown Madrid that operated into the wee hours every night. We also frequented the elegant Hilton Hotel and the inexpensive Officers Club in Madrid, when we had a date. George AFB was a big disappointment for dancing, but we soon discovered that it was a short drive to LA and the nightclubs in Manhattan Beach.

JUNE 28, 1966
ROLLING THUNDER MISSION #44

Our flight was assigned to the Pack One Park for what I had hoped would be a temperate contest. However, we discovered that the resident Skunk Teams were gaining additional combat training and becoming more aggressive on the field. I had completed several low altitude attacks under the night-lights hunting for shy moles before several bad-tempered stinkers watered my eyes. Their injurious fire-balls nearly scored a direct hit on our bird as we flew low over the ground. Maybe the fearful moles had taken refuge in the town of Dong Hoi, but our ground rules would not allow us to compete on their home field. I was pissed at the bad tempered skunks and eventually scattered our bombs on a suspected den.

I gathered my flight for our usual hung ordnance check and headed straight towards the Clubhouse for breakfast. However, Home Plate informed us that the Ubon runway was closed. We were then directed to proceed to Korat. Bill dialed in the Korat TACAN station for direction and mileage. We had never flown to the F-105 base located about 180 miles to the west of Ubon. We contacted Korat tower when we were fifty miles away and received clearance for a straight in approach, with a full stop landing, as we were running low on fuel. We discovered, after stopping in the dearming area, that the Korat ground crew knew nothing about F-4C Phantoms. We finally waved them away and decided to pin our own equipment, after we shut down on their transit ramp.

We hoped to find some empty cots, to rest on, until we were notified that Ubon was opened for our return. However, the Quarter Master sent us away without even offering a pillow or blanket—they said there were no rooms available. It was apparent that they could not be bothered with wayward Night Owls. We finally talked the Air Police into allowing us to reside in the closed Officers Club. We needed to get under cover for the night since rain was possible. I thought the OClub might have a few couches but there were only hard wooden chairs, tables, and a long bar.

I soon discovered that even a hardened Night Owl could not get comfortable on the inflexible floor, small chairs, or by lying on the bar. It was impossible to rest so I just wandered around the club and waited for word from Ubon to come home to roost. We finally walked to the parking ramp at first light to wait by our birds for affirmation that Ubon was open for our return.

Mission Summary: 0 trucks. (1+35 night)

RTL Summary: 2 trucks.

We finally received clearance to return to Ubon at first light. I decided to accomplish a wing takeoff because I had not taken off in the wing formation position for over a year. I soon discovered that I was out of practice, when I boomeranged around, but managed to get my "Hummer" airborne without running off the runway. I recognized that I needed to practice wing takeoffs, unless I wanted to be embarrassed in front of my teammates.

I learned, after landing at Home Plate, that five Rookies had joined our squadron and eight experienced owls had departed for the States. I was officially promoted to the position of flight leader and designated a mature Night Owl. My flight commander only needed eight more missions and Bill needed seventeen, before they could treat their teammates to 100 free drinks.

Mission Results: 1+00 day.

Mission Notes: Our teammates at Korat were not friendly toward Night Owl players.

20

We had a precarious escape tonight near Ron Ferry, because I was not paying attention to an opposing Team. Our narrow escape started after I led my flight to the ferry crossing and pickled off four flares over the field to hunt for slippery moles. Bill and I were behaving like dumb inattentive competitors while we slowly maneuvered around the flare pattern. We carefully searched for shy transit moles while the resident skunks were quiet. I suddenly decided to bank sharply to my right when I thought I had seen movement. I was immediately jolted from my complacency during our steep turn. Numerous bright flashes illuminated the cockpit and shocked us! An opposing 85mm AAA site captured my full attention with four white sizzling fireballs that exploded close to our left wing. I surmised that we would have been blasted from the air if I had not initiated my steep turn. The deadly fireballs exploded exactly where we would have been flying!

I immediately broke away from the fireballs and quickly changed altitude before we could be knocked out of the battle—it was obvious that the AAA site was using radar to lock onto our little bird. The 85mm shooter had come extremely close to us. The nefarious den had our exact altitude, but was just slightly to the left of our Phantom. The accomplished Skunk Team had done an excellent job of measuring our exact ground track and altitude but my fortuitous turn had saved our tail. We were very lucky to be alive. We could have easily been taken out of the battle due to my laxness. Maybe the Big Boss was bestowing a wake-up call and a clear sign to start paying attention, if I wanted to complete a hundred missions. To make matters worse, we never discovered any trucks in the area so I had my flight scatter our bombs in a suspicious area where the 85mm skunk den might be hidden.

I informed wing Intelligence that the enemy was moving radar directed 85mm AAA sites to the Ron Ferry Crossing. I speculated that it would not be long until radar-tracking AAA sites were also positioned around Quang Khe and Dong Hoi. The incorrigible Skunk Teams might have more dens than they needed around Hanoi and were now sending them south.

Mission Results: 0 trucks. (1+10 night & +20 weather)

RTL Summary: 2 trucks.

Mission Notes:

-North Vietnam had positioned 85mm radar guided AAA sites at Ron Ferry.

-Never fly straight and level anywhere in Pack One.

Captain Bob Frasier (Quick Draw) was buying drinks at the Club tonight as his wife had just given birth to a baby boy—it was their third. Bob was known for his skill at drawing a lucky card when he needed it and his luck was still holding—he would soon be leaving for the States.

JUNE 30, 1966
ROLLING THUNDER MISSION #46

My flight participated in a well-directed battle on the hostile fields near Quang Khe tonight. Our bombs accidentally hit an area that resulted in a huge explosion when we were trying to crater the road going through the town. It appeared that we had struck a gasoline storage area, because the flames were high and bright—then the fire spread to the town. We never intended to start a deadly large fire in the town. We never targeted buildings. It was common knowledge that the Fans hid most of their supplies in the villages, but I always tried to be observant and only attacked valid targets. I anticipated that we had contributed moderately to the war effort tonight, but we had probably put many residents out on the streets. Now the malicious Fans had even more reasons to cut us into little pieces if we were shot down in their Park. I speculated that an increased number of young males were now ready to travel south and murder our teammates.

Mission Results: 0 trucks. (1+05 night & +15 night weather)

RTL Summary: 2 trucks. (46 missions)

The 497th switched back to the late schedule, which gave me the opportunity to compete in a double-header, as we were short of competitors for our team roster. I learned that the big important mission, that I had not been able to participate in, was against the second biggest petroleum depot in North Vietnam. Intel indicated that the Thuds from Korat and Takhli had dropped 72 tons of bombs on the depot. Nevertheless, I questioned why the "Big Buffs" had not bombed the target, instead of our little fighters carrying a few bombs. I wondered when the Target Master was going to allow the "Big Boys" to compete in the NVL—we needed some heavy hitters.

JULY 1, 1966
ROLLING THUNDER MISSIONS #47 & 48

We completed another impotent mission in Pack One with no visible results. I used my final flares to locate a generic piece of jungle that might have been the Umpire's truck park for our ordnance. I asked the Wing Intel players for a copy of their dog-eared truck park photo, so I could frame it for a war souvenir.

I was required to spend duty time in the tower immediately after landing and completing our short flight debriefing. Bill was a thoughtful friend and brought me a sandwich with French-fries. I was starving—there had been no time for my usual breakfast. I was scheduled to brief in twelve hours for my second NVL contest, and was looking forward to a double header. I learned that we were fortunate to have completed our first event. The 497th had to cancel a number of missions.

Mission Results: 0 trucks. (1+15 night)

RTL Summary: 2 trucks.

We blasted off on time for another routine contest in the Pack One Park. I was gratified to be able to search for reticent moles without using flares, as we lifted off just after sunset and could see the trail clearly. I scrutinized miles of road, but could not discover any moving targets, despite receiving a sore neck from scanning in all directions. We never spotted a single slippery mole, and even the conniving skunks stayed in their holes. I speculated that the elusive Mole Teams were concealed in the tall grass and the bad-tempered Skunk Teams had taken the night off to sleep

We also tried to identify at least one of the 2,000 road cuts, described in the TIME article, but we could not even discover one crater. I wondered where the highway system of the article was located. I had only seen numerous deserted dirt roads that were well graded.

It was apparent to me that the devious moles were not aware that they should participate in our contests. I had only discovered two trucks during 48 missions, and those vehicles may have been decoys. However, the loathsome skunks were always ready to compete and immediately took the field to fling sizzling fireballs at us when we arrived. It was hard for me to believe that I had never spotted a secretive skunk opponent! They were experts in using camouflage and possessed an uncanny ability to stay out of sight in their dens.

We only noticed a few sparkers during our recce run and they were probably from Fans heading home from the fields. It never ceased to amaze me that every belligerent resident possessed an operating weapon with loads of ammo. I finally directed my flight to strew our bombs on the usual deserted truck park and retired for the night.

Mission Results: 0 trucks. (1+05 night & +10 night weather)

RTL Summary: 2 trucks.

The ordnance equipment shortage was improving as each F-4C was now carrying more rockets and bombs. I learned that our Wing had recently received a shipment of napalm. We were gaining additional Rookie players in the 497th, which meant I might not be able to participate in another double-header. The majority of our experienced Owls had departed for the States—with a smile on their face. I was not familiar with any of the new aircrews as many of the youthful Rookies were right out of pilot training or from another type aircraft. The lack of realistic training, and little flying time in the Phantom, would make it difficult for them to compete in our demanding night battles.

Major Paul Blease, Captain RL Penn and I were the only initial 497th Night Owl teammates remaining in the squadron. I was surprised to learn that I had flown eight more missions than Paul had, although he had been here for a longer period. RL required an even larger number of missions due to a medical problem that originated during a lively night hubbub at the Clubhouse bar with Ed. The precious coins in my little tin can were slowly accumulating but I still needed 52 valuable pennies before I could buy 100 drinks.

JULY 2, 1966
ROLLING THUNDER MISSION #49

The weather was nice when Bill and I departed the squadron for our usual two-bird flight to the Pack One Park. I checked in with my teammate, received clearance from ground control to taxi, and joined with my wingman, who followed three hundred feet behind. I was nearing a remote section of the field when I noticed a long mottled green object ahead that stretched completely across the taxiway. I finally realized that it was an enormous snake, about the size of a fire hose, and it was not moving out of my way. I calculated that the tires of our 55,000-pound aircraft would leave three large deep ruts in the half-witted snake, if it remained on the taxiway.

I was surprised and confounded when we rolled over the extensive snake! It felt like I was rolling over a very solid object—our tires made a definite thump instead of my assumed "squash" sensation. I radioed my wingman to see what had transpired. I assumed that he would see three prodigious indentations in its stretched body. I was thunderstruck when he told me that there was nothing on the taxiway! It was incredulous that my aircraft had not injured this super sized snake! I definitely never wanted to encounter a reptile similar to this one in the jungle, or on my bike at night! I was convinced that I would just stay in the top of a tree to wait for the Jolly Green or Air America Teams if I had to eject.

We spent the evening searching for movement on the coast trails from Ron Ferry down to Dong Hoi but never discover any trucks or ferries. I finally had my flight scatter our ordnance on some suspected skunk dens near the Quang Khe ferry crossing before we returned to log a short 1.2 mission.

Mission Results: 0 trucks. (1+10 night)

RTL Summary: 2 trucks.

JULY 3, 1966

There was an extensive all night party that continued into the day with free booze at the Clubhouse as numerous 497th and 433rd teammates completed their 100 missions. I decided to avoid the noisy crowd. There was nothing more obnoxious than drunken teammates who had finished their tour. I was also reminded that I was only half way to the magic number. The Clubhouse had recently opened an excellent new annex. The new room was now packed with ecstatic former contestants and anyone else who desired free drinks. There must have been umpteen gallons of booze splashed on the new floor, as it ended up a wet mess and appeared to be warping in various places. I assumed the Club would have to close their attractive new annex for repairs after this night of merrymaking and amusement.

I spent the afternoon in the air conditioned library and found an exceptional article in the June 27th edition of U.S. News & World Report titled; 'Has the U.S. 'Missed the Boat' in Vietnam". It confirmed my unfavorable suspicions and should be required reading for the High Rollers and Senior Managers. It explained that North Vietnam was making itself knockout proof by dispersing all the plants, fuel dumps, and supplies—it was also increasing their antiaircraft intensity to that of WWII. The article displayed pictures of bicycle convoys, ox-carts, and handcarts, used to move supplies to South Vietnam.

I felt that Maj. Gen. Roy Lassetter, Jr. was right on target when he indicated to Congress that the bombing of North Vietnam merely slowed the flow of men and arms. He felt that the Communists had the capability of transporting all of the ammunition, weapons, and troops into South Vietnam that was necessary for victory. I certainly concurred with his assessment, as our aircraft were not slowing the flow of supplies to the South. I also agreed with him when he said that the North Vietnam transport system could not be paralyzed no matter how much the bombing was stepped up. It was obvious to me that the dirt trails were repaired each night, and truck convoys were easily hidden in the jungle from our birds. I surmised that it was a complete waste of time and money to hunt for trucks along jungle roads with our fast moving fighter aircraft.

It was disturbing to read in TIME that North Vietnam had 90 SAM sites but the report insinuated they were not very effective—only 14 had scored hits. I wondered how the analysis would feel if he was flying in one of the birds that had been knocked down. I would be delighted to take him along on a mission to Pack Six, or any of our leaders, so they could fly over all of those "ineffective" missile sites at night with no warning gear.

I was in accord with the comment that "History will show that we pulled our punches in February of 1965 when we should have gone in swinging-or not gone in at all". I felt that the article was correct when it observed that there was no victory in sight and maybe there was going to be an endless escalation. Even more reason to never be taken prisoner—this was a wanton battle that might continue forever. The U.S. had already lost 260 warplanes over North Vietnam, but the High Rollers and Senior Managers never seemed to be concerned. I wondered what it would take to get the attention of leaders who fought from behind the safety of their desks.

JULY 4, 1966
ROLLING THUNDER MISSION #50

I would finally reach the half way mark, towards the 100 required contests, but there was no joy in Mudville. It was the 4th of July, and we would soon have our own personal fireworks display in the Pack One Park. I speculated that my flight might be able to participate in an effective contest today, because we were going to blast off before dark. We would be afforded daylight to search the roads and rivers for transit moles, barges, or ferry activity. The numerous antagonistic Fans could be expected to provide deadly bright sparklers when we arrived in their park—they usually disapproved of our playing performance with bullets. The residents could be counted on to always participate in our contests with their automatic weapons but we stayed out of their slaughter zone. Bill and I made it a point to fly over three thousand feet above the unfriendly Fans to stay out of their constant small arms fire during the daytime.

The 37/57mm stinkers only took a few spray shots at us today, with luminous red fire balls that never came close. I was amazed that I had completed 64 contests without spotting a skunk den, despite being on the receiving end of a thousand fireballs. The opposing stinkers were very experienced competitors, as I could not spot them even when they were right under my nose. I was miffed at our devious competitors and directed my flight to spread our ordnance on an area that might have contained several skunk dens near the Quang Khe ferry approach. We returned to Home Plate to score another completed contest with no hits.

Mission Summary: 0 trucks (+40 day & +30 night)

RTL Summary: 2 trucks. (50 missions) (4% playing average)

Mission Notes: My mole destruction average was only 4% for 50 contests—that was embarrassing to say the least

It was a listless quiet Fourth of July, except for the fireworks observed during our day/night contest. There was nothing happening at Home Plate—it was another lonely day in Mudville. I decided to celebrate the holiday by attending the movie to see an old Alan Ladd flick that proved to be enjoyable. The old flick reminded me of an evening dancing with his daughter, Alana, at a party in Madrid. Our Squadron Executive Officer was dating Ava Gardner, which helped get us invited to a few notable parties. Alana was an excellent dancer, and I wanted to ask her for a date, as we seemed to be enjoying each other's company. My hopes were dashed when Kip told me that she was dating a bullfighter. The 497th invited Alana and some other celebrities out to our squadron for a party and a tour of our squadron. We later lined-up on our flight ramp by our Deuces so they could walk by. This was a treat for me as I received a big smile from Alana and a quiet greeting—I sure missed those momentous days in another life, but still had my memories to sustain me.

JULY 5, 1966
ROLLING THUNDER MISSION #51

The weather was outstanding tonight, with a moon so bright that I never had to deploy our flares to see the ground. This was the ideal weather for night contests but the resident skunks also had a momentary view of our birds—they sprayed more than usual but never came close. It was almost like flying during the day, and we spotted several speeding moles that immediately disappeared into the tall grass when they heard us coming. I ordered my flight to scatter our ordnance where the trucks had departed the trail. We were rewarded with our efforts—I observed one explosion with three fires. I felt confident that we had at least wounded some wary moles but could not confirm if they had been killed.

Mission Results: 0 trucks. (1+10 night)

RTL Summary: 2 trucks.

I checked the flight board, after debriefing, to see if the frags had come in for tomorrow's missions, but they were not posted. I learned that the 497th had been assigned four more Rookies and Major Paul Blease was designated as my new flight commander. I was contented to work for Paul, as I liked and respected him.

JULY 6, 1966
ROLLING THUNDER MISSION #52

Bill and I were still competing in the local contests on the fields of Pack One, but I knew that these quick events would become more infrequent. It was evident that we would soon start battling in additional high PRF night engagements north of Hanoi against a zillion pissed off skunks. The Old Pros were pleased to pack their bags and depart before the squadron participated in deadly night contests on the Six Pack playing fields.

We departed on time and completed an uneventful night engagement under a bright moon in the Pack One Park. We spent an hour searching for the timid moles, while avoiding nasty skunks, but our contest ended in a scoreless tie, with no hits by either side. However, we enjoyed flying along the well-groomed mole trails and peaceful rivers in the moonlight—it was a beautiful night. I had my flight scatter our ordnance on a suspected skunk den, instead of the designated truck park. It seemed a shame to disturb the silent night.

Mission Results: 0 trucks. (1+25 night)

RTL Summary: 2 trucks.

The word was out that the 497th would start flying more missions up north of Hanoi in Pack Six very soon. It would certainly elevate the pulse rate frequency of all the unlucky players scheduled for the long distance contests. Our Intel teammates indicated that North Vietnam had been adding SAM and Skunk Teams at an increasing rate in Pack Six. It appeared that the evil investors in China and Russia were working overtime to supply them with more playing equipment.

Our unproductive missions were beginning to aggravate me, and I was angered to learn that the military had now lost more than 260 fighters bombing questionable targets. Maybe there would come a day when the owners of the Rolling Thunder League would get infuriated at the High Rollers for throwing money down an empty mole hole. It would be interesting to know what it had cost the taxpayers for the four trucks, or decoys, that I had destroyed during 64 missions.

It was nearly impossible to attack trucks that we could not even detect—they disappeared into the jungle within seconds. I presumed that it might be possible to destroy a few trucks on the coastal road when they traversed through rice patties with little jungle for cover. It should be obvious to our civilian and military leaders that it was impracticable to stop the movement of supplies or enemy troops traveling to South Vietnam. We should be assigned a new mission that would contribute to the war effort instead of scattering bombs on empty truck parks. I was very surprised to read a U.S. News & World Report that indicated there were SAM sites near Dong Hoi! Our squadron was operating there every night, and no one had ever seen or heard of a missile in that area.

JULY 7, 1966
ROLLING THUNDER MISSION #53

I was scheduled for tower duty before I led my flight to a night contest on the Pack One fields. I was disappointed that my short events were coming to a halt and I would have to fly to the distant north. It was a pleasant night as only one resident skunk attempted to contest our presence, and he must have been a rookie. I decided to spread our bombs in the middle of a well-manicured mole trail—the ground maintenance players needed to earn their keep and fill in the holes.

Mission Results: 0 trucks (1+20 night)

RTL Summary: 2 trucks.

My flight commander, Major Wilkins, completed his final mission and headed to the bar to buy 100 drinks. I never had to buy a drink of booze, as over-joyed Night Owls were finishing every night and departing for the States ASAP. Two Rookie Owls arrived today and placed on our team roster. It brought the 497th close to full strength. I realized that now I had to lead most of our missions and would get more than my fair share of the high PRF contests in "The Valley of Death". I received some good news when the squadron changed our mission from Pack Six to Pack One due to bad weather up north.

I stopped by the pool to soak up some sun but also managed to sprain my ankle when I tried to dive on what was a sorry excuse for a springboard. Once upon a time, I could complete a few diving maneuvers, but it was obvious that all my spring and flip had gone down the drain. I now had to hobble around on an injured foot, but I was not going to let that bother me. I had no qualms about strapping on my equipment and crawling to my bird, if necessary, to participate in tomorrow night's contest.

Maybe one of the reasons that we seldom located trucks was that there were only a small number to be found. I speculated that there were thousands of residents available to carry supplies to South Vietnam on their back or using push-carts. North Vietnam could also employ hundreds of the little wooden fishing boats that dotted the rivers to ferry supplies down the coast. I had flown over thousands of acres of fertile rice patties in Pack One that were available to feed their troops.

I recalled reading that my ancestors had pushed a handcart over a thousand miles across the American plains—the enemy had a much shorter distance to South Vietnam. Our family records indicated that my Great Grandmother, Martha James, from Pinvin, England, had pushed a handcart for 1300 miles from Iowa to Utah. Her parents departed England on May 3, 1856, for America, with Martha and her seven brothers and sisters. However, the baby girl died and was buried at sea while the family endured six weeks of rough weather on a sailing vessel. They finally arrived in New York, on June 17, and immediately traveled by train to Camp Iowa to prepare for the long demanding expedition to Utah. The family only had sufficient funds to purchase a small wooden handcart to carry the tent, provisions, and baggage, for the lengthy trek across the plains. They departed Camp Iowa on July 15, pulling the hastily constructed handcart or walking along side the inadequate cart in the rough terrain. They were almost trampled to death by a massive herd of buffalo that covered the landscape. Hostile Indians menaced the party and later drove off the few cattle in the assemblage. The poorly assembled handcarts were always splintering during the long excursion and required constant repair with very limited materials. They soon discovered that their provisions were not sufficient for the trip, and only a little nourishment could be allocated each day.

On October 23, 1856, the exhausted and famished family finally arrived at a stream called the "Last Crossing" at Fremont, Wyoming. The fatigued family was forced to stop on the riverbank—they were unable to ford the swift water. Her father, William James, strength finally gave out and he died by the river in the severe cold. Her mother and the remaining children were freezing, starving, and needed help to raise their tent for shelter from the bitter weather. Some conscientious members of the party came to their rescue and helped them until assistance could arrive from the Salt Lake City settlement. The ravenous shivering family arrived in Salt Lake on November 9, 1856. The elders allotted them a small wooden shack for a temporary shelter. The fatherless children had to reside with other charitable families in order to survive the bitter winter. I admired my ancestor's strength, dedication and courage, to complete a burdensome lengthy journey to an unknown region. It was difficult for me to imagine the anguish they had to brave while pushing a wobbly handcart 1300 miles across hostile territory. I certainly had no reason to complain about my trifling concerns, when I recalled what my ancestors had encountered long ago.

JULY 8, 1966
ROLLING THUNDER MISSION #54

It was a pleasant night for Night Owls to fly. We searched for activity along lonely dirt trails but we never discovered any transit moles. I assumed that additional aggressive skunks had recently arrived. It appeared that added dens were spreading over the Pack One fields. It was very frustrating to battle against detestable skunks that I could never see—their camouflage was too good. They were always spraying us with sizzling fireballs and I wanted to retaliate by hitting them with a bean ball, but they never came to the plate. I was mindful that I needed to keep my tail moving and never get careless, or I could be taken out of this contest for good.

I speculated that the Mole Teams were placing worn out trucks on the road for our attention. We would end up wasting all our time attempting to hit the small targets with our ordnance. This strategy would keep our birds occupied trying to hit a decoy, while the loaded trucks were most likely speeding south. Other flights might report that they had destroyed the identical trucks. Then the bean counters could provide trumped up numbers to McNamara. The reports would indicate that fighters were destroying numerous trucks, but in reality, we were probably doing very little to halt the supplies heading south.

Mission Results: 0 trucks (1+10 night)

RTL Summary: 2 trucks.

I played poker until sunrise and then adjourned to the dining room—the Club's chef had just baked a cherry pie that I topped with vanilla ice cream. I was pleased with my delicious treat, but then I felt guilty and donned my swimming suit to work off some of the fattening indulgence in the pool. I departed the pool and rode to the squadron to check the team lineup for the next contest. I learned that we were scheduled for an early battle tomorrow that would allow a daylight departure for a change of pace.

JULY 9, 1966
ROLLING THUNDER MISSION #55

I led my flight to the Pack One fields for a twilight contest where we had some luck. Our flight managed to surprise three trucks driving north in an open area. I immediately maneuvered to attack the trucks with a low rocket pass in the dim light. I was lucky and managed to hit tail end Charlie with our rockets although I had fired at the lead truck. The other two speeding trucks reached cover and quickly disappeared into the tall grass before we could attack them. It was amazing how fast they could just flat vanish into the jungle, as if there was always a nearby hole to dive into and hide. I was fortunate that we had time to complete our pass before they disappeared. The trucks usually drove into the tall grass before we could even start our attack. I was aware that we had to be ready to pounce as soon as we spotted a truck, or they were gone in a flash. I was gratified to finally tell our Wing Intelligence teammates that we had destroyed a moving truck, although it was heading north and probably empty.

Mission Results: one truck (+35 day & +35 night)

RTL Summary: 3 trucks.

I pulled an uneventful mobile control duty after my mission and then enjoyed a leisurely breakfast. Then I had to bite the bullet and visited the flight surgeon for my required typhus shot. I limped to the pool for some rays and chatted with Ed Collins, who had just returned from his LA vacation. I learned that he had an enjoyable time visiting his girlfriend, who flew for Continental Airlines. Ed affirmed that he would not be leaving Ubon until late in November, due to his second tour in the front seat.

I had not seen a lot of my old friend, Captain John B. Stone, since his arrival from George AFB—he was flying in the other squadron. JB and I had participated in some notable sporting events when we were stationed at George AFB. I recalled that we had arrived at George AFB, before the base was scheduled to receive Phantoms from the factory. We were fortunate that we were current in the T-33, as the Wing maintained several of the old birds for pilot proficiency. On August 21, 1965, we managed to sweet talk the Wing scheduler into assigning us a T-33 for a weekend cross-country flight that almost resulted in our demise. Someday the Air Force might realize that it was never a good idea to allow two bachelors, who drove high speed sports cars, to fly a T-Bird on their own.

We had decided that I would fly in the front cockpit to Buckley Air Base, in Colorado, to spend the night and visit some old friends in Denver. We rented a room in a local motel, had an exceptional time in the city, and even managed to get a few hours sleep before returning to Buckley for our next sortie. JB commanded the driver's seat for our flight to Las Vegas, where we would try our luck at the gambling dens on the strip.

We agreed that it was an absolute necessity to check out the bottom of the Grand Canyon en route to Vegas. We were still slightly numb from our night's activities, but we were resourceful enough to look on our maps to discover where the power cables crossed the canyon. Then we filed an instrument flight rules

(IFR) flight plan, that we would later cancel and switch to visual flight rules (VFR) when we arrived at the Canyon.

It was not very demanding for two highly skilled bleary-eyed fighter pilots to find the Canyon—it was very wide and spectacular with gorgeous colors. I canceled our IFR flight plan as JB rolled inverted and pulled the T-Bird's nose straight down towards the canyon. We leveled out of our high-speed dive at a very low altitude and headed south, deep in the canyon. It was proving to be a noteworthy sightseeing flight and was not costing us a penny of our own money. We were having the best of times admiring all the scenic beauty and never considered that other aircraft might be flying in the canyon. I was relaxing in the rear seat enjoying the view to my right when a blue and white civilian aircraft flashed before my eyes heading north and was less than 100 feet away. I decided to believe that JB's keen eyes had seen it coming, and he only wanted to water my eyes with a near miss. However, I doubted that I would ever know if he had failed to spot the prop job. A fighter pilot would never admit that a bogie could sneak up on him in the air.

Maybe the civilian aircraft had not noticed our little silver jet, as we never received any transmission on guard about a military aircraft flying in the Grand Canyon. We mutually agreed that maybe it was an appropriate time to complete our scenic tour of the canyon and fly on to Nellis, AFB, located just north of Las Vegas. A dedicated fighter pilot would never let a little thing like a close mid-air slow his future fun and games on the Strip. We had reserved a room at the Nellis BOQ, where we could shower, shave, and don our civilian clothes for the exciting games in Las Vegas. There was an outside chance that some friends might fly in from LA to bring us luck. I was also looking forward to attending some spectacular floorshows, along with competing on the craps tables.

I jumped into the front seat of the T-Bird on the 24th, after an exceptional weekend in Vegas, for an extremely low altitude flight over the desert, when we returned to George AFB. We were happy and relieved to note that there were no authoritative officers waiting on the flight line for a couple of worn-out fighter pilots after we landed. We surmised that the other aircraft in the canyon had never glimpsed our bird and had no idea that we had almost hit them.

JULY 10, 1966
ROLLING THUNDER MISSION #56

We participated in an easy Pack One contest tonight. We searched for moles on miles of trails, but never glimpsed a single dark tail. It was so peaceful that I thought we were in the States conducting a nice cross-country flight. Not one nasty stinker bothered us. The countryside looked very nice with no hostile Fans to shoot at us, but I was dispirited about terrorizing their kids. I could understand why the residents would want to kill me if they could get their hands on me.

I carefully placed my bombs in the middle of a mole run and then flew back to Home Plate for a hot breakfast. I relaxed and let Bill fly most of the mission. I was sure that he would be gratified to upgrade to the front seat after he returned to the States.

Mission Results: 0 trucks. (1+20 night)

RTL Summary: 3 trucks.

I was thrilled that I had deposited twenty-five precious coppers in my old tin can during the last 25 days. I thought my performance on the hostile fields had been satisfactory, and I might survive this League with any luck at all. I attended my first party at Ubon when one of the doctors on base gave a party for all the 497th aircrews—I appreciated his thoughtfulness. The nightly indulgence at the Clubhouse bar continued with an overabundance of free drinks, after each lucky aircrew completed 100 missions. My fun and games came to a screeching halt when I learned that we were scheduled for a distant night battle north of Hanoi tomorrow night.

JULY 11, 1966
ROLLING THUNDER MISSION #57

My luck held for another night as the long ass-busting battle north of Hanoi was canceled due to weather. I was gratified when my Coach directed me to lead a backup mission to the Pack One Park. I was fragged to carry six napalm canisters, along with our two flare pods. This would be my first mission with the newly arrived napalm. I realized that we would have to attack under the flares. Napalm canisters were not equipped with fins for guidance and tumbled all over the place once dropped. I was not thrilled that we had to get close and personal for delivering the distasteful napalm. I endeavored to consider trucks as just a projected target, with no human association, but napalm changed that. It was necessary to attack close to the ground, in order to drop right on the target. I was not delighted about torching trucks—the drivers would be burned alive if they tried to stay with the vehicle. However, I realized that it would be a more effective weapon for liquidating speedy moles, since it spread hot liquid fire over a large kill zone.

These irrational battles were really starting to grate on me, and I would not be appeased until the conflict was completed. I questioned if it was righteous to kill

Fans who might not be "Bad People", or a threat to our way of life. I never dreamed that I would be defending my country by hunting elusive trucks and fighting against deadly guns in a poor country with little indoor plumbing.

Bill and I discovered two trucks heading north in the lowlands north of Dong Hoi, after we dropped our flares over the coast road. We were fortunate because the drivers had just stopped in the middle of the road, and there was no tall grass available for cover. I hoped the operators had already made a mad dash for cover when we attacked with our six cans of napalm. The bad-tempered skunks sprayed wildly in the air during our low-level attack, and later as we circled the flare pattern. I assumed the resident stinkers were just guessing at our location. It appeared to me that we were safer operating under the flares than when flying around the flare pattern. Nonetheless, I had to be very careful not to run into the ground during our attack. The darkness and shadows made depth perception extremely difficult. It was extremely distracting to pull off the target in the bright flare light and abruptly revert to the black sky during the recovery. I could easily be stricken with overwhelming vertigo when coming off the attack if I failed to transfer my attention to the flight instruments. I was gratified that we had destroyed two trucks, while avoiding the nasty skunks that were participating with vengeance. I recalled that we had not seen any drivers, and the trucks were stationary. They were probably a flak trap.

The new Rookie aircraft commanders were going to have a difficult time attacking under flares unless they were excellent instrument pilots—it was extremely difficult to tell up from down. The lights on the ground could be confused with stars in the sky and cause the aircraft commander to become disoriented. It was extremely critical for one teammate to stay on the gauges if you wanted to survive night contests.

Mission Results: 2 trucks. (1+15 night)

RTL Summary: 5 trucks. (57 missions)

Mission Notes: My destruction average had improved to almost 9%!

JULY 12, 1966
ROLLING THUNDER MISSION #58

I thought we were playing in an old war movie tonight! We observed exploding flak and red tracers on all four sides of our poor bird. I was positive that it would be impossible for me to observe a firework demonstration again without recalling the displays that we viewed every night free of charge. However, there was a slight difference as hostile skunks wanted to make a fireball of our poor bird. I was convinced that North Vietnam was deploying additional AAA sites to Pack One. I was not thrilled to see that it was getting hotter than hell all along the coast, and particularly heated around the ferries.

The worst part was that we never found any devious moles and just scattered our ordnance around the ferry crossing with the possibility there was something of significance in the area. I made it a practice to attack toward the water, whenever possible, in case a sharp-shooting skunk got lucky. I thought that we had participated in a tough contest tonight against a bad-tempered Skunk Team. It was obvious that the stinkers were becoming more aggressive and wanted to knock us out of the competition. I thanked the Big Boss for any assistance that may have come our way tonight during our tough high PRF contest against atrocious skunks.

Mission Results: 0 trucks (1+15 night)

RTL Summary: 5 trucks.

It had been 90 days since the B-52s bombed North Vietnam. I was disappointed that they had never returned for a repeat battle. I assumed our astute High Rollers had never read their history books. I recalled that we had not won WWII by bombing the enemy to death with fighters.

JULY 13, 1966

I visited the Wing Intelligence shop to study Route Package Six A. My Coach told me that that I would be assigned to lead innumerable missions up there. All but a few of the "old heads" had departed for the States. I was now one of the most experienced pilots in the squadron. I surmised that I could look forward to a distant battle north of Hanoi every fourth night. I figured that I could be competing in at least ten high PRF events, as I had 42 more missions for the magic 100. Bill only had to complete three more missions before he departed this conflict for good. I would then have to fly with Rookies, who would be weak teammates until they had a few tough contests under their belt. I would not mind competing in the Pack Six Park if the Target Master assigned a target of importance, but I would be pissed if he ordered me to route recce deserted roads or railroads.

My Intelligence teammates indicated that our target would most likely be the distant Northeast railroad that extended from the Chinese border to Hanoi. Moreover, we had to fly through numerous SAM sites in order to reach the railroad that was protected by hundreds of AAA sites. The NVL had placed a zillion skunk dens along the railroad tracks to shoot down Thuds during the day. Now they would have a chance to fireball me at night. One big bitch about flying at night was that every perceptive skunk was looking for only one or two birds to spray with all their blistering fireballs. I was well aware of the fact that we had to fly so low that their radar could not lock on to our bird or we were in deep shit.

To make matters worse, the Intelligence players seldom had any current photos of Pack Six, but I knew that our recce birds were flying F-101's over North Vietnam. I recalled that one of their recce birds had almost run me down—where were the photos. I speculated that all the pictures were probably sitting on the desks of the High Rollers and Senior Managers. I was disappointed that current photos were seldom available for the users. It would be nice to know where those 90 SAM sites were located. Notwithstanding, that was asking too much—McNamara and the Generals required the photos for their news briefings.

I figured that we had to fly between three to five hundred feet above the ground during the complete mission to be safe from missiles and radar controlled AAA sites. I left Wing Intelligence feeling depressed and lonely. Flying north of Hanoi at night was not going to be a piece of cake. There was no possibility of rescue if we went down in Pack Six, so I would load my pistol with six hard-nosed bullets.

I rode to the library to read what the experts were saying about the war. I never seemed to know what the hell was going on in this conflict. The 11 July TIME and U.S. News and World Magazines were current and printed a few reports on the war in North Vietnam. One article mentioned that the Thud raid against the oil depot was successful, but one aircraft was lost and the pilot taken prisoner.

I read that McNamara finally acknowledged that the round-the-clock surveillance of the Ho Chi Minh trail had not checked the infiltration from the North. The article stated that North Vietnam had built and camouflaged new roads to the South for an estimated 15,000 trucks and indicated that truck traffic had doubled this year. It was incredulous to believe that the enemy had that many trucks—I could seldom find even one. I could not fathom how they knew that truck traffic had doubled, unless the High Rollers had spotters sitting on the road. A photo in U.S. News & World displayed a 51-truck convoy moving at night, but I was not able to recognize the area. At least my suspicions were confirmed, as I now knew why we never had a chance to see the latest pictures. The article also stated that Hanoi had begun dispersing and burying gas storage tanks along the Ho Chi Minh Trail. I speculated that they were using some of the fuel tanks that we had dropped during our air defense missions.

The analysis figured that the North Vietnam had an estimated 200,000 workers employed for road-repair gangs. I could certainly believe that assumption as the roads were always in great condition with no evidence of craters or wrecked vehicles. I was very disappointed to learn that the High Rollers were not interested in using B-52s to bomb North Vietnam.

JULY 14, 1966
ROLLING THUNDER MISSION #59

I led my flight to the coast in Pack One and we got lucky for a change. We surprised two stationary trucks on a road near Dong Hoi that appeared to have been driving north through some rice patties. I made a quick attack and splashed them with six cans of napalm but there was no sign of drivers running for cover, which indicated that they might have been a flak trap. The disagreeable skunks had 23mm fire hose sprayers in the area that gave us fits. It appeared that they were night blinded and never pulled lead when we attacked under the flares. I remembered a time when the offensive skunks sprayed sporadically but now the menacing fireballs had increased and were more accurate.

Bill just had two more missions to complete, and then he would be on his way to the States. I hated to see him go. It would be harder for me since he pulled a great deal of the nightly load. I would have to fly the plane more and be extra alert, as the new Rookies were very inexperienced at night flying. They would eventually learn how to compete against hostile skunks, but first they had to survive a few contests to obtain experience. It appeared to me that they had not received realistic training in the States for combat in our area—especially at night. We debriefed with Wing Intel and declared that we had destroyed two trucks heading north, but it might have been a flak trap.

Mission Results: 2 trucks. (1+20 night)

RTL Summary: 7 trucks. (59 missions)

I rode over to the Clubhouse for breakfast and noticed two round-eyed women in the dinning hall that had wandered in from parts unknown. I never had a chance to talk to them. They were getting more attention than they could handle from my teammates. It appeared that they were just wandering around Thailand and had dropped in to see what was going on in Ubon. I lost interest in them and decided to spend a few hours at the library reading the latest war news.

I found a July 11 article in U.S. News & World Report stating that President Johnson had the final say on which targets in North Vietnam were hit and which were to be left alone. That confirmed what I had been told and explained why we had such asinine perplexing targets to attack in North Vietnam. The report also stated that the war had drained the Tactical Air Command (TAC) in the States and another emergency could bring a call-up of the Air National Guard. I thought that General Disosway's comment about TAC being "right down to bedrock" was a correct and mindful comment. It was obvious that many experienced fighter pilots would be leaving the military for the airlines, if they survived their tour. I was not aware of any teammates requesting orders to return to the Tactical Air Command, and I agreed with them.

It would be interesting to see what the High Rollers were going to do now that they realized it was impossible to stem the flow of supplies to the south using fighter aircraft. I was convinced that the Target Master needed to use bombers to eliminate any strategic targets and demolish the supply lines to China. It was impossible to stop the flow of supplies unless the country was invaded, as there was too much dense jungle for cover. It was very discouraging to read what the experts had to say about the war—it looked like a deep tar pit to me. Then to make matters worse, I had to ride home in a dense pouring rain that was like standing under a waterfall.

21

It was a joyous night for Bill when we finished our quick contest on the Pack One fields for his final mission. We were careful to avoid all the fiery skunk dens and spent our time looking for shy moles far from the hot ferry crossing. It was a peaceful night with no scorching fireballs from the resident skunks. We concluded our mission by strewing our six 500-pound bombs on a designated truck park with the same unknown results. I speculated that we had been using the same few truck park photos for all our contests, but it was hard to tell because they all looked the same to me. I theorized on who had decided that it was a truck park, and concluded that it was a target planner who had only seen North Vietnam on a map.

We were disappointed when we checked in with Home Plate. The weather was the pits and we had to divert to Korat again. We were both exhausted when we landed at the Thud base, but it was still impossible to relax on the floor, tables, chairs, or on the bar. Maybe our pointy nosed teammates were not amenable to visiting Night Owls, but we really meant them no harm. We simply wanted a place to rest our weary bones. It was a relief when we finally received clearance to return to Home Plate, so Bill could celebrate surviving his hundred missions.

Mission Results: 0 trucks. (1+35 night)

RTL Summary: 7 trucks.

I was gratified to fly in the daylight for a change but soon realized that I had not missed it all that much. I now considered the darkness to be my friend. Of course, it was usually preferable to see the ground, but the disagreeable Fans could locate you quicker if you were shot down during a day contest. The Jolly

Green or Air American Teams could possibly rescue aircrews at first light, if they ejected at night and were able to hide in the darkness.

Summary: +45 day with a 0-7 mission.

The Squadron placed me in the lineup for a contest on the Northeast railroad tomorrow night. I would be flying with my roommate, Lt. Mac Hardwick, who still required a few missions before he completed his 100. Mac was certainly an accomplished pilot, but I had not flown many missions with him. I was not anxious to battle in the Pack Six Park without Bill, but it was impossible to talk him into extending—very smart of him. It would be a long hazardous mission with no chance of rescue if we went down. I had not been on one of the real tough ones but this was the fourth time that I had been scheduled for it. I was always a little leery of competing on strange dangerous fields far from home.

We were getting low on players for the team roster. All the "Old Pros" had departed with a smile on their face. It was obvious that our squadron had to reduce our nightly schedule until the new Rookies arrived around 1 August. It would be tough on our new teammates, as they had no combat time, lacked experience, and had only participated in few night attacks.

JULY 16, 1966
ROLLING THUNDER MISSION #62

I climbed out of the sack at 1600 and noticed that our distant high PRF mission was canceled due to weather, but I never complained to our Coach. The squadron then changed the game plan and assigned me to a different mission that I could lead with a Rookie GIB in the rear cockpit. We were assigned an easy contest in the Pack One Park that would allow the Rookie to become accustomed to competing on our local fields. I always warmed the new players up slowly and showed them where the bad-tempered stinkers battled. My favorite skunk den was a huge cave complex that was probably loaded with supplies, because it was situated on a river that flowed from the north to Quang Khe. It was always possible to tease the vigilant skunks around the cave into tossing a few fireballs if you flashed your lights or cycled the afterburner. It was a worthwhile night display for Rookies on their first orientation mission; they were exposed to a variety of colorful tracers.

We were able to visit most of the Pack One Park, but not one timid Mole Team wanted to participate. I finally deployed our final night-lights and completed several dive bomb attacks to crater the road leading to the Quang Khe ferry. The multiple attacks allowed my new teammate to become accustomed to calling the correct pickle altitude under the flares. I was not pleased with my

Rookie's performance and decided that he required additional night missions, before he was assigned to a new aircraft commander. It was obvious that he should be crewed with an experienced aircraft commander but few adept teammates remained.

Mission Results: 0 trucks. (1+10 night)

RTL Summary: 7 trucks.

My old friend, RL Penn was the acknowledged Night Owl Skunk Exterminator for our squadron. He had been at Ubon since December but was behind me in missions flown due to a fling at the Clubhouse bar. RL had a "fireball theory" that explained how it was difficult for a stinker to spray a bird at night. He explained that the AAA sites were just firing at an object, or light in the sky, and the shooter's eyes could not provide accurate depth perception at night to adjust their red tracers. He was confident that the sizzling red fireballs would always miss his bird, so they were of no consequence to him. RL liked to torch his afterburners at night to get a reaction from the repulsive skunks. He indicated that there was nothing so exhilarating as being shot at without effect. I decided to leave the pointless skunk games to RL. I had learned a long time ago to leave the loathsome critters alone. It was impossible for me to strike a motionless mole with a bomb, much less a repulsive skunk den that I had yet to see.

JULY 17, 1966
ROLLING THUNDER MISSION #63

My Coach assigned me to fly on the wing of a semi-experienced captain in order to prepare him to lead night missions. This was a good idea, because there were only a few experienced aircraft commanders remaining to lead our team. We certainly needed assistance from the FNG's. It was another uneventful mission to the Pack One Park until my Rookie leader prepared to deploy his flares north of Dong Hoi. I was approximately a mile west of his bird when he radioed that he was dropping several flares. We were intently looking for a tiny sparkle as the flares released from his bird but the sky was suddenly awash with two pods of rockets firing from his Phantom! It certainly got our attention, but I immediately recognized what our Rookie had done. It was a design deficiency in the F-4C.

It appeared that not one of the McDonald Douglas (MD) engineers ever envisioned that their Navy Interceptor might be utilized to carry flares and rockets at the same time. Otherwise, they might have designed a different armament setting for rockets and flares. I had observed several Phantom drivers make this same ordnance release blunder when using the station selector on the armament panel (dog bone). To make matters worse, the eagle-eyed designers had not illuminated the armament panel sufficiently for pilots to see the switch settings. I learned the hard way to use the Phantom's floodlights, or my personal flashlight, to read the armament selections.

The unexpected burst of rocket fire usually scared the piss out of all the participants in the air and possibly on the ground, when they suddenly lighted up the sky. I never wanted to be the target of this senseless mistake. I made sure that my tail was never in front of any flare bird when the night-lights were supposedly being released.

I determined that the resident skunks thought that we were using a new weapon. The stinkers never even gave us a hosing all night. My Rookie teammate finally managed to release his flares correctly but we never located any trucks. I assumed the moles had sufficient time to hide in a hole after our fireworks display. I completed several napalm attacks on the Quang Khe ferry crossing for my Rookie GIB. I decided that his performance was commendable.

Mission Results: 0 trucks. (1+15 night)

RTL Summary: 7 trucks.

I learned that Bill had not gotten his assignment. He was still at Home Plate but had packed for an immediate departure to the American League.

JULY 18, 1966
ROLLING THUNDER MISSION #64

Our squadron scheduled Mac Hardwick for an easy counter to Pack One for his last contest. I was pleased to participate in his final mission for this conflict. I led our flight to the coast to hunt for trucks, but never sighted a single vehicle. The resident skunk dens were not interested in competing with us tonight. They stayed in their well-concealed dens. I decided to scattered our bombs on the approach to the ferry crossing with multiple attacks. I assumed that it would give the ground maintenance teams something to do. Then we headed home after completing Mac's last contest in the Rolling Thunder League.

We had bad luck at Home Plate! We had to divert to Korat, since there was a Rookie in the arresting gear again. It was obvious that many of the new aircraft commanders had never landed on a short wet runway and were not braking correctly. We had our usual uncomfortable stay in the Korat Officers Club until we received clearance to return home.

Mission Results: 0 trucks (1+35 night)

RTL Summary: 7 trucks.

It was a short 45-minute flight back to Ubon from Korat. Mac headed directly to the OClub to start providing 100 free drinks for all. I told him that I would be there shortly to sip a few cold brews. I was now losing my roommate, and that was unfortunate, as we had gotten along well for many months. Only a few experienced Night Owls remained in our squadron, and I was feeling alone. All my familiar teammates had departed on the Freedom Bird. I had not recognized any of the new Rookies coming into the squadron, and I was not impressed with the preparation they received for our treacherous contests.

I reviewed the schedule and learned that I had another high PRF mission north of Hanoi tomorrow night with Paul Blease leading. I was assigned a new GIB for this contest, as both Bill and Mac had finished. I was not delighted to break in a Rookie on the menacing Pack Six fields, but there was no choice in the matter.

JULY 19, 1966
ROLLING THUNDER MISSION #65

I met Paul at the squadron to brief for the distant high PRF contest. The weather looked good and that was OK—I had to fly to the distant battleground sometime. Paul was one of the few Field Grade officers participating on the Pack Six fields, and I respected him for leading us to the railroad. We had ample time before our briefing to discuss the rationale for this mission. It was my opinion that we were just participating in a modern day "Charge of the Light Brigade". We were ordered to fly through numerous hostile SAM sites and in close proximity to Kep airfield. A rumor was circulating that top Russian pilots might be flying the all weather Russian MiGs at Kep. I was not delighted that the harmful SAM Teams had the opportunity to fire at us—both to and from the target area. I fantasized that a certain General, who had told reporters how it was easy to outplay a missile, could fly with us to demonstrate how to defeat a deadly missile at night. I theorized that the MiGs would not attack us when we were in-range of the surface-to-air missile sites. They had not scored any kills at night.

I had no idea why the Target Master wanted us to scatter a few bombs on a railroad protected by a zillion skunk dens. We knew that the skunks could concentrate all their fireballs on our two birds. I could not even imagine how much it costs to scatter a few bombs on deserted railroad tracks that would be repaired immediately. I speculated that some of the 200,000 enemy maintenance troops, which McNamara had talked about, would be available to repair the tracks quickly.

No wonder North Vietnam was not interested in ending this conflict. We were doing very little damage to them while throwing all our money down empty mole holes. It seemed bizarre that few of the Senior Managers ever visited Ubon to observe the contests that they ordered for the Rolling Thunder League. Our shrewd Generals should be required to participate in, or at least watch our missions, because it had to be costing the taxpayers millions of dollars each day. Of course, we also contributed to the exorbitant expenses. I would earn an extra two dollars tonight if we survived. I wondered if any fearless civilians desired to battle in the Pack Six Park for a couple of bucks.

As usual, the eighth TFW's excellent maintenance and ordnance ground crews had our Phantom ready for battle and loaded with six 750-pound bombs. The dedicated hard working ground crews were always on the ball but received little appreciation for working around the clock every day of the week. I had experienced very few aborts on the ground and only one emergency in the air when I lost an engine over Laos. I felt extremely fortunate to have such dedicated professional crews taking care of our equipment.

Paul led our flight to the departure runway where we released our brakes and torched off the AB's to take us to our distant contest in "The Valley of Death". I always wondered if my "Hummer" would struggle into the air with a heavy load so I always pumped the stick for good luck. I was gratified when our tough old owl easily lifted off before we reached the end of the runway. Paul radioed to change channels to our battle frequency, as we were completing our after-takeoff checklist. I told my Rookie GIB to shake the stick if he wanted to fly the bird, while we slowly joined with lead during our climb towards Danang. We would maintain a route formation position on Paul's right wing, until we refueled with our KC-135 teammates over the water. We crossed over Laos and the northern portion of South Vietnam at 20,000 feet during our flight towards the Gulf of Tonkin. We cruised along at 360 knots, since we were not worried about hostile missiles along this route. We had to opportunity to relax until we reached the tanker.

I looked down at the jungle, as we flew over South Vietnam, and was concerned for all our ground teammates competing below us. I mentioned to my GIB that I was anxious about our teams on the ground—they might not want to be there but were captive competitors. I surmised that they were not thrilled to always battle against the home team on foreign fields. It had to be horrendous to be competing in the tall grass against a lethal team that used their own advantageous ground rules. It was very difficult for me to imagine all the horror and misery that was going on in that dark green mass of foliage. I knew that it would be extremely difficult for me to battle in that impenetrable jungle for a year against a murderous home team. I just wished that we could extend more help to our ground teammates that were forced to participate in South Vietnam. We would try to help tonight by competing in Pack Six against the enemy.

We completed a routine join-up with the KC-135 Team, but Paul was unable to receive all his required fuel due to a malfunction in his refueling receptacle. It was impossible for us to continue the contest without his flares—we had to abort the mission. Paul radioed that he had insufficient remaining fuel to divert into Pack One for our secondary mission and then return to Home Plate. We had no choice but to contact Danang Approach for an individual ground controlled approach for recovery at their base with our bombs. Danang Approach cleared us for landing and alerted us to sporadic firing near the base, which was not what I wanted to hear. Our flight finally touched down safely and we followed taxi instructions from ground control before shutting down on the transit ramp. We were fortunate that Danang had experienced F-4 ground and ordnance crews—there were Air Force and Marine Phantom squadrons operating on base.

Our Wing had warned all aircrews to remain with their bird if forced to land at Danang. We were briefed that the Marines were master scavengers and would strip our aircraft of anything that could be removed for their own F-4s. One of our aircrews had diverted into Danang and later discovered that the inner refueling mechanism was missing when they tried to refuel. We played it safe and took turns going to the dinning hall so one of us could guard our Phantoms on the dark ramp. I was pleased with the Danang refueling and ground crews—they were super efficient and had us ready to depart in short order. We cranked up, taxied, and blasted off for our nice friendly little base in Thailand where we could enjoy apple pie and ice cream.

Mission Results: 0 trucks. (2+10)

RTL Summary: 7 trucks.

Mission Notes: My fifth scheduled mission to "The Valley of Death" was called off.

We finally returned to Ubon after a long frustrating mission that was unproductive. We were not sure how to score the event—it may not be a counter, as we never dropped our ordnance. I noticed that our Coach rescheduled me for another engagement in the Pack Six Park tomorrow night. I had obviously not completed my contest to his satisfaction.

JULY 20, 1966
ROLLING THUNDER MISSION #66

We heard some good news! Our Wing decided that we could count the mission last night, since we were over North Vietnam for part of the flight. Then I was delighted to learn that my sixth scheduled battle in the Six Pack was canceled. I was then tasked to lead a mission to the Red River in Pack Five, with a refueling in north Thailand. I was very pleased for this change—it was a shorter and less risky mission than going to Pack Six.

I briefed our flight and blasted off on time for the Red River contest with Lt. Bert Finzer as my new GIB for this mission. Bert was a Rookie but was on the ball and operated the radar with skill and cunning. He was right on the money when he called for the Tanker Team to turn for our refueling contact. Bert was lucky to find the KC-135 on radar! I had to keep dodging thunderstorms coming from every direction. We finally joined with the tanker team and then I immediately assumed the refueling position with scary lightning flashing all around us.

We had a challenge refueling as the tanker crew had to keep alternating their heading to avoid the raging storms. I had a difficult task because I was forced to refuel in a 30-degree bank while flying in and out of the weather. It was not long until I had a bad case of vertigo, which was always troublesome and even more so when refueling at night. I had no idea when our wings level. I could not look at my instruments, and I was always in a steep bank in my mind. Our experienced tanker team played well and they finally found a clear area for my flight to finish refueling our birds.

We departed the tanker and I joined my flight near Udorn before crossing over Laos into North Vietnam. I directed my flight to the northern portion of Pack Five and illuminated the roads coming out of China with my flares. We only received light skunk spray during our search of the lonely dirt roads. We never discovered any spoor—there was too much dense tall grass for cover. I finally decided to strew our bombs on the well-maintained road when we were down to our last flares.

We had a rough flight to Home Plate due to a solid line of furious thunderstorms. We finally radioed approach control and learned that we had the choice of diverting to Korat or landing in the middle of a heavy thunderstorm. It was an easy choice for me. I was not in favor of reclining on the uncomfortable chairs at the Korat Officers Club. The rain was so heavy and impenetrable on final that the ground control radar lost contact with our bird. However, I was able to catch a glimpse of the strobe lights just before I started to abort the landing. I immediately corrected towards the runway and planted the legs of our tough bird just past the strobe lights while deploying the drag chute instantly on touchdown. The runway was covered with water but I played the anti-skid system to perfection and managed to stop without taking the arresting gear. My wingman also managed to find the runway but ended up in the arresting gear.

Mission Results: 0 trucks (1+00 night weather & 1+00 night)

RTL Summary: 7 trucks. (66 missions)

I was pleased when our Coach placed in the lineup to fly in the rear seat tomorrow due to a shortage of GIBs. I never enjoyed competing from the rear seat, but it counted towards the magic 100 and freedom. The mission was also an opportunity to assist my Rookie aircraft commander by providing pointers on how to survive this war. Mac was still residing in our room but had packed his gear and hoped to be leaving in a few days. Bill was completely packed and ready to roll, but had not received his new orders.

JULY 21, 1966
ROLLING THUNDER MISSION #67

I was in the rumble seat tonight for our mission to Pack One. We were lucky to have gotten off the ground. Only four missions departed before the base experienced a bad accident! I learned that an ill-fated "Hummer" from the 433rd Squadron had crashed off the end of the runway. The Wing immediately canceled all the remaining flights and attempted to rescue the unlucky aircrews. We were still close to the base when we heard about the accident on Guard channel. It was obvious that we might have trouble recovering at Home Plate after our mission.

We had to fight the miserable weather all the way to the coast. Our flight had to fly in and out of clouds or the entire mission. We hunted for wary moles under the flares, which was very difficult due to the bad weather, and the critter's reluctance to participate. The resident skunks were in their usual hostile mood. We watched numerous 37/57mm fireballs flash by our Owl when they spied us flying under the clouds. We finally scattered our bombs on a suspected AAA site, after we were down to our last flares. We checked each other over for battle damage before heading for Home Plate, but I knew that we probably had to divert to Korat.

As expected, we were told to redirect for Korat. The base had not recovered the aircrew from the crashed Phantom. Nevertheless, I had planned for that eventuality and we had sufficient fuel to divert safely to Korat. I wondered if we would receive a nice welcome from our pointy nosed teammates. The weather was disturbing all the way to the Thud base where we had to land in a dense rainstorm. It was difficult to sit in the rear seat and watch a Rookie aircraft commander land long and hot. It appeared that he had limited knowledge of applying the anti-skid system on a wet runway. We were able to stop after many thousands of feet—Korat had a long runway for their ground loving birds with bomb bays.

The Thuds needed miles of dirt to safely take off and land; I assumed that was why some teammates labeled the F-105 as the "Ultra Hog".

Mission Results. 0 trucks (+45 weather & 1+25 night)

RTL Summary: 7 trucks.

We experienced another distasteful evening at Korat! The base was unwilling to give us anything of comfort, while we waited for clearance to depart. Maybe we should have been thankful that we were allowed to wait inside the Officers Club, with the luxury of a hard chair. It was still raining, with standing water on the runway, when we landed at Home Plate. My aircraft commander ended up in the arresting gear again! I realized that I was going to spend a lot of time at Korat, if all the Rookie aircraft commanders kept taking the arresting gear every time they landed. It appeared that they had never landed on a short wet runway in an F-4 and certainly had no idea on how to use the anti-skid system correctly. However, the base construction crews were working hard to extend the runway a few thousand feet, which would help immensely.

We returned to our squadron and learned that one pilot had been killed in the crash. The other crewmember, who had also stayed with the "Hummer", was alive. None of my teammates had any knowledge of what had caused the fatal accident. I was convinced in my own mind that I would never try to stay with a "Hummer" that could not get airborne. I always briefed my GIB to eject us both if we were still glued to the pavement when we reached the end of the runway.

Bill departed today, after he finally received his assignment. He seemed satisfied to be going to Homestead AFB, Florida. I would miss him greatly as we had participated in many exciting and demanding missions during the last five months. It would be more painstaking to survive the next 33 missions. The rookie rear seat pilots were enthusiastic teammates but had little experience at night. The treacherous nightly contests were becoming more forbidding. It appeared that additional stinkers were spraying us with better aimed fireballs. The majority of our experienced Night Owls had departed Home Plate, except for RL and Paul. I thought that our Rookies were going to experience a tough learning curve, before they became accustomed to competing in aggressive night battles over North Vietnam.

July 22, 1966
ROLLING THUNDER MISSION #68

I was gratified to be competing from the front seat tonight, although the weather was still miserable. I had a horrendous time trying to deploy my flares to search for fugitive moles without getting our tail feathers singed. We noticed lots of skunk spray along the coast. I could see the fireballs coming up from the ground, but I could not pin point their dens on the black playing fields. We sprinkled our bombs in the vicinity of the red spray, and then headed back to Home Plate in turbulent weather.

We learned that the storm had increased in size and moved directly over Home Plate. We were forced to fly in dense clouds once we reached the holding pattern. I received clearance for my wingman to start his penetration immediately and hoped he would stay out of the arresting gear. I then entered the holding pattern at 20,000 feet indicated altitude until we received further clearance from approach control.

I never liked to fly for long in a holding pattern during night weather. It was easy for me to get vertigo if I was careless with my head movements. I was never comfortable when the ground controllers requested us to change our Identification, Friend or Foe (IFF) squawk, before we penetrated due to the position of the black box. Some perceptive cockpit designer had managed to place the IFF control device in the far right rear corner of the cockpit. The installation of the IFF controller in this location was unfortunate, as the aircraft commander had to turn his head to the right and down to dial the correct code. To make matters worse, it was also difficult to read the numbers on the black box due to marginal cockpit lighting. I knew better, but I was careless when I made the dial change, while in a 30-degree bank turn, and ended up with a bad case of vertigo. I rolled out of my turn but now my senses indicated that I was still in a 30-degree bank although I was now flying straight and level.

Now I had to fight all my senses that were screaming to me that I was in a turn, but my instruments correctly indicated that I was flying straight and level. It was extremely troublesome and always a challenge for me to fly in this predicament—I felt like my whole body was leaning. It was strenuous for me to hold my head level in the cockpit although the aircraft was wings level. This unbalanced mental situation continued to progress to the point that I placed both hands on the stick and told myself that the instruments were correct. It took all my will power to overcome the urge to make an improper correction that could put the aircraft out of control. I could easily understand how pilots without adequate instrument training could get insidious vertigo in weather and crash. It was obvious that your senses could lie to you. You unconditionally had to rely on your instruments or you would lose control of your bird.

Approach control finally instructed us to change frequencies for the GCA. I instructed my GIB to change the radio because I was not going to take my eyes off the instrument panel or my hands off the controls. I had a formidable time trying to fly the correct heading and altitude, as my mind indicated that I was in a disastrous descending left turn. Our GCA controller instructed me to begin my descent for landing just as we entered a heavy rainstorm. I was not thrilled with our situation because the rain in Thailand during the monsoon season was horrendous—I felt like we were flying under an extensive waterfall. I could only see a few feet ahead of our Phantom and we were flying over 150-MPH.

The F-4C was equipped with a rain clear system that blew high-pressure air over the front windscreen, but was ineffective during monsoon rains. I finally spotted the splendid strobe lights on the approach end of the runway and my vertigo cleared in a flash. However, I was unable to catch a glimpse of the dark pavement of the runway through the solid rain. No matter, I planned to plant the Phantom just beyond the strobe lights and immediately pop the drag chute. I had no intentions of going to Korat! I just wanted to land and deposit another precious copper in the tin can after a nice hot breakfast.

I continued to fly our drenched bird to the strobe lights and descended to where the runway should be located. I finally sighted the gloomy runway and firmly placed our wheels on the end of the dark pavement. I was thankful to the Navy that the F-4 had very strong landing gear that could take a hard landing. I deployed the drag chute immediately and would need every inch of the runway if I wanted to avoid using the arresting gear. I monitored the 1000-foot runway marker lights, as they flashed by each side of the canopy, and they helped me to remain in the middle of the runway. The brake system had to be played perfectly while braking. I had learned that the best method for me was to brake to the anti-skid cycle before releasing and starting over. The anti-skid system worked well on a dry runway by flooring the brakes and letting the system stop the aircraft, but I had discovered that this procedure seldom worked for me on a wet runway. Again, thanks to the Navy, the F-4 was equipped with a rugged tail hook, to engage the mid-field arresting gear, if you had doubts about stopping a "Hummer". I had never been required to engage the arresting gear for one of my landings, but I had been in the back seat when a Rookie used the hook.

I felt fortunate that we were able to stop on the waterlogged runway and relieved when we pulled into the dearming area at the end of the runway to meet the ground crew. We completed our after landing checklist during our return to the ramp. I was sympathetic for our crew chief, as he was waiting in the heavy rain to steer us into our parking area with his flashlights.

Mission Results: 0 trucks (+45 day & +45 night weather)

RTL Summary: 7 trucks.

JULY 23, 1966
ROLLING THUNDER MISSION #69

It was another discomforting Pack One night contest in wretched weather that would not go away. I was thankful that there were no devious SAM Teams around—it was impossible to see what the hell was taking place most of the time. The clouds were down to around two thousand feet, and that was too low to compete unless we were near the coast with no mountains to consider. We had to fly close to the flare pattern and then attack under the lights to drop our napalm, but this allowed the wicked skunks to glimpse our bird and spray us. The resident stinkers were becoming more proficient with their aim, as we noticed numerous scorching fireballs flashing by our canopy. I had been getting too complacent about malignant skunk spray, because I had been ignoring it lately, which was not smart!

We were fortunate and surprised a couple of wet moles high tailing it north of Dong Hoi. The truck drivers probably thought we could not operate in this abominable weather and were safe on the road. I immediately attacked and released all six canisters of napalm, in the pair's mode, with three delayed pickles on both trucks. We pulled out of the attack and noted that the resulting fire had encompassed the trucks. I was not pleased that we had to use firebombs, but they were one of the best weapons for killing speeding moles. We scored two unquestionable kills, because they were moving when we knocked them out of the contest. I never dreamed that I would be protecting our country from the "Bad People" by torching trucks in a poor country.

I tried to avoid the numerous thunderstorms on the way home but we were still thrown all over the sky. We were also dazzled with awesome lightning bolts that were more alarming than skunk spray. I radioed Ubon approach control near the Thai border. They instructed us to recover at Udorn due to severe weather at Home Plate. I was pleased to land at Udorn, because I had flown over the field numerous times and was curious about the base. It was a relief to finally shut down on the transit ramp at Udorn and get away from the high PRF thunderstorms.

Mission Results: 2 trucks (1+30 night)

RTL Summary: 9 trucks. (69 missions)

We were fortunate to catch a ride to the Udorn Officers club, which unlike Korat was open, and the mess hall was serving hot food. I was surprised to meet one of my old instructors from Perrin AFB, Texas. We relaxed together and enjoyed an appetizing breakfast while reminiscing about the good old days. I reminded him of our swinging party at Lake Texoma after I had finished my F-102 interceptor course. It was a great time for me as I had received the Distinguished Graduate award for Class 62-A. The honor also granted consideration for an appointment to the Regular Air Force. I was lucky to have finished first as Robert McIntire (Mac), David L. Ferguson (Fergie), and Robert C. Ettinger had been tough competition. I was able to choose the 497th TFS in Torrejon, Spain, which I thought was the best assignment in the Air Force.

I was never a big drinker but that night was a special happening for me, and I over indulged. I had become slightly numb during the night and sprawled out on the ground near the fire to sober up. All at once, an instructor's wife plopped down on my outstretched hand, and I was at a loss on what to do. I could visualize her jumping up with a scream as if I was trying to grope her, and then I would be in trouble. I decided not to budge, just lie low, and hope she would move on to a softer spot. However, she never changed position and then my arm started to go numb. Finally, I decided to quickly roll away while pulling my hand back, and declaring that I was getting sick. I quickly left before she could utter a word. I left the party immediately, and that was the only time I had ever driven a car drunk. I finally staggered back to the BOQ in one piece. I was thankful that I had not lost my assignment and destiny that night.

We blasted off at first light for Home Plate, after briefing a quick game of unauthorized air-to-air combat during our return. We were pleased to practice air combat maneuvers, because it was impossible during our night contests. I enjoyed playing our one-on-one game in the daylight, as we attacked each other and managed to avoid a mid-air collision. I had almost forgotten what it was like to fly during the day and have the opportunity to practice air combat maneuvers. Maybe someday, I would be able to contest a hostile MiG Team in a belligerent arena, instead of a neighborly teammate over friendly fields. I checked our lineup, after landing, and was pleased that my Coach had scheduled me to lead a mission to Pack One with a Rookie aircraft commander on my wing.

I rode to the library and read the latest newsmagazines about how the war was progressing before retiring. There was an article in the 18 July, U.S. & World Report, about the air war over North Vietnam. The narration included an interesting analysis about how the conflict was growing bigger and bigger. The writer indicated the oil storage facilities that had been hit by the Thuds, were 55% destroyed. I questioned if that would slow the trucks down, as they had probably positioned all our dropped centerline fuel tanks along the roads for fuel storage. The article stated that 113 missions were flown on July 6 but never indicated if anything was accomplished. I speculated that McNamara was only interested in counting sorties, so he could rattle off statistics for the reporters.

I was upset to see pictures of POWs being paraded around Hanoi! I assumed that some of my teammates were there and undergoing torture. I questioned if my Commander in Chief was doing everything possible to end this senseless conflict, because he was not using B-52s to destroy the few important targets in Pack Six. I wondered if our leaders had any authentic knowledge of our battles—they never visited our base.

I had completed 69 day and nights missions over North Vietnam and had not discovered any significance targets. Our Senior Managers insinuated that there were thousands of trucks in North Vietnam, but I could not believe their assertions. I had searched numerous dirt roads, during day and night missions, but I could seldom find even one truck. I speculated that the enemy had a low number of trucks that they could easily hide in the jungle.

JULY 24, 1966
ROLLING THUNDER MISSION #70

It was an uneventful night in Pack One—we searched all the coastal trails but never spotted a truck. However, my Rookie GIB received a taste of our nasty night contests when he was exposed to deadly fireballs along the coast. I used the last flares to scatter our napalm in the vicinity of a disgusting skunk den, but we could only guess where his dugout was located.

I had learned to radio Home Plate early during our RTB, to see if a Rookie was in the arresting gear or if the weather was below minimums. My fears were justified, as we were told to divert to Korat again which was definitely a pain in the ass. Our base had gotten very leery about letting Rookies take off or land in marginal weather after the recent fatal accident. I wished my new teammates would learn to land on a short wet runway soon—they were making my life miserable! However, I knew the Home Plate construction workers were laboring day and night to extend the runway and that would be a big help. I was beginning to feel like an old exhausted competitor who was running out of 'Go' juice. I realized that I had to stay on the ball and keep battling in a resourceful manner, if I wanted to survive this war.

Mission Results: 0 trucks. (1+30 night)
RTL Summary: 9 trucks. (70 missions) (Average .0129

There was not a gesture of sympathy or any food, blankets, cots, etc, at Korat, which was no surprise—I had expected this banal reception. It appeared that the Thud Managers never wanted us to visit their precious base with its long runway.

I thought that it would be difficult to feel concern for our unfriendly needle-nosed Thud teammates again. I was able to get our flight airborne at first light, but the weather was still grubby at Home Plate with more heavy rain. I imagined that the apprehensive moles probably loved this bad weather, as they were free to run up and down their trails, but it sure made our life miserable. My roommate (Mac) was leaving today, but the squadron was almost back up to full team strength.

JULY 25, 1966
ROLLING THUNDER MISSION #71

My luck was still holding, as I succeeded in getting my flight airborne before our Wing canceled the remainder of the missions due to lousy weather. It was another troublesome night of in and out of the clouds while searching for trucks. The malicious skunks threw sizzling fireballs at us when they glimpsed our bird—we had to fly close to the flares. I finally illuminated two trucks on the coast road that were heading north, but I was leery of shy moles sitting motion-less in the middle of the road. However, my wingman and I made several napalm attacks under the flares, and left the trucks burning in a sea of flame. It was obvi-ous that the enemy had positioned multiple aggressive skunk dens along the road that sprayed blistering fireballs in our direction. I speculated that the trucks were worn out shells and were being used as a flak trap.

The belligerent skunks never seemed to be short of hot fireballs to send our way. The spray never seemed to bother me anymore, but I still tried my best to avoid the stinkers. I speculated that the enemy had an extensive network of little wooden boats going up and down the coast to ferry ammo for the AAA sites. Their use of small vessels would negate the requirement for numerous trucks and save valuable gas. Nonetheless, I had been unable to catch sight of any of the nar-row black craft along the coast—the diminutive one-man skiffs would be very difficult to see under our flares.

We started our egress for Home Plate and quickly learned that our field was closed due to the wretched weather—no surprise. I was prepared for this eventu-ality and had saved adequate fuel for our diversionary flight to Korat. I ques-tioned where we would be directed to go if Korat was also closed, as sometimes we were on fumes when we landed at the Thud base. There was another Thud complex at Tahkli, but it was 120 miles west of Korat, and we could not fly that distance with our remaining fuel. It was possible for us to divert to Udorn, which was approximately 200 miles north, but that required an immediate redirect with no playing around.

We received a big surprise at Korat! It might be time to start feeling sorry for the Thud drivers again. I was pleased that we were finally allowed to use several small iron cots in an old plywood building. This luxury was really appreciated—I was delighted to receive a pillow and blanket for a few hours rest. I was exhausted and managed to get a few hours sleep before we blasted off for Home Plate at first light. I noticed when we taxied out that the Thud Teams were all gearing up for a strike. I wondered where the Target Master was sending them. I was not aware of any consequential targets, other than a few airfields and large cities.

Mission Results: two trucks. (1+20 night & +25 weather)

RTL Summary: 11 trucks. (71 missions)

The miserable weather must have blown past Ubon—it was decent when we landed at Home Plate. Our efficient hard working maintenance teams were pleased to have the Phantoms back—they needed to ready them for the next battle. I marveled at how the Wing could constantly perform so skillfully, in a multitude of hostile day and night contests, during this disagreeable weather. Numerous Phantoms diverted to Korat, and then, the maintenance crews had to wait until the aircraft returned before they could get the birds in the air again. Our dedicated maintenance and ordnance teammates were doing an outstanding job while competing in the tough Rolling Thunder League.

My roommate (Mac) departed this morning, which left me alone in my hootch, but probably not for long, as Rookies were arriving daily. I decided to skip my usual breakfast and attempted to catch up on my sleep. I was way behind on my rest and wanted to snooze for the next 12 hours. I noticed that my Coach had placed me in the line-up to lead another flight to the Pack One Park tomorrow night, with a Rookie in the back seat. I was gratified that our squadron required experienced teammates to familiarize the Rookies on the Pack One fields.

JULY 26, 1966
ROLLING THUNDER MISSION #72

I briefed my Rookie GIB and a new wingman for our nightly contest in the Pack One Park and tried to give them the benefit of my combat experience from 71 missions—I wanted them to survive their treacherous tour. I explained that they would be on their own to take the field in hostile parks when the last of the "Old Pros" left. Our Squadron Coaches and Wing Managers were available, but they seldom if ever participated in the Pack Six contests. I told them that they were free to compete against the wicked Skunk Teams, but I personally never played one-on-one with a vicious stinker. I had never been able to spot their well-camouflaged dens during 72 missions, and decided not to battle hidden nasty varmints that possessed menacing fireballs. I told the Rookies to respect the deadly Skunk Teams and be very careful—they were aggressive and growing in number. The stinkers were harmful opponents that could knock you out of the contest with a well-aimed lethal fireball.

I was not pleased with my rear seat teammate during our mission. I thought that he was nervous and reacted slowly, but I knew that he was trying his best. I tried to be pleasant, since it was his first flight, but he had to get with the program. I had to chew him out a few times, because he was not playing well enough to stay in the contest for the long haul. I attempted to get his attention by pointing out that a half-witted error could scratch him off the team roster.

We were never able to locate any elusive moles, so I used some of our flares for an instructional flight. I decided to make numerous attacks on suspected skunk dens that had fired at us. I deployed the night-lights and attacked the stinkers' whereabouts with our napalm. I released one can of napalm on each pass that allowed my Rookie to become familiar with calling the release at the correct altitude. I stressed that it was critical for him to remain glued to the gauges and be ready to help his aircraft commander at all times. It was easy for his teammate to get vertigo when exiting the bright flares into the darkness—he had to be ready to take control of the aircraft if necessary.

We were fortunate that it was pleasant evening in North Vietnam. I had time to show my Rookies the Pack One fields with a delightful river rippling to the coast. I explained that you had to be watchful and never become complacent, as vicious skunks could see your bird in the evening sky. The country was very pretty at dusk, and, sometimes, I just toured around the fields to enjoy the scenery, when the skunks were tranquil. I personally thought that maybe someday there would be hotels on the sandy beaches and the country might become a tourist attraction. It was difficult to grasp what the fighting was all about—I had flown 72 missions without seeing a menace, except from argumentative skunks and unfriendly Fans in their fields.

I was pleased to recover at Home Plate, since I needed to get some rest for a fierce contest north of Hanoi. I advised our Coach that his new GIB needed additional experience in Pack One, before going to Pack Six with a Rookie aircraft commander. I noticed that I was in tomorrow's lineup for a risky Six Pack contest with Lieutenant Benjamin B. Finzer. I was pleased to fly with Bert, as I had flown with him in Pack One and was impressed with his readiness.

Mission Results: 0 trucks. (1+15 night & +15 weather)

RTL Summary: 11 trucks.

JULY 27, 1966
ROLLING THUNDER MISSION #73

I checked the squadron missions schedule, after I had awakened, to see if the Target Master still wanted to send us to "The Valley of Death". Everyone knew that LBJ personally approved all our missions over North Vietnam. It appeared that my Commander in Chief wanted our Wing to attack the rail line extending from Hanoi to China, and my Coach selected me to lead the mission. We were all aware that your military career was ended if I anyone bombed an outhouse that was not approved by the Master.

I noticed that our distant high PRF night attacks were obviously for junior aircrews—I had never seen a Lt. Colonel or Colonel on the schedule to battle in Pack Six. I had never even participated in the same battle with a Lt. Colonel since arriving at Ubon. Colonel James C. Covington was our only Wing teammate that I had observed taking part in Pack One contests with our squadron. However, that was OK with me, as tough night contests were for young competitors with quick reflexes.

I located my slightly experienced Rookie GIB studying our mission's tasking that was displayed on our scheduling board. We visited the Intelligence shop for a briefing on the latest information that was usually of limited or no use. I was surprised to learn that there was little guidance from our Umpire. I assumed that it was up to me to formulate the strategy for searching out the railroad after departing the tanker. Then I had to use my own judgement on how to battle back to the tanker and refuel before returning to Ubon.

We discovered that there was little current data available on Route Pack Six A. It would have been nice to know where all the SAM sites were located, and I was pissed that we were not equipped with missile warning gear. I was told that our Photo teammates had flown over Pack Six, but the snapshots never seemed to get to the users.

There was no reason to even consider that the Jolly Green Teams could rescue us in Pack Six, as they would not have the legs to reach up there. I knew there were HU-16 amphibious Albatross rescue aircraft available in the Gulf of Tonkin for day missions, but they were not available at night. However, our Navy teammates had helicopters available for day or night rescue operations in the Gulf. I was delighted about our Navy support—it was a big plus if we had to eject during a night event. The Wing Intel players warned about possible barrage balloons north of Haiphong. I thanked them for the timely information, but, how the hell were we going to be able to see balloons at night?

I gathered my apprehensive flight for a detailed briefing to discuss how we were going to conduct our distant mission. I was pleased to be leading the flight with the freedom to devise my own game plan. We had to plan carefully, because it was a long mission with a refueling before and after the attack. I briefed that I would lead us to a lighthouse north of Haiphong, after we refueled with our tanker. We should easily locate the lighthouse as it was usually illuminated for ships going into the port. I explained that I would "hack" at the lighthouse to start our 10-½ minute low altitude run to the railroad, and my wingman could fall in trail at that time. I decided that I would fly close to the 25-mile buffer zone that extended from the Chinese border so we could use the mountains along the border for protection. The missile and AAA sites would have a difficult time painting us on their radar, as the high terrain would shield us during most of the way to the railroad. I told Bert that I needed him to follow the ground track on our map because we had to fly between three to five hundred feet above the highest terrain. I had no qualms about flying lower if I could see the ground, and there might be some moonlight to help us. I explained that we would probably be greeted with an unfriendly missile if we flew too high. We had to watch for missile launches and any bright lights in the sky, but I had no idea how to defeat a missile at night.

I briefed my wingman that I would expend all my flares during my initial pass in an attempt to find the railroad. I was sure that we would receive a spectacular fireball demonstration from bad-tempered skunks once the flares illuminated. Intel had briefed that we could expect to receive extremely heavy flak from an innumerable number of 37/57/85mm AAA sites. I instructed my teammate to remain 6-7 miles in trail during our approach to the railroad and be ready to roll in immediately after the flares illuminated. It was critical for them to immediately locate the railroad and release their bombs in a shallow dive. We had to stay low as the offensive skunks or SAMs could paint us on their radar if we flew above 500 feet. I briefed that I would exit my flare drop to the west and promptly roll in for a low angle attack after their bombs had exploded.

Then we would both depart the railroad heading to the east and haul ass for the coast as fast and low as our "Hummers" could speed. We would return to the tanker using our own game plan, but I had decided that I would again hug the mountains to foil the radar sites. I explained that the missile and AAA sites with radar could give us a lot of menacing heat if we climbed above 500 feet, so it was critical to stay low and fast. Little that could be done if either of us took a hit and had to eject in Pack Six—rescue was impossible. I would do everything possible to make it to the water, because I was not going to eject in Pack Six, but Bert was free to eject if he thought it was necessary.

I also briefed our secondary target, the Ron Ferry Crossing, in case our primary mission was cancelled. I warned my teammates about the 85mm AAA site located in that area—it was manned by a sharp shooter. I reiterated that Night Owls should never fly straight and level in North Vietnam if they wanted to survive this conflict.

We blasted off on time and had completed our refueling with the Tanker Team, when we received word that the mission was canceled due to weather. Our secondary mission on the Ron Ferry in Pack One was completed without encountering a single truck or the 85mm AAA site. I finally had my flight scatter our twelve bombs on the road leading to the ferry. I realized that I had missed my seventh chance to compete in a high PRF contest on the Pack Six fields. Nonetheless, I was not disappointed to have lost the opportunity to battle with a zillion stinkers and missiles at night.

Mission Results: 0 trucks. (2+00 night & +20 night weather)

RTL Summary: 11 trucks.

Mission Notes: Maybe I was "not meant" to battle in the Pack Six Park tonight.

JULY 28, 1966
ROLLING THUNDER MISSION #74

I was content to compete in a expeditious contest in the Pack One Park tonight. I was pleased to resume battling on the near fields after trying to attack the northeast railroad in Pack Six. We hunted along the roads leading to the Quang Khe ferry complex, but there were no elusive moles running on the trails. I saved my final flares to light the Quang Khe Naval complex. I was very surprised and pleased when our flares ignited. There was a large vessel docked in the small port area! My wingman had already expended his ordnance on a suspected skunk den, but I still carried six cans of napalm.

I made a command decision and declared that it was not a Russian ship—it could bite me in the rear later. I rationalized that it was most likely a North Vietnam vessel, as it was docked in of their coastal harbors. Nonetheless, I was aware that the Target Master would have his Managers rip the wings off my chest if I had made a bad decision.

I immediately positioned for a low altitude pass under the flares and ignored the several bad-tempered skunks there were spraying some red fireballs. I released my first pair of canisters close to the vessel on the first attack—it should have been an excellent hit—but we never observed a fireball during the recovery. I immediately repositioned and made another diving attack to release two more cans of nape right on top of the craft, but again there was no fireball and that really pissed me off. I then deployed my last flares exactly over the boat so I could get a super good look at the target for my final attack. I dropped my last two cans at mast level and we could clearly see the supplies on the deck of the vessel. However, it was not my night to score a hit. I had missed a large target again, or the nape never ignited. I was very upset to have missed the mark with each of my attacks, but I had done the best that I could. Maybe God had not wanted that vessel torched tonight.

It was very frustrating to have finally discovered a material target and then let it get away. I was also upset that were not equipped with an internal gun for additional attacks. This was the first time that I had ever seen a sizable vessel anywhere along the coast, and I could not even get one canister to light. It was troublesome to realize that every can of napalm had missed or failed to ignite. I had attacked with the best of my ability, using very low releases right over the ship, but the napalm had not exploded. I could not radio for other Night Owl teammates to attack the target—we were the last flight of the night.

We debriefed with Wing Intelligence after landing at Home Plate. I recommended that the Umpire frag a mission on the target, but I doubted that the vessel would still be there in the morning. I was upset to have missed hitting the only meaningful target that I had observed in 74 missions over North Vietnam. We checked the scheduling board and learned that our Coach had scheduled an early hour team meeting in our squadron briefing room. I decided to ride to the Clubhouse for a good hot breakfast before retiring after an exasperating night.

Mission Results: O trucks. (1+15 night)

RTL Summary: 11 trucks.

22

I competed in a short routine Pack One contest from the back seat with Captain Kenneth D. Robinson. Ken was a Rookie aircraft commander who had already flown several missions in Pack One. Our Coach wanted me to assist in upgrading him to flight lead.

We deployed all our night-lights looking for shy moles and finally scattered our bombs on a suspected truck park to end an unproductive contest. I told Ken to plan for recovery with sufficient fuel to divert to Korat—our Rookies still had problems landing on the short runway. We broke away from our wingman, when he started his approach to land. We then entered the holding pattern to await our turn. Ken had just started our penetration to land when we were instructed to divert to Korat—our wingman was in the arresting gear. We were ready for this eventuality, it was no big surprise, and we had sufficient fuel to divert.

We were well on our way to Korat when our tower teammates radioed us to return as our wingman was now out of the arresting gear and the field was open. We reversed course and were number two to land when the "Hummer" in front of us took the barrier. I was upset, but I was aware that our Rookies had a lot of trouble landing on a 5800-foot runway. Ubon tower again radioed us to divert, but now there was insufficient fuel to reach either Korat or Udorn unless we jettisoned all our external stores. My hurried computations indicated that we might have just enough fuel to reach Korat, but it would be close.

I told Ken to declare a low fuel emergency and informed tower that we had to clean our bird of all external stores. Tower gave us clearance to jettison our scarce equipment worth thousands of dollars—but who was counting money at this point in time! I found the jettison area, which was a small lake, by following a radial off the Ubon TACAN station. Then Ken depressed the emergency jettison

231

button, in his cockpit, when we were over a lake that we could see in the moonlight.

We immediately started a low fuel profile flight for Korat but it was soon evident that we could not reach the Thud base with our remaining fuel. Ken was doing a great job flying the bird, while I was computing time, distance and a fuel analysis. I determined that we had to either land at Home Plate, or we would have to eject when we ran out of petrol. Ken radioed Ubon that we had to return and land ASAP—we could not make it to Korat.

The Ubon ground crews must have heard our distress call. The efficient ground crew snatched the other Phantom out of the arresting gear in record time. We started our final approach with little fuel showing on the gauge. I was ready to eject both of us if the engines flamed out. There was less than five hundred pounds showing on a fuel gauge that was unreliable at low readings, as some of the fuel was not useable. Ken immediately shut down an engine after landing and was ready to use emergency braking if the other engine flamed out. I praised Ken for doing an excellent job flying the aircraft! I was impressed with his performance. He had maintained outstanding aircraft control while we were playing musical bases.

We were told after landing that our Wing Director of Operations (DO), Colonel John S. Clarke, Jr., wanted to know why we had to jettison scarce expensive gear in the local lake. The 497th thought that I should be the one to justify our decision, as he had been my squadron commander in Spain. Colonel Clarke was not dazzled by my song-and-dance routine about our dire circumstances, but he understood what we had to do.

Mission Results: 0 trucks. (1+30 night)

RTL Summary: 11 trucks.

I rode to the library and read in the Stars and Stripes that a woman pilot crashed with golfer Tony Lema aboard. It appeared that the plane might have run out of gas—sounded familiar. I speculated that I should get a job flying celebrities around the world. It would be a piece-of-cake after these hostile night engagements and experience with landing on short runways.

The squadron scheduled me to battle in the Pack One Park, and I was pleased to see that I was going back to the front cockpit. I seemed to have trouble competing from the rear seat. I had flown four missions in the rear cockpit and had been involved in my only arresting gear engagement, along with almost running out of fuel. I admitted that the Rookies were making life a lot more thrilling, but I had no desire for additional excitement during my final missions. I noticed that our squadron was scheduled to return to the late schedule in three more days.

I had some tough luck with my bike as both tires went flat, after I had just pumped them full of air. I later discovered that the local bikes had high maintenance valve cores that broke if the tires were over-inflated.

JULY 30, 1966
ROLLING THUNDER MISSION #76

I crawled out of bed at 1230 to attend our squadron meeting and then learned that it had been canceled. I was pissed as I had only gotten six hours of sleep, rather than my normal 12 hours! I returned to my nice cool bed for additional rest, but it was impossible to go back to sleep. I finally gave up and rode to the Club for breakfast, before heading to the library. I read my novel in the cool library, until it was time to brief for our routine contest on the Pack One fields.

We blasted off on time and hunted everywhere for the slippery mole teams, but they were a no-show for the contest. It was a very quiet night. Even the indecent stinkers ignored us while we searched the Pack One fields. I used our last flares to light the Quang Khe Naval Complex, but the ship was no longer at the dock. I then had my flight scatter our bombs where the ship had been docked—some supplies might still be in the area. I really enjoyed leading flights, and was not disappointed that there were never any Coaches or Managers around to bitch about my performance.

It was raining hard when we returned to Ubon, but we were allowed to land. Wet field landings were no problem, if you just played the brakes correctly and stayed out of a skid. Still, it was nice to know that every "Hummer", thanks to the Navy, had a big iron tail hook to use if necessary.

Mission Results: 0 trucks. (1+20 night)

RTL Summary: 11 trucks.

The squadron offered to give me the day off tomorrow, but I told them that I wanted to fly. I wanted to battle every night before I ran low on "Go Juice". It was still pouring down with vengeance! It appeared as though our Home Field would never dry out. I questioned how the natives were able to survive in a hot steaming shower with high humidity that sapped your energy. This rain was really getting to me. I might have to take the five days of rest and relaxation (R&R) that was coming up on the fourteen of August. I was mindful that I had sixty days of leave accrued that I would use it for entertainment, if I survived the Target Master's war.

I received word that my old roommate Lt. Tom (Tomas) Boyd would not arrive until 1 September. I hoped that Tomas had relished his final days in the States and had not gotten married to just any girl before he departed the real world. I figured that he would arrive about the time I finished league competition. I hoped to be off the fields and out of the Parks by the end of August.

JULY 31, 1966
ROLLING THUNDER MISSION #77

We attempted to compete in a routine contest tonight in the Pack One Park, but the Mole Team was a no-show. However, numerous Skunk Teams wanted to complete and seemed to have an unlimited supply of sizzling fireballs. I noted that our Rookie aircrews could never see any elusive moles on the trails either, so it was not just my eyes. The skunks might have been training some rookies tonight—their fireballs were wild but they had lots of ammo for practice. I speculated that the enemy was moving additional AAA sites to Pack One and using experienced shooters to train the rookies. I wanted to be off the playing field and long gone before they learned how to accurately toss sizzling fireballs at Owls. It would not take long for the rookie skunks to become precise with all the practice allotted to them. I was not thrilled to know that I needed to complete 23 more missions against improved competitors that were increasing in number every night.

We returned to Home Plate after scattering our unproductive bombs on a suspected skunk den near Dong Hoi. I was pleased to land at Ubon, because there were no Rookies residing in the arresting gear for a change. I contemplated that our Umpire might question me for not dropping on his designated truck parks, but I could take his heat, and I would like to express my opinion on his target calls.

Mission Results: 0 trucks. (1+15 night & +10 night weather)

RTL Summary: 11 trucks.

It was sad to say adios to the last of my experienced teammates when they turned in their gear after the final mission. Nonetheless, there was more free booze than you could ever imagine, as the "Old Pro's" bought drinks for all. I would be the next combatant to finish—followed by Paul and RL. The drinks were free, but I never felt like drinking a great deal of booze when I had to fly every night. I was pleased to just sip on a beer and congratulate my exhilarated teammates for a series well played. I decided to leave the cheering crowd to attend a movie that proved to be regretful. I was able to view several recent sports reels, with hot buttered popcorn, as a consolation prize.

I rode back to the squadron after the movie and noticed that our Coach had scheduled me to participate in another high PRF contest tomorrow night, with RL leading the way. It was always a striking experience to compete with RL—you never knew what the squadron skunk exterminator was going to do next. My squadron had not received any word on my new assignment. I decided that those orders would determine whether the Big Boss wanted me to stay in the service. I received a notice from military finance that I would receive a whopping big pay raise of eighteen dollars a month! I would probably be a millionaire many times over if I just had a penny for every bullet fired at me during our belligerent battles.

I decided to check for war news at the library before retiring and read a long article in the July 25 U.S. News & World Report titled "Is End of Vietnam War in Sight?" The article indicated that supply lines to the South were still open and operating with no crippling shortages of arms or ammunition. The analysis also stated that it was impossible to stop the flow of supplies with fighters—I agreed. The article explained that Americans were flying 800 daily strikes, with 300 against North Vietnam, 400 in the South, and 100 against infiltration routes in Laos. The article failed to mention that numerous strikes were ineffective and never explained why B-52s were not flying against material targets in North Vietnam. The article confirmed my grievous suspicions when it stated that supplies were possibly moved with the help of porters and pack animals, such as horses or elephants.

I assumed that our Senior Managers had finally realized that it was impossible to find enemy trucks or troops going to South Vietnam. I was convinced that aircraft could not stop the flow of supplies, because there was cover all the way from western China to South Vietnam. I agreed with the estimate of the article that it would be a long war and might last for over five more years if we played by the current ground rules. I could not believe that Congress would let the Target Master continue his expensive losing game plan.

23

August 1, 1966
PACK SIX MISSION WITH R.L.
ROLLING THUNDER MISSION #78

RL briefed our distant high PRF Pack Six mission that included the usual air refueling over the Gulf of Tonkin, both before and after striking the target. I was crewed with a Rookie, but I had already flown with him, and he had his act together. RL was carrying six 750-pound bombs, two flare pods and a center line fuel tank. I was surprised to see that my Phantom would be loaded with seven 1,000-pound bombs. I had never seen this ordnance before. They would be the heaviest load that I had ever hauled.

We inspected our frag, which instructed us to recce the northeast railroad from China to Hanoi. However, we had to observe the 25-mile buffer zone with China and the 30-mile ring around Hanoi. We were authorized to recce the remaining 26 miles of track for rolling stock. We decided to start our ingress to the target from the lighthouse north of Haiphong, with each of us flying our own route to reach the railroad. RL would illuminate the railroad when he arrived, and then I would join him to search for rolling stock. We would cut the railroad, if we never discovered any targets on the tracks, and then fly our own route back to coast. We were aware that we each had to avoid the numerous AAA and missile sites using our eyes, as we had no electronic warning equipment. We finished discussing our strategy, signed out, and went to our heavily loaded birds on the ramp in front of our squadron.

I inspected our aircraft flight records and confirmed that our Phantom was ready for our distant night contest in the Pack Six Park. We were required to carry our checklists when we inspected our aircraft and ordnance, but no one ever looked at them—we had memorized them long ago. It was another senseless regulation that we had to follow as we played by the ground rules. A teammate never knew when a Coach or Manager might be watching but they were seldom out at night.

I inspected our bird, while my GIB inspected the ordnance with checklists opened to the correct page. The bombs and flares were safeguarded with pins, until we reached the arming area just short of the departure end of the runway. My aircraft was equipped with two wing tanks, two sparrow missiles, and seven bombs, which was close to the maximum takeoff weight of 58,000 pounds. I was mindful to check the landing gear closely—a blown tire on takeoff could spell disaster.

I inspected my ejection seat and pulled all the numerous pins in the Rube Goldberg contrivance, except for two. Then we let RL know that we were ready to crank on our squadron's discrete radio frequency. RL switched our flight over to Ubon ground and requested clearance to start our engines after we checked-in. We completed our usual start procedures and checked the refueling receptacle, located behind the rear cockpit, for proper movement and illumination—we had to refuel twice on this mission

We received clearance to taxi and followed three hundred feet behind RL to the arming area, where the ground crew pulled all the ordnance pins. I wondered why we always carried missiles that were useless at night, as I tuned the two unnecessary Sparrows. Another ground crew gave us a final check for leaks and general aircraft appearance. Then RL used a visual signal to switch to tower frequency. RL requested takeoff instructions with a 30-second delay between aircraft—it was idiotic to make a wing takeoff with a maximum bomb load. The tower cleared our flight onto the runway and instructed us to hold for further release.

I ran each engine up to 100% and examined each gauge closely, as I wanted a healthy bird with no suspicious readings on this mission. We never checked the afterburners on the runway as the brakes could not hold the Phantom in place, but they had to light immediately or I would abort. My GIB finished reading the before takeoff checklist, and we were then ready to roll.

The tower cleared our flight for takeoff, RL acknowledged, released brakes, and selected both afterburners. I hacked our clock to get the 30-second timing. I pushed our throttles up to 100%, checked the engine readings again, released the brakes, and shoved the throttles outboard to the afterburner position. The nozzles operated correctly and the airspeed indicator was monitored for correct acceleration, as we counted the runway markers.

I was convinced that it was impossible to stop a fully loaded F-4 on the Ubon runway once we exceeded one hundred knots. I always instructed my GIB to eject us if we were not airborne by the time we reached the end of the runway. The F-4C had tremendous power, but I was still concerned as we accelerated down the runway attempting to reach takeoff speed of around 175 knots. We had computed the go-no-go speed and the refusal speed, which I consider of little use, because I knew when the "Hummer" was running right. I was sure as hell not going to try and stop a 28 ton bird at the 160 knots refusal speed on this short runway. I pumped the stick a few times for luck, made sure I had full back stick, and watched the runway markers rapidly disappear.

Our huge weighty bird finally lifted off the runway in good shape. I immediately raised the gear and flaps to reduce drag. We turned to the east and I pulled the throttles out of burner at 350 knots, as we slowly joined with lead. I decided to relax and let my GIB fly our bird while we maintained route formation on RL. We settled into a comfortable formation above Laos. We would also fly over South Vietnam on our way to the Gulf.

We locked on to the Danang TACAN station and used the navigational aid until we reached the Gulf. We then turned for our contact point with the KC-135 Team that was coming from the Philippines to refuel our birds. The tanker would remain on station, until we returned from our attack on the railroad, because we required additional fuel to return to Ubon.

We changed to our refueling frequency, checked in, and gave our tanker teammates a call. They responded with the information that they were already in the preplanned orbit and ready for action. Both of us painted the tanker on our radar and computed an intercept course to close with them. RL instructed the tanker when to turn, and he was on the money—we rolled out less than a mile in trail. We completed our join up on the tanker, with RL moving directly to the refueling position. I flew to their right wing and maintained a close formation position until it was my turn to refuel.

RL took the tanker's left wing position after he had refueled. Then the tanker driver cleared us to the refueling position. I opened our refueling receptacle and slowly maneuvered to a position below the tanker's tail, just behind the refueling boom. The tanker was arrayed with color-coded refueling lights on the bottom of the fuselage that directed refueling aircraft into the correct position. The boomer could also verbally position the refueling aircraft using color-coded markings on the boom. Our boomer teammate radioed that we had a good contact and there was good fuel flow to our bird. I had to fly smooth precise formation on the tanker, using the boomer's window to hold position. It was necessary to increase power to remain in position as the F-4 refueled. I finally had to select one afterburner and used the other throttle to maintain my refueling position during the final top-off of fuel. Refueling at night was like making love to a porcupine—all movements had to be closely controlled with smooth techniques. It was difficult to see anything, as the tanker only had a few position lights, and the rest of the world over the sea was pitch black. We were all aware that the slightest error in judgement could cause a mid-air collision.

The Tanker Team wished us good luck when we departed to the northwest. I wondered if they would be bored stiff flying in circles until we returned—with any luck at all. I extinguished our navigation lights, and initiated our decent checklist procedures. I took spacing behind RL during our easy let down toward Haiphong. We had agreed to fly to the railroad on our own, but we had to observe the buffer zones. We would meet over the railroad, after he dropped his flares to locate any targets on the tracks.

I used our radar altimeter, after leveling, to keep us approximately one hundred feet above the ocean. We watched for missiles during our flight to the lighthouse just north of Haiphong harbor. I wanted to stay as low as possible, since the malicious SAM Teams could easily paint our birds when flying over water. Wing Intelligence warned us of possible barrage balloons anchored with heavy cables in the area, but it was a murderous hazard that we could not see to avoid. There were many large ships in the area that would have been easy prey, but the Target Master would not allow us to strike them. It was not contented to fly past ships unloading missiles and ammunition that was used to kill us. We were involved in a war where the enemy was allowed to do what they wanted and we could not retaliate. I knew that we were putting our ass on the line in order to try and find a railroad at night in the middle of over a hundred skunk dens. I was confident that we would find the rail line deserted, if we survived any missiles, as the enemy knew we were coming. I took a few minutes to make some choice comments about our Commander in Chief to my GIB.

I had to watch for missiles outside the cockpit and monitor the radar altimeter to maintain 100 feet over the ocean. We both punched our clocks, when we passed north of the lighthouse that was nicely lighted for ship traffic. We had estimated it would take us exactly ten and one half minutes to reach the railroad at four hundred twenty knots ground speed. It was critical for me to keep my head out of the cockpit as much as possible. I had to keep from running into the ground and watch for missiles. I always found it hard to believe that our military leaders had never provided any electronic warning equipment for the F-4C. My teammate operated the throttles to maintain precise ground speed. He was also required to precisely track our position on his map. We had to know the terrain along the route, as I would pop-up above the highest point within a mile of us if we ran into weather.

We were extremely lucky to have a full moon, thank you God, which allowed me to fly within 100 feet of the ground. I could even fly low in the valleys, which greatly contributed to keeping us out of the launch parameters of the SAM sites. Of course, the full moon would also allow the enemy aircraft to locate us more easily once we departed the missile rings.

I was astonished to spy an extensive convoy of trucks coming south from the Chinese border on the coast road with their lights on. It was a long convoy and reminded me of the U.S. News & World narrative where McNamara displayed a 50-truck convoy photo to reporters. The truck drivers seemed to know that we would not attack them—they made no effort to extinguish their lights. I assumed that the enemy had scads of time to hide any rolling stock on a railroad that would be extremely troublesome to locate.

I had to admit that it was exhilarating to fly so close to the ground in the bright moonlight! I surmised that it was impossible for the enemy radar to paint our bird at this altitude. It gave me a feeling of gratifying invincibility to know that we could fly undetected anywhere in North Vietnam, under a full moon, and our rivals could not see us. It was exciting to watch the moonlit ground, as we flew very low through the valleys and sped toward the railroad. I turned south toward Hanoi, exactly as planned, at 10 ½ minutes to meet RL. We were looking for the railroad tracks in the moonlight, when a spectacular fireworks demonstration ignited in the sky towards Hanoi.

We observed an extraordinary sight miles to the south! The whole sky was suddenly awash with flaming red fireballs and brilliant white flashes! It was immediately obvious that RL had riled an enormous den of vicious 85/100mm skunks, along with the smaller disagreeable 37/57mm varmints. It appeared that RL had decided to release his flares at the southern end of our authorized railroad near Hanoi. He was very close to, or maybe even over, Kep Airfield where innumerable disgusting skunks operated. The Target Master had not authorized us to bomb Kep, but maybe RL merely wanted to let the MiG Teams know that we were available to compete with them on their field. Of course, RL had managed to piss off every deadly AAA site in the area and there were hundreds. I thought that the "Skunk Exterminator" was going be lucky to escape intact from this deadly battle. The sky continued to light up with bright white 85/100mm fireballs. We could also see flaming streams of 37/57mm spray flowing up from the ground in unending quantities.

I assumed that we would have to locate the railroad on our own—RL was engaged in trying to stay alive! I explained to my teammate that we were not going to get involved with any of his pissed off skunks. We continued to fly south toward Hanoi, while heavy 37/57mm fireballs arouse from the ground, but the stinkers were only guessing at our position. As I had expected, there was no sign of rolling stock on the railroad. I decided to drop our bombs, one at a time, on the railroad to maximize the damage to the rail bed, if we never located any rolling stock. I planned to release our bombs, at the lowest possible altitude, that would keep us out of the frag pattern, in order to avoid radar guided missiles, or AAA sites. We finally had to drop our bombs, and I felt each bomb release during our pass on the railroad. Now we would not require a hung ordnance inspection on the way home. I immediately broke for the coast after the last bomb was released and descended back down to 100 feet above ground level to avoid the enemy radar. I thanked God for the good weather and a bright moon, so we could operate on the deck to avoid deadly missiles. I was sure that every SAM site in North Vietnam had been anxious to throw a fiery missile at our bird in an attempt to knock us off their fields tonight.

We figured that RL had finally ended his battle with the loathsome skunks and dropped his bombs somewhere in the Six Pack Park. The disgusting stinkers were still trying to hit them with red fireballs, as they made their way to the coast. RL finally contacted me and indicated that they had experienced a hot time in the Park tonight, but none of the noxious skunks had managed to hit them with a bean ball. I was not worried about missiles or guns during our recovery to the coast—we were flying too low for them. I assumed that any MiG Team would be after RL, since he had competed near their field. I assumed that we were so close to the ground that the enemy could not see us streaking for the coast. I was convinced that we could attack any target in North Vietnam with minimum exposure when the moon was full.

I relaxed and came out of my high PRF mode, when we reached the safety of the coast. I started to climb and turned to the southeast for our rendezvous with the tanker. We discovered that RL had already refueled with the KC-135 and immediately departed. The tanker crew was surprised that both birds returned—they had witnessed the colossal fireworks exhibition. We repeated our usual refueling procedures and received enough fuel for a safe return to Home Plate. We thanked our tanker teammates for their excellent service and departed to the west. The flight to Home Plate seemed to take forever. I requested an immediate penetration when we checked in with approach control. We had been in the air for a long time, and my two-hour ass was sore.

I berated our Intelligence teammate, during our debriefing, about having to ignore worthwhile targets, but I knew they had no say in the matter. Maybe I should have bombed the long convoy of trucks coming from China, even if they were in the buffer zone. I might have justified the attack by saying that I thought I was over the railroad, but that would be stretching it a long way. I was upset that we could not attack ships going to Haiphong or truck convoys coming from China—we could not do what was right.

Mission Results: 0 trucks. (2+40 night)

RTL Summary: 11 trucks.

Mission Notes:

-It was possible to fly very close to the ground under a full moon.

-AAA and SAM sites were not able to see or paint us on radar when below 300 feet AGL.

-We had to ignore a large convoy of trucks, and bomb empty railroad tracks, due to half-witted ground rules.

-B-52's, not fighters, should be bombing the Northeast Railroad with thousands of bombs.

-I finally completed a mission to Pack Six after eight times on the schedule.

We debriefed with RL and learned their bird was near Kep Airfield when the flares illuminated. Intel estimated there was 208 AAA sites ringing the field. It appeared that they all fired into the air when the night-lights came on. RL had a formidable task trying to avoid a spectacular array of deadly red and while fireballs that materialized from the ground. I was surprised that his bird had escaped the blistering fireballs that filled the air. I assumed that RL released his bombs on another target that may or may not have been the railroad. I thanked RL for generating the most dazzling fireworks demonstration that I had ever seen! He had provided a visual memory that I would retain forever.

We adjourned to the Clubhouse to discuss what we thought of our distant contest in the hazardous "The Valley of Death". It was evident to me that we could use cluster bombs to destroy any SAM site or MiG field on a moonlit night, as flares would not be required. However, the Buffs should be bombing the railroad at night. We could protect them from SAM, Skunk, and MiG Teams with cluster bombs. It was senseless to send fighters, with no warning devices, to bomb a railroad with a few bombs. One B-52 was capable of dropping over a hundred bombs on the railroad—which might get the enemies attention!

I thanked my Rookie GIB for an outstanding performance and called it a night. I was extremely glad to return to my little wooden hut. The mission had taken almost three hours with a hell of a lot of stress.

I was thrilled to have tossed 31 coppers in my old tin can during July. I had also flown six additional flights returning from Korat. I had earned my $65 monthly combat pay! I felt that I could see a faint light at the end of the tunnel—I only had to participate in 22 more NV League contests. The unfortunate component was that I would be scheduled to fly at least seven more high PRF missions to "The Valley of Death".

I was angry when Wing Intelligence briefed that 43 aircraft had been lost over North Vietnam in July. My impression, from what I read at the library, was that no one in the States seemed to give a rat's ass about our losses. The only people that seemed to care were the families of the missing pilots, and many never knew if their loved ones were dead or prisoners of war. Our losses were probably just a footnote in the newspapers, or just a casual comment on the evening news. I wondered why our leaders never allowed any reporters on base to hear our comments about this war. I speculated that they were probably pleased that we were captive players, with limited contact to the outside world. I could not even make a telephone call to the States, if it was not for Bert, and I assumed there was a reason for this isolation.

I had now flown 78 mission over North Vietnam and 14 over Laos with very little accomplished. There had only been a few targets for me to attack. It had been extremely difficult to contribute anything meaningful to the war effort. It was obvious that B-52's could obliterate all the important targets in the North Vietnam in less than a month, and they would get more attention from the enemy—the few bombs we dropped were unproductive. I felt that we were just targets for the largest flak traps in the world and their AAA sites were becoming the best shooters in the world. I could see that the enemy was improving their defenses daily. It was obvious that we were going to lose an infinite number of fighter pilots. I hoped to depart this conflict before l was knocked out of the battle, but my exposure time was extremely dangerous in Pack Six.

AUGUST 2, 1966
ROLLING THUNDER MISSION #79

The 497th returned to the late schedule and placed me in the lineup for a 0400 contest. The weather was bad, but we finally blasted off an hour late and were in atrocious weather all the way to the coast. It was my turn to compete in a night contest with an aircraft commander assigned to my back seat. I discovered that it was not an enjoyable event. Major J.E. Barrow occupied my rear cockpit for a mission in Pack One near Dong Hoi, and he complained constantly about the way I maneuvered around our flares. The Major thought that it was not necessary for me to vary my heading and altitude so often, as the resident skunks were not firing at us. I tried to explain that the reason the skunks were not firing was that they could not get a reliable radar analysis of our flight path. I speculated that he never flew under the flares attacking trucks. I noticed that he kept his mouth shut and breathed heavily during several passes under the flares searching for skunk dens. I mused that he might lose some tail feathers one day, if he thought he could fly straight and level around heavily defended areas with radar-tracking AAA sites.

It was a bitch trying to land at Home Plate! It was raining too hard to even see the runway, and I had to use the strobe lights again. I really valued the genius who invented those crucial lights—they were a lifesaver for me. I managed to stop our "Hummer" on the short wet runway but questioned if the good Major appreciated my skill and cunning. I never wanted to fly with him again, as he out ranked me and I had to bite the bullet about his insinuating comments.

Mission Results: 0 trucks. (1+15 night)

RLT Summary: 11 trucks.

It appeared that I might not get to fly tomorrow night—the weather was minimal with a heavy storm moving into our area. I was disgusted to be out of our line up for even one night, and it might get worse as the weather was becoming horrendous.

AUGUST 3, 1966

The weather was so wretched that not one Night Owl flew tonight, as a severe storm affected our base with extensive turbulence. As usual, the rain came down in torrents. I was not pleased with my free time. All the poker players had left for the States and none of the Rookies was interested in playing cards. I was so bored that I visited our small Base Exchange, which proved to be a waste of time. The store seldom had anything to purchase, except for local gifts of jewelry and wooden teak elephants with sapphire eyes. I only needed a few minutes to scan the few shelves of merchandise, so I splashed over to the library in the drenching rain to see if any new magazines had arrived.

I read an article that discussed the Domino Theory—it never made sense to me. I recalled disagreeing with the pseudo intellectuals at Squadrons Officers School, who were adamant that this theory was correct. My viewpoint was not appreciated, and I received low marks for expressing my opinion about the conflict. I told my instructors that I was not convinced that I had to fight in Vietnam to save the world. I was going to war because my Commander in Chief had ordered me participate in the conflict—I had no other options. I reflected that I had decided to remain in the military to defend our country from the "Bad People" and not to shove our way of life down some poor farmer's throat that probably just wanted to grow rice.

I read an article in the July 29 TIME that reported U.S. pilots in Vietnam were laughing off the dangers they faced each day in enemy skies. I wondered who these fearless teammates were, and if they had flown through SAM sites at night with no warning gear to attack north of Hanoi. The magazine indicated that 303 U.S. airplanes had now been lost over Vietnam while bombing bridges, trucks, trains and barges.

I had flown 79 missions; with out seeing a threat to our way of life, over a country that appeared to have few targets of consequence. I had only seen one vessel along the coast and had observed no significant industry in Pack One or Five. However, there were hundreds of small wooden boats in the rivers that could be used to transport supplies. Nevertheless, it was true that every enraged Fan possessed an automatic weapon, and appeared to have unlimited amounts of ammo to fire at Night Owls. Still, I would have fired at foreign planes flying over Idaho if they were attacking my country!

AUGUST 4, 1966
ROLLING THUNDER MISSION #80

The rain was coming down in sheets, but I still hoped to compete in the Pack One Park near Dong Hoi. There was plenty of time for my usual breakfast. I had a late departure at 0430 for our contest along the coast. I waded to the squadron to brief my flight after a hot meal of eggs and bacon.

We blasted off on time, and I led my flight to the seacoast where it was quiet and peaceful. We hunted high and low, but there was no sign of activity on any of the dirt roads or ferry crossings. We shattered the stillness, when we scattered our ordnance on the designated truck park.

We returned to Home Plate and I landed first because I had no desire to divert to Korat if my wingman fouled the arresting gear. I noticed that our Coach had scheduled me for another distant Pack Six battle tomorrow night, but that was to be expected. I was not going to let competing in "The Valley of Death" trouble me—my fate was up to the Big Boss.

Mission Results: 0 trucks. (1+20 night)

RTL Summary: 11 trucks.

AUGUST 5, 1966

It was another detestable day at Home Plate. The deluge of water continued and our Wing canceled my ninth scheduled mission for Pack Six—maybe God was assisting me. I then briefed to lead a flight to the Pack One fields for a short contest. However, it poured down with such intensity that the runway was covered with water. The whole base was half under water! Our squadron truck even became waterlogged as we were driving to the OClub. We had to abandon our vehicle and underwent a soggy hike the rest of the way in standing water. I kept rationalizing that the furious downpour could not possibly increase in power, but it magnified during the night and pounded down on my tin roof.

I enjoyed breakfast and then waded to the library to see if any magazines had arrived through the violent storms. It was always interesting to read how our leaders were justifying a conflict that we could not win using the current ground rules. The Aug 1 U.S. News & World Report quoted a Top U.S. military man who stated, "if infiltration through Laos is to be stopped, it will have to be done on the ground". The article went on to explain that strategists figure this blockage will require from three to five U.S. divisions strung out across the waist of Laos from Thailand to Da Nang. I thought this concept was a good honest assessment, because the impenetrable jungle extended from the Chinese border all the way to South Vietnam. It was impossible to locate vehicles or troops from the air—they easily vanished into the dense foliage. The article also stated that there were 40,000 enemy troops laboring to keep open the major rail lines, leading from China to North Vietnam. That verified my hypothesis that the few bombs we dropped on the railroad were not effective. I thought that B-52's were needed to destroy the tracks.

I talked with Paul Blease who was not agitated about competing in the distant contests in the Pack Six Park, but was disturbed because his family had problems in the States. I learned that he had to move his family, as the owner of their rental house had returned and wanted to reoccupy his home when the lease expired. Paul needed to request leave for returning to the States to move his family, but the military had not informed him of his new assignment.

I realized that it was hopeless to consider relaxing around the pool—it rained constantly. There was nothing going on at the OClub, as all the poker players had returned to the States, and my good bridge partner, Crash Pollard, was long gone. It was very lonesome and depressing when I was not battling against the North Vietnam competitors. I would rather take the field to hunt elusive moles and battle filthy skunks, than sit around the Clubhouse doing nothing. Whenever I started feeling sorry for myself, I tried to remember my ancestors who had it a lot tougher during their lifetime.

The most daring of my ancestors was my Great Grandfather Daniel Ross, who was born in Helenbourgh, Scotland, on January 22, 1826. He left home with his brother when he was ten to become a cabin boy in the merchant marines of Great Britain. He visited all the significant ports of the world and completed several arduous excursions by walking across the Isthmus of Panama to catch a ship on the other side. Barbarous pirates captured him and his brother and held them as slaves for two laborious years, until the U.S.S. Frigate "Constitution" (Old Ironsides) came to their salvation and liberated them. They showed their gratefulness to the United States by enlisting in the U.S. Army and served in the war against Mexico. They later returned to their home in Scotland, after they were honorably discharged from duty with Army.

The venturous brothers returned to the sea when they heard of gold in California and again hiked across the Isthmus of Panama, with another party pursuing the gold fields. They were extremely fortunate in California and unearthed $20,000 in gold nuggets, after a year of forceful work. The brothers abandoned the gold fields and rode a stagecoach to the Mississippi River, where they boarded a riverboat going to the Gulf. They located a ship sailing to Scotland and purchased tickets for the long journey home. After returning home, they used a portion of their hard-earned money to bring the entire family to America on a sailing ship. Then the family traveled to the mid-west where they purchased a wagon, with an ox team, to pull them across the plains with the Cutler Company in 1851. I was in debt to a daring "Scott" for conveying my ancestors to Utah.

AUGUST 6, 1966
ROLLING THUNDER MISSION #81

It was still raining torrents when we blasted off at 0430 for the Pack One Park. Daylight was approaching by the time we left the battleground. The obnoxious skunks had thrown numerous sizzling fireballs our way, but fortunately for us, they were inaccurate. I speculated that the stinkers were just training rookies for new dens that were arising all along the coast. We never found any moles on the trails in the Park, so I had my flight scatter our bombs in the general area of a skunk den that had fired at us. I was tired of wasting my time attacking the Umpire's deserted truck parks.

Mission Results: 0 trucks (1+15 night)

RTL Summary: 11 trucks.

The 497th TFS promoted me to Assistant Flight Commander—I outranked many of the new contestants who were usually First Lieutenants. I was gratified that I was no longer required to sit in the tower for many hours during the night. Now I had to spend a longer period behind the small counter in Squadron Operations watching over the flight schedule, until all our birds were down. I seemed to lose all concept of time when we flew the late schedule. It was always dark and I never seemed to know what day it was. It was another cloudy miserable day, and I was in the lineup for my tenth scheduled mission to the distant Pack Six Park. The 497th had been tasked to fly additional night missions in Pack Six, and it was obvious that I would be scheduled to lead them. Nonetheless, our Coach could only schedule me for 19 more high PRF battles, before I completed the magic 100. I would be the next Night Owl to finish—with any luck at all.

AUGUST 7, 1966
ROLLING THUNDER MISSION #82

I was fortunate that the weather was wretched in Pack Six. Our Coach changed the game plan and ordered me to lead a flight to Pack One to initiate a Rookie rear seat teammate. We never found any evasive moles, but I encountered several disagreeable skunks that were tossing 37/57mm fireballs in the air. It was a good opportunity for my Rookie to witness the red fireballs. I explained that I had never seen the exact location of a skunk den during eighty-two missions in North Vietnam. It was always feasible to see the brilliant bloody tracers emanating from the black ground, but I could never spot where the gun emplacements were actually hidden. It appeared that the wicked stinkers disappeared into a tunnel or cave once they tossed a few blistering fireballs. I would have to ask RL if he had ever spotted one of the little frightful critters, as he was the squadron expert on every known skunk species.

Mission Results: 0 trucks. (1+15 night)

RTL Summary: 11 trucks.

I made an adjustment in my dining routine tonight and ordered a nice steak with freshly made cherry pie and vanilla ice cream for desert. Sometimes I felt guilty when I thought about what my ground teammates in South Vietnam were eating, but then I remembered that I had to battle in Pack Six at night. I had not received my new assignment—maybe some desk jockey thought that I might not survive this reprehensible series.

The resourceful Edsel Kid and his clever crew had come up with another illustrious scheme for our Wing to attempt. The Kid had a brainstorm and designated two fighter squadrons to share 18 aircraft for day and night operations, instead of each squadron having its own 18 aircraft. Our two squadrons had been selected as the guinea pigs to execute a strategy that was already coming apart at the seams. It appeared that trying to fly the same plane day and night was running our maintenance crews into the ground. I was concerned that the Kid's new scheme would victimize our squadron—we were already losing missions for lack of aircraft parts. Nevertheless, the Wing always had aircraft available for the high PRF Pack Six battles, and I was in the lineup for my eleventh scheduled try for the railroad.

AUG 8, 1966
ROLLING THUNDER MISSION #83

It was still raining hard—it looked as though there was always a dark cloud hanging over Home Plate. It reminded me of a character in the "Lil Abner" comics that had an everlasting cloud over him. It appeared that the Big Boss had not wanted me to compete in my eleventh scheduled high PRF contest in Pack Six, as the distant ass-busting mission was canceled. The weather was marginal at Home Plate, but we still blasted off for an engagement on the Pack One fields.

I led our flight of Rookies to the coast after they received my usual lecture about leaving the offensive skunks alone. I illuminated a speeding truck heading north on the trail near the Quang Khe ferry crossing, where there was no jungle for cover. We had six canisters of napalm, which was sufficient to nail the vehicle, but I still felt troubled about using it. The sight of my deadly napalm destroying a moving truck was a vivid memory that I would have to live with for the rest of my life.

The destructive skunks were trying their utmost to protect their fellow moles with numerous scorching fireballs that flashed by our cockpit. My Rookie GIB received a bang-up training contest tonight, as we were under fire for a good portion of the mission. I felt sure that we had earned our generous combat allowance tonight, but there was no place to spend all that money, except for high quality booze.

Mission Results: one truck. (1+15 night)

RTL Summary: 12 trucks.

My Coach placed me in the lineup to lead my twelfth scheduled Six Pack mission. At least we still had moonlight that would be of great assistance. However, I was convinced that our battles would be a lot more troublesome when we lost the moon in a few days. The Thuds lost five birds today! I could not conceive of any target in North Vietnam that was worth that many teammates.

I enlightened our Rookies to the fact that we had limited contact with the outside world because there were no telephones available for our teams. It was a sad state of affairs when you had to rely on a renegade telephone operator to have any contact with the outside world. I read that the airlines were hiring and that might be a good option if the Big Boss allowed me to change my Destiny.

AUGUST 9, 1966
ROLLING THUNDER MISSION #84

Maybe God was still looking out for me—the weather was too bad to compete on the Six Pack fields. I was delighted that we were still able to blast off for our substitute contest in Pack One, as it was still pouring down on Home Plate. I was confident that I could compete in Pack One contests under almost any circumstance, but it was probably foolish to be so anxious to get on the field. We received numerous blistering fireballs from offensive skunks under the clouds and near the flares, but I just ignored the nasty critters. They eventually left us alone. I told my Rookie GIB that the resident stinkers would have a very difficult time hitting us with their red piss balls as long as we kept moving our tail around. I never worried about the sinister critters, unless a pack of them sprayed us at the same time. I had my flight scatter our ordnance around the Quang Khe ferry and naval complex, as I suspected that there was a ferry hidden in the area.

I was delighted when we touched down safely at Ubon, as all I observed on final approach were the strobe lights. We were also extremely lucky—I stopped the "Hummer" without engaging the barrier. It was a good decision to land first. My wingman ended up in the arresting gear—maybe someday the Rookies might learn stopping on a short wet runway in a monsoon.

Mission Results: 0 trucks. (1+20 night)

RTL Summary: 12 trucks.

The 433rd lost a bird during the day yesterday and had another badly damaged. The unlucky teammates bailed out of their wounded bird, but the Jolly Green Team could not locate them. I theorized that it might be safer flying at night—the Fans and Skunk Teams could not get a good shot at us. I had not flown a day combat mission since the 24th of July, and that was just fine with me. There was no need to look at the schedule to know that I was in the lineup to lead a distant tail busting high PRF mission to the Six Pack Park tomorrow night.

AUGUST 10, 1966
ROLLING THUNDER MISSION #85

My luck was still holding—my thirteenth scheduled distant battle was cancelled due to weather. I was gratified to lead a flight of Rookies to the Pack One Park, for a quick contest against the usual skunks. We finally observed vehicle activity on the trails—the enemy must be receiving more trucks from China. I caught sight of my first large convoy of trucks in Pack One on the road going south out of Mu Gia Pass and several of them could not get off the road. The convoy was protected with SU-23mm multi-barreled guns that were mounted on two trucks but their solid stream of scorching fireballs missed us. We attacked quickly and aggressively under the night-lights, but had to avoid a solid stream of sizzling red balls. My wingman and I dropped our napalm directly on three trucks and verified that they were all burning as we departed. It was thrilling to have finally won a hard fought engagement after 85 battles over North Vietnam. We had finally pitched in and helped the troops in South Vietnam, as we knocked three trucks out of the game. However, it was a bad sign to see that the North Vietnam might be acquiring large numbers of trucks to deploy supplies or troops to South Vietnam.

Mission Results: 3 trucks. (1+15 night)

RTL Summary: 15 trucks.

I was surprised to see that my Coach had scheduled me to lead four Night Owls to a leaflet drop on Haiphong tomorrow night—it would be a new event for me. I had never led a flight of four Owls to attack the enemy at night. It seemed a shame that we were only carrying toilet paper to antagonistic Fans. I wondered who had dreamed up this peculiar battle, as it seemed like a complete waste of our time and effort.

I noticed in the Stars and Stripes that an airliner had crashed—I hoped that none of my friends was on the bird. There was no rain last night, for a change, and I thought that I might see the sun, if I could find the energy to stay awake that long. I returned to my little plywood hut and added another precious penny to my tin can.

24

LEAFLET DROP ON HAIPHONG
ROLLING THUNDER MISSION #86

I rounded up my teammates for our night leaflet drops on Haiphong. I concluded that it should be an easy mission for the Rookies. I was looking forward to our engagement. All my teammates were inexperienced, which meant that my game plan had to be very detailed to cover every aspect of our contest. We had to refuel in the Gulf of Tonkin before attacking Haiphong with our toilet paper, but it would not be necessary to refuel again after the drop. I was aware that I had to closely monitor every move of my three Rookie Night Owls, as they fluttered around the KC-135. Refueling at night could be difficult with just two players, and it would be an extra challenge to monitor three Rookies who had never refueled over the water. I would have to be extremely alert and make sure the young Owls stayed in proper position to avoid a midair collision.

I planned to depart the tanker and descend to approximately 300 feet for our approach to the harbor. I intended to keep my flight out of the effective range of the SAM sites during our approach, pop-up, and release, of the leaflet canisters. I tasked my teammates to get busy computing the correct altitude and airspeed to release the leaflet canisters, so they would open over the city. It would be interesting to know if the residents could read the leaflets. The Fans probably needed all the toilet paper that we could pitch in their direction—it was probably in short supply during a war.

I managed to get my flock of birds in the air on time and gathered them up in a loose flying formation for our flight to the tanker. Our comfortable formation would also allow the back seat pilots to enjoy some stick time that was hard to obtain in combat. The GIBs had to battle in tough contests from the rear seat, and follow the coaching of their aircraft commander. I recalled that I had recently participated in a few events from the rear cockpit, and had not enjoyed that position.

We continued our flight from Home Plate toward the Danang Tacan before turning north in the Gulf for the KC-135 refueling track. The Tanker Team was waiting for us—they were always on time, and ready to participate in our contests. I speculated as to why any KC-135 driver would remain in the Air Force past his military commitment, since he could fly the same type aircraft in the airlines for more money. I was elated with the enlisted sergeants that refueled our birds—they were skillful and professional. I had never seen a Boomer play a bad game or make a single error—tonight was no exception. Nonetheless, it made me nervous to watch my teammates playing touch and go with a Tanker Team at night, as an error might be disastrous. I had briefed each aircraft commander that he was not to move his tail, until I cleared his bird into the refueling position or for returning to the tanker's wing.

The Rookies performed successfully. Only one teammate had trouble pumping fuel, but he eventually settled down, before I had to divert his tail to Danang. I thanked the Tanker Team for a game well played and gathered my teammates to my wing for the descent toward Haiphong. I radioed for a descent check and requested each teammate to confirm that his external fuel tanks were feeding correctly. I could clearly see the lights of the city and harbor—they probably knew that the Target Master never allowed us to attack them. I mused that the port participants were probably busy unloading missiles and ammo for the SAM and Skunk Teams to fire at us. It was difficult to comprehend that we were really in a war. All the lights were on and ships were freely going in and out of the port.

I radioed my teammates to take spacing and arm up for our deadly toilet paper attack. North Vietnam looked very peaceful with lights illuminated all the way to Hanoi. We had planned to make our own pop-up and release the canisters toward the city. I maneuvered our bird to arrange for a release that would toss our leaflets directly towards the harbor. I hoped that one of my metal canisters might hit a Russian ship that was probably full of guns and missiles. The enemy SAM and AAA sites never entered the battle because we recovered outside of their effective firing range. I monitored my teammates carefully as they slowly returned to my wing during our return to Home Plate.

I was gratified that my Rookies had participated in a nice easy event and experienced their first refueling at night over the Gulf of Tonkin. However, it was obvious that we had participated in a bizarre and illusive battle against a target that was off-limits except for toilet paper.

The weather and runway at Home Plate were excellent, and none of my teammates had to engage the barrier. I conducted a quick debriefing and then headed to the Clubhouse for my usual breakfast.

Mission Results: 0 trucks. (2+10 night)

RTL Summary: 15 trucks.

Paul Blease and I had not received our new assignments, which ruffled our feathers. Paul had more time to wait—he was nine missions behind me. I was surprised to see that the squadron had scheduled me for a contest in the Pack One Park tomorrow night.

I rode to the library and found an article in the 8 August U.S. News and World Report titled "Air War in Vietnam: is it Worth the Price?" The article acknowledged that 50 planes had been lost over the North in the past seven weeks and that 310 had been shot down since February 1965. It also stated that these losses struck some military observers as high for the results obtained. The article also indicated that transportation routes had been disrupted, but I had not seen any evidence of that. Some Air Force Colonel tried to justify the use of fighters to hunt for trucks as acceptable, because of some basic concept relating to what the target was worth to the enemy. I calculated that it has been four months since the Buffs bombed Mu Gia Pass, and it looked as though I would never fly cover for them again.

AUGUST 12, 1966
ROLLING THUNDER MISSION #87

My Coach was easy going tonight. He let me participate in an expeditious contest in Pack One with a Rookie GIB. It was necessary for experienced owls to check-out the new rear-seat teammates and four more arrived today. I led the usual two-bird flight to Dong Hoi and made a command decision to attack what appeared to be a large storage area. I realized that this target may not have been in accordance with the Target Master's rules, but I decided to go for it. I attacked by employing a low angle release under the flares to make sure I only hit the storage area with all six cans of napalm. We were surprised to see that our attack produced a massive explosion that illuminated the dark night for miles. It must have been an ammo cache or fuel storage depot, because we observed a tremendous fireball with smoke boiling up to over two thousand feet. Every resident skunk den around Dong Hoi was pissed and sprayed a stream of sizzling red fireballs into the air. However, none came close, as they were just shooting around the flares in hopes of a lucky hit.

Our mission provided excellent combat time for my Rookie GIB. He observed many hot fireballs while we participated in an exciting event under the night-lights. I explained that the only effective way to strike a target was to attack under the flares. It was impossible to release ordnance above the flares and even come close to a target. Maybe some of the departed "Old Pros" had not believed in dropping under the flares, but I could not agree with that philosophy—it never got the job done. The sun was just coming up as we landed at Home Plate. It looked like it might be a nice day for a change.

Mission Results: 0 trucks, 1 storage bldg. (1+20 night)

RTL Summary: 15 trucks & 1 storage bldg.

I received some wretched news, after we signed the score sheet! We learned that RL and Bert Finzer had been sprayed with deadly fireballs in the Six Pack Park tonight. Still, it was no big surprise; RL had no qualms about going head to head with any stinker. They were very fortunate to have flown their wounded bird out over the Gulf of Tonkin before they were forced to eject. I was reasonably sure that our Navy rescue teammates already had them out of the water. Their efficient rescue helicopters were always on alert. Our Coach would have to change the lineup for my mission to the Pack One Park tomorrow night. I was scheduled with Bert and my teammate may not be available for another contest.

AUGUST 13, 1966
ROLLING THUNDER MISSION #88

I participated in a very late contest tonight with another Rookie GIB who was recently assigned to the 497th. It was an excellent training mission for him, as we surprised two nervous moles with our flares at the Quang Khe ferry crossing. They were waiting at the ferry crossing heading south, with no holes to hide in, when we deployed the night-lights. The noxious skunks tried their best to protect the moles, but we completed an accurate napalm attack under the flares without taking any hits. I sure hated to use napalm, but it was an ideal weapon for trucks as long as you were close to the vehicle when you released the canisters. We released the nasty firebombs very low and directly on top of the trucks with good results—they really blew up. I speculated that they might have been carrying ammo to South Vietnam. It felt righteous to assist our ground combatants, but I also hoped the drivers had left the trucks and were not slowly burning to death. It appeared that North Vietnam was sending more trucks south, as we were discovering more of them during our night contests. I mused why the enemy would drive trucks down the coast road—they had to cross numerous rivers and there was little foliage for cover. North Vietnam could send trucks from the Chinese border in Pack Five to South Vietnam and always have jungle for a disappearing act. However, it was quicker to come down the coast, and the enemy appeared to have more trucks available to transport supplies. North Vietnam might have changed their strategy. It appeared that they were willing to sacrifice trucks on the coast road to quickly supply their troops in South Vietnam.

It was a good initial contest for my Rookie. He had gained vital experience competing against the Mole and Skunk Teams. We were able to land at Home Plate although the downpour was almost impossible to see through. I had to use the life saving strobe lights to locate the runway.

Mission Results: 2 trucks. (1+20 night)

RTL Summary: 17 trucks, 1 storage bldg. (88 missions)

I was placed in the lineup to participate in my fourteenth scheduled contest in Pack Six. I was sad to learn that the full moon was gone. Now we had to fly higher, which would allow the radar directed AAA and SAM sites an opportunity to blast us out of the air! I mused that all my personal effects would easily fit into my footlocker if my luck ran out. I was really feeling down tonight as Bill, Mac, Crash, Braz, and all my old teammates from Spain had long departed. There was no one available for playing cards, and I seldom saw Ed Collins—he was in another squadron. RL was the last of my teammates from Spain remaining, and I was not sure if he was coming back to Ubon, after his ejection into the Gulf. I decided that I could either ride over to the Clubhouse, to down a few two-bit drinks, or stay in the hootch and look at my old year books from when life was good.

I decided to reexamine my 1959-college yearbook and reminisce the priceless times in college when I was working at four jobs. I turned to a picture of my small 22 member Theta Chi Fraternity, and I wondered what my good friends Larry Hattemer and Dean Gentry were doing. We had received a national charter for our fraternity during my junior year, and I was elected to be the treasurer. It was interesting that the Air Force ROTC pages never acknowledged my presence on campus—I was not a Distinguished Cadet. I recalled that only a few students from my class managed to finish flight school.

I read that I had lost the opening Pacific Coast Conference baseball game to the University of Washington—I had struck out 12 batters but we had eight errors. I recalled that I preferred to pitch against the best teams, and won my fair share, but sometimes the errors were tough to overcome. It was always a challenge to pitch against the Oregon and Washington teams. The big schools had numerous athletic grants—we only had several grants that were divided.

I recalled an ideal summer when I played semi-pro ball for the Pack River Lumber Company at Sand Point, Idaho. My baseball coach at Idaho, Clem Parberry, had obtained a working position for me with the lumber company to play for their ball team. Cotton Barlow coached the team that consisted of all-star players from Idaho and Spokane, Washington. I remembered the outstanding players from Gonzaga University in Spokane that included Nick August, Greg Briggs, Duke Gaffney, and Terry Cossette. My catcher, Larry Koentopp, was also from Gonzaga and was the best catcher that I had ever played with in baseball. I retained several old newspaper clippings that showed I had earned seven wins with one loss in league play. I was pleased to review an article in the Spokane Paper pointing out that I had pitched our team to victory for the Spokane Twilight League championship. It was one of the few times in my life that I had ever played on a winning team, and it was an honor to be named to the all-star team. I also had an exceptional following year pitching for the University of Idaho. I had wins against Oregon State and knocked Washington State away from the northern division baseball title by winning a 10-inning game.

My only claim to fame against a Major Leaguer was when I won a 4-1 game opposing Ray Washburn, when he was pitching for Whitworth College in Spokane, Washington. I always scanned the St. Louis Cardinals box scores in the Stars and Stripes to see if he was winning his games. I finished reviewing my precious publications, containing my happy memories, and recognized that I was now playing in a different league with tougher ground rules. I was well aware that an error in this series might send me to the showers and out of the game forever.

25

AUGUST 14, 1966
LEADING AN ATTACK ON THE NORTH EAST RAILROAD
ROLLING THUNDER MISSION #89

I had acquired essential knowledge regarding the Six Pack fields during a previous battle. Now I would use that experience to attack the railroad north of Hanoi. I wholly realized that it was critical to fly below 300 to 500 feet AGL, or run the risk of taking a missile up our Phantom's tail from one of the many deadly SAM sites. I also acknowledged that I had to release my night-lights, quickly attack, and speed away, or we would be blasted with a thousand blistering fireballs. We had to contend with the Target Master's miserable ground rules that restrained our approach to the railroad. Regardless, none of the Senior Managers or High Rollers was going to be near the Park tonight to watch our performance on the field. I decided to approach the railroad close to the Chinese border, as it was difficult for the SAM sites to detect us when we used the mountains for masking. Wing intelligence pointed out that an EB-66, stationed off the coast, would alert us if any MiGs tried to participate in our contest.

I had a semi experienced Rookie GIB in the rear cockpit, Lt. Sammie Hoff was going to participate with our team tonight. I had flown with Sammie before, and I felt comfortable competing with him, he was an excellent teammate. We would be flying over the aggressive playing fields of numerous SAM Teams during our 10-½ minute run that started from the lighthouse north of Haiphong. I would fly at 300 feet AGL, if I could see the ground, but I would climb to 500 feet AGL if I lost sight of the terrain or ran into weather. I was aware, from my earlier contest that the Skunk and SAM Teams could not attack us if I stayed below 300 feet; but I was not sure what might occur at 500 feet. Sammie had to interpret our map very closely. It was critical to fly approximately 300 to 500 feet above the closest high terrain. I would be soaring and descending and watching for missiles during our approach to the railroad. I could only afford to glance inside my cockpit, so Sammie had to operate the throttles and nail the 420 knots ground speed.

We would have to turn on time, as there was no moon tonight and it would be impossible to find our target without flares. I would use the F-4C's radar altimeter to keep us at the desired altitude above the ground, but the instrument could not measure what was ahead of us. Sammie would use our radar to paint any high object in front of us. The inertial navigation system could help us find the railroad, yet it was not always correct. We had to descend as low as possible if a missile was fired at our bird—I had no chance of out maneuvering it at night. We had to fly so low that it would strike the ground!

I knew that it was critical to immediately deploy my flares and attack the rail-road with a single pass. There was a zillion skunks dens in the area that would flood the air with dangerous fireballs when the flares ignited. I briefed my wing-man to make a solitary attack under the flares, to bomb whatever was there, and then haul ass for the coast. I thanked God that we were not ordered to fire rock-ets, as they would illuminate our bird and the evil skunks would probably knock us out of the contest. I recalled that I had almost been hit firing rockets over Dong Hoi when less than a dozen skunks were firing at me.

After our wingman's bombs detonated, we would complete our lone attack—unless we noticed any rolling stock to hit. I made it clear that each of us would only make one attack. There would be hundreds of hostile skunk dens waiting for our arrival at the railroad, and they would be extremely anxious to blast us out of the air.

I told Sammie that I would do everything possible to reach the water if we took a hit, but I would not bail out as long as our "Hummer" was flying. He was free to depart our bird whenever he felt like it, but I was dead if I had to eject, as I would not be taken alive.

The frag ordered our ordnance teammates to load my bird with two flare pods, centerline tank and six 750-pound bombs. My wingman carried seven thousand-pound bombs and two wing tanks, which was a maximum load for his Owl. I cautioned him that he would have to use the increased thrust of one after-burner during our refueling with the KC-135. We needed to receive all the fuel we could pump—the contest might last three hours if we all battled successfully and returned home.

We checked the weather, as it was a critical factor tonight since there was no moon for us. It would be an extremely dangerous situation if we flew into any weather, because it would be impossible to see a missile coming at us. It would also be hazardous to deploy our flares over the railroad if there was weather in the area. I assumed that the skunks might see us outlined against the clouds.

I told my teammate to break off the attack, if we hit weather, and then he would have to decide what to do with his bombs. They were briefed to remain seven miles in trail, after we departed the lighthouse. This position placed their bird one-minute behind us, which allowed time for them to reverse course if I encountered weather. I would turn toward Hanoi and try to drop my bombs somewhere on the tracks, if the target was obscured. I was not about to return my bombs to Home Plate after risking my life to reach the railroad. However, we had to remain outside of the 30-mile buffer zone around Hanoi and stay away from Kep Airfield. We all knew that the Target Master would have our ass if we hit one of his off—limit fields.

I warned my teammate that we were not allowed to bomb convoys coming out of China, but it would be tempting to accidentally release our bombs on the trucks. The enemy had considerable time to clear the railroad of any rolling stock, so I never expected to discover any by the time we arrived. It appeared to me that the High Rollers were just sending us on a very high-risk mission to harass North Vietnam. The Skunk Teams were allowed to use us for target practice and the SAM Teams would fire a missile up our ass if we flew too high.

My wingman had never flown with such a heavy load or refueled using afterburner—it might be a challenge for him. He was free to do what he wanted on takeoff with a max load, but I instructed Sammie to eject us if we were not airborne by the time we reached the end of the runway. There was ample time for my teammate to join up on the way to the coast, but he had to let me know if he was not closing, so I could reduce power. We finished our briefing, recorded our aircraft tail numbers, and signed out for a long and dangerous battle with very iffy weather. This may be the most strenuous event in which I had ever participated! I was aware that we could be scratched from the team roster if I made an error.

We blasted off on time and climbed out on an easterly heading that would take us to the Gulf to meet our Tanker Team. The KC-135 crew was waiting for us as usual. They had already established a refueling track to meet us head on. I instructed the tanker driver to initiate his turn when we closed within ten miles, which placed us less than a mile in trail for our joining. I instructed my teammate to join on the tanker's left wing. I would drink first as he might have trouble refueling, and he required more JP-4. I topped off our tanks, cleared my teammate to the refueling position, and settled on the right wing. He experienced a few problems when he had to use one afterburner to stay in position, due to the seven thousand-pound bomb load. Our tanker teammates were instructed to remain in orbit over the Gulf while awaiting our return. We would require additional fuel for returning to Home Plate. Our tanker teammates wished us good luck, when we departed towards Haiphong for the little lighthouse.

It was pitch black and we could not see any lights on the ocean or over land which was not a good sign for our traveling team. Sammie and I agreed that it looked like bad weather ahead, which was unacceptable for competing with SAM Teams at night. I was not thrilled that we had to battle missiles in the weather with no warning gear. We had computed that it was exactly ten and one half minutes from the lighthouse to the railroad at four hundred and twenty knots ground speed. I was apprehensive about flying through uncounted active SAM sites with no electronic warning equipment of any kind in our Phantoms. My teammate took his spacing during our approach to the coast. We would later see him over the railroad with any luck at all. The radar altimeter was initially set at one hundred feet during our run to the coast. Then we would climb to maintain three hundred feet AGL as long as I could see the ground.

We hacked our clock passing a lighthouse that was always lit up for the Russian ships supplying the enemy in Haiphong harbor. I gave Sammie the throttles to maintain 420 knots ground speed, while I kept my head out of the cockpit to watch for missiles and to avoid hitting the ground. I just glanced inside the cockpit to check my altimeters and warning lights—it was critical to maintain my night vision.

Sammie followed our track on the map and updated me on what altitude to fly to remain three hundred feet above the ground. He was also doing an excellent job monitoring the aircraft's radar for obstacles ahead and nailing the ground speed. We had to remain exactly on our preplanned ground track, as we were close to the mountains and could not afford an error by flying too far north. It was very difficult to see the ground and it was impossible to see any lights to the south towards Hanoi. I had a gut feeling that we were in trouble! The view toward Hanoi indicated that there was unfavorable weather ahead of us. I told Sammie that we might run into the soup soon and then we were going to be between that proverbial rock and a hard place.

My fears were justified when we entered the clouds just 30 seconds from the railroad! I immediately radioed our teammate to let him know that we were in the weather, but I would still turn south as briefed, in an effort to find an open area. I instructed him to cancel the contest, and avoid the weather if possible. I decided to remain at 300 feet, although I could not see the ground. At least we were turning away from the mountains towards the flatlands.

I was now firmly entrenched in a super high PRF mode! We were obviously in a critical situation! We could be tagged with a missile if I flew any higher, or we would run into the ground if I lost excessive altitude. I initiated a steep high-speed turn to the south in the weather at the 10-½ minute mark when we were theoretically directly over the railroad. I told Sammie that there was nothing more spine tingling in life than making a momentous turn in the weather at 300 feet over one of the world's most dangerous flak traps. We were aware that numerous missiles could be thrown at our bird from SAM sites that would be impossible to see in the weather. We also realized that there were hundreds of AAA sites trying to obtain a radar lock-on so they could spray us. I had a queasy feeling that my destiny might be terminated tonight, unless we received some consideration from God. We were in deep shit!

I rolled out of our crucial turn heading toward Hanoi and told Sammie that we would deliver our bombs, even if we never cleared the weather. I knew that we were in distress, but had to keep battling with all our skill. Maybe we would get a lucky break. I realized that I had to release our bombs and break to the east before we neared Kep. I made a command decision and told Sammie that it appeared to me that there were railroad tracks under us, although I could not see shit. I flew our streaking "Hummer" straight and level, while I rippled off our bombs, before breaking hard towards the coast to avoid the frag pattern. The exacting level turns in the soup at 300 feet were mind boggling! We finally got a marvelous break when we cleared the weather a few minutes later. Sammie was now painting the coast on our radar and we were going as fast as a "Hummer" could fly without using afterburners.

I finally called my teammate to see if he dropped their bombs and if they had remained clear of the weather. He radioed that he had remained clear of weather, and found a target of opportunity. He also indicated that he was well on his way back to the Tanker Team. We finally received a radio transmission from the EB-66, orbiting in the Gulf, advising us of possible MiG activity. I had to laugh at the advisory. It was impossible for me to imagine that other idiots were playing games in this crap. It was still high PRF time, as we had to fly directly over many deadly SAM sites. It would be painful to compete against a disagreeable missile at night. Sammie indicated that we were now tracking over the flatlands and we could go lower if necessary. I eased our altitude down to 200 feet AGL and maintained 500 knots while scanning the sky to see if there were any bright white dots tracking our bird. We were fortunate; the SAM sites never fired a missile at our bird.

Our teammate met us at the tanker for our post refueling and then we headed back to Home Plate. I thanked the Big Boss for riding shotgun—our survival was in doubt for a few minutes.

We signed our score sheet at the squadron to show that we had completed a night weather contest in the Pack Six Park. It was interesting to note that we were so busy trying to survive our jeopardous competition that I never even had time to be scared. We earned our $2.10 combat pay tonight! I explained to Wing Intel that I had dropped my bombs on a suspected railroad half way between Hanoi and the Chinese border. I was also pissed at whoever sent us out in this bloody weather.

I thanked Sammie for his skill and cunning—he had kept his cool and greatly assisted me during our charge into "The Valley of Death

Mission Results: 0 trucks. (2+15 night & +15 night weather)

RTL Summary: 17 trucks, 1 storage bldg.

Mission Notes: I detested competing, in the weather, against murderous Skunk and SAM Teams.

With any luck at all, I would only have to lead three more of these high PRF ball breakers during my final eleven missions. I was surprised to see that RL and Bert had safely returned to Home Plate and placed on the flying schedule for another mission. I had the impression that RL thought he was in the Battle of Britain, and it was crucial for him to get back in the air to defend his country. However, maybe he just wanted to return to the Pack Six Park and bomb the skunk dens that had shot him down.

AUGUST 15, 1966
ROLLING THUNDER MISSION #90

My Coach finally gave my tired ass a rest from the noxious Pack Six Park and let me participate in an easy contest with a Rookie GIB on the Pack One fields. I now considered myself an experienced Pro, with lots of exposure time, and capable of showing our Rookies the layout of every Park. I briefed my new GIB to stay on the gauges whenever we came off a target and be prepared to help in case I became disoriented. I instructed him to be ready to grab the stick and assume command if our bird appeared to be going out of control. It was essential for him to call the proper release altitude on the altimeter to insure that we recovered from our dive before entering the frag pattern. I stressed that many of the Rookie aircraft commanders were very inexperienced. He had to be prepared to pull his weight during every mission. It took a conscientious team, using great skill and cunning, to survive one hundred missions over North Vietnam.

I was concerned about the training received by the Rookies in the States—it appeared to me that they were not ready for competing in our aggressive contests under the night-lights. I believed that our Wing was going to encounter increased losses until the Rookie aircrews accumulated crucial night experience. They needed some "Old Pros" to get them oriented in the hostile contests, but there was just three of us remaining and I hoped to depart the field before long.

We never sighted any fugitive moles along the coast, so I turned our mission into a training exercise for my Rookie. I flew several controlled attacks under the flares to cut the road as my new teammate need to learn how to compete in a new night environment. We even managed to get a foul skunk den to lob a few scorching fireballs our way—they were way off target. My FNG also received good weather training when we executed a vertigo inducing weather penetration with a low visibility landing.

Mission Results: 0 trucks. (+40 night & +35 night weather)

RTL Summary: 17 trucks & 1 storage bldg.

I was pleased to see RL and Finzer at the Clubhouse—they looked excellent for having just ejected in the Gulf at night. I learned that they were fortunate to have been rescued by a Navy Chopper shortly after landing in the water. RL said he would tell me all about his ejection and recovery later, as they were already assigned to fly another mission tonight. We had to have dinner by candlelight when the power went off—I hoped it was not due to enemy activity.

I hit the pad earlier than usual, as some General was going to be on base for a few hours and we had to be available for him. The 497th wanted all the aircrews down to the building at 1300 in case the Senior Manager had generously allotted time to give us a pep talk. I was not going to hold my breath for him to meet us. The only other General that visited here just stayed a few hours. I wondered if anyone really wanted to know what was going on during our night contests.

The 497th placed me in the lineup for a short Pack One battle tomorrow night, but that event would be followed by another Six Pack venture. At least I had finally reached single digits for the remaining missions.

AUGUST 16, 1966
ROLLING THUNDER MISSION #91

The visiting General lived up to my expectations and never bothered to meet with our tired expectant aircrews. All the Night Owls had wandered around the squadron for over an hour trying to look busy and appear professional in case the General had time for us. The squadron finally allowed me to return to my hut to get some rest, but I was pissed-off by the General's snub. I could not get back to sleep, as I was upset and felt that I was coming down with a cold, which was not needed at this late stage.

I met with another Rookie GIB for our mission and welcomed the opportunity to instruct him on how to compete safely on the Pack One fields. I felt confident that I could provide many tips that just might save his tail during his 100-mission tour. We blasted off on time and reached the Dong Hoi fields, just before dawn, where the resident skunks were delighted to welcome us with a few misguided fireballs. My Rookie GIB was nervous when the unfriendly stinkers entered the contest and sent sizzling fireballs flashing around the sky. I showed him that it was no problem competing with indecent skunks as long as we constantly moved our tail during the contest. We were lucky and spotted trucks, when I deployed our flares. The vehicles were stranded on the road near a ferry crossing, with no foliage available. I made an immediate napalm attack and splashed the two trucks with six canisters of liquid fire. My teammate missed the burning hulks with his bombs, but ignited an apparent gas fire, when they exploded near the vehicles. We finally departed the field of combat with two trucks burning and a possible fuel depot on fire.

We learned after landing and debriefing that our Night Owls Teams had been unusually successful in Pack One. Our squadron had apparently destroyed numerous trucks along the coast. This was the first time that our unit had scored numerous hits during my tour. I wondered why trucks were suddenly traveling in open areas with no cover. I assumed the enemy required critical supplies for a big attack in the South.

Mission Results: 2 trucks. (1+05 night & +10 day)

RTL Summary: 19 trucks & 1 storage bldg.

Mission Notes: North Vietnam appeared to be sending more trucks south.

I met with RL at the Clubhouse and he related his story about the numerous AAA sites that had almost blasted him out of the competition. He explained that he was leading a mission to the Northeast Railroad with Lt. Bert Finzer and it was Bert's first contest on the distant Pack Six playing fields. They attacked the southern portion of the railroad and managed to flare near Kep Airfield field again. I speculated that RL just wanted a return engagement with the revolting Skunk Teams at Kep—he liked to play hardball with the contemptible critters.

However, this time they received the short end of the stick! They were hit hard during the contest and their poor bird lost some feathers from a profusion of scalding fireballs. Their Night Owl was severely wounded! The bird had become very sluggish, and it was hard to hold the nose up. He indicated that there was no apparent fire and the flight controls were still functioning, but very sloppy. They immediately turned for the coast, but noticed that their fuel was dropping so rapidly that they decided to jettison all the external stores. The wounded bird managed to fly to the ocean, and grasped for the awaiting tanker, but their fuel was almost depleted. They approached the KC-135 tanker with their refueling receptacle open, but their engines flamed out before they could latch onto the boom. The Phantom instantly turned into a flying brick and plunged straight down toward the ocean.

RL indicated that Bert immediately prepared to exit the aircraft and ejected from the rear cockpit with a loud explosion. RL pulled his face curtain, which initially blew his front canopy, but then came to a programmed mechanical stop. He had not expected an obstruction that required an increased pull on the face curtain before firing the rocket seat. It was an unfortunate situation for RL as the unplanned additional exertion moved his arms, head, and shoulders. This extra physical activity moved his vertebrae and caused a problem—his spinal column was not straight when he ejected. RL had a safe descent, but indicated that it was very difficult to find his raft after he splashed down in the water. He mentioned that it was extremely troublesome to function in the wet pitch-black darkness before the Navy rescued him. His back was sore from the ejection, but an injured spine was not going to stop him from battling in additional engagements.

AUGUST 17, 1966
ROLLING THUNDER MISSION #92

Maybe the Umpire had finally listened to my comments about trying to battle in high PRF events when the weather was unfavorable. I was satisfied when I heard that my fifteenth scheduled Pack Six battle was canceled due to bad weather. I was assigned to our secondary mission in Pack One. My Coach appointed three Rookies to my care as none of them had competed in an engagement over North Vietnam. I briefed my new teammates about what I had learned from months of competing in the North Vietnam. I described the numerous AAA sites located around the ferry crossings and towns. I explained how the stinkers liked to use trucks for decoys and then placed numerous skunk dens around the trap. I mentioned that the resident skunks usually tossed a few fireballs at us when we were around the flares, but hey seldom came close if we kept changing heading and altitude. I rarely noticed any accurate fireballs, when we flew through the flares, since the shooters had insufficient time to acquire an owl speeding through the light. I explained that I thought the most horrendous problem at night was from running into the ground due to vertigo.

We blasted off and flew directly to the Pack One border where we hunted for evasive trucks on the dirt trails leading to the coast, but failed to notice any movement. It was fortunate that I saved some flares for the ferry crossing at Quang Khe—we surprised the first ferry that I had ever seen. Of course, it could have been a flak trap, but I suckered in anyway and deployed my last flares to allow one attack for each bird. I followed my wingman's attack for a low angle pass and released each bomb separately, as I wanted to get a large bomb footprint. We might have destroyed the ferry as neither of us could see it in the water after the explosions had subsided.

As usual, it was pouring when we returned to Home Plate. I thanked the strobe light mastermind again for his greatly appreciated invention. I noticed that the runway construction to lengthen the runway was almost completed—maybe the Rookies could finally stay out of the barrier. I informed Wing Intel that I might have finally destroyed my first ferry after 92 missions.

Mission Results: one ferry. (1+15 night)

RTL Summary: 19 trucks, 1 ferry & 1 storage building.

Maybe I was "not meant" to fly my sixteenth scheduled high PRF mission tomorrow night—the battle was canceled and my feelings were not the least bit wounded. My Coach then assigned me to an event in the Pack One Park. I was gratified to know that I may only have to compete in two more battles in Pack Six. I was thrilled to learn that the runway extension was finally completed!

I rode to the Clubhouse where I found an old Stars and Stripes newspaper that had an article about an airline strike in the States, but I had little sympathy for them. The crowd movers obviously never realized they might be paid too much for sitting in a large conformable cockpit and reading gauges for a few hours each week. I mused that my monthly combat pay would not even cover an evening out for underpaid pilots that desperately needed more money. I enjoyed my usual hot breakfast and finished reading the paper with only a cup of coffee for company—all my old friends were long gone.

I visited the library to read several articles from the 12 August TIME and learned that the oil storage tanks near Hanoi were 90% destroyed. I believed the destruction of their storage complex was not important, as we were detecting more trucks than ever on the trails. It was interesting to read that American planes were pounding the Ho Chi Minh trail and had destroyed 41 smaller fuel depots, bridges, flak sites, along with 230 barges. The statistics appeared ridiculous—maybe they considered a secondary explosion from our cluster bombs as a fuel depot. I could not believe that 230 barges had been destroyed—I had never seen a barge and only one ferry during 92 missions. Maybe I had very poor eyesight because I had never visually acquired even one of the numerous AAA sites that were supposedly destroyed. I speculated that it would require a very slow moving aircraft, in an undefended area, to detect some of the targets they claimed. I knew that it was flat impossible for me to find a camouflaged target, while flying more than 400 knots, with deadly fireballs flashing by my cockpit.

I questioned the comment "Never before had tactical air power been used so intensively to help fight a ground war." The article stated that the American campaign from the skies was running some 670 sorties a day over both North and South Vietnam. However, it never mentioned that a large portion of this massive air campaign was against small elusive targets or deserted truck parks. The report went on to declare that over 300 aircraft had been shot down but failed to mention that most of the losses were from attacking low value targets. I personally thought that it was costing us one fighter for each truck destroyed. I was upset about the loss of 300 fighter teammates, as the Bomber Teams were capable of eliminating all the significant targets within a few weeks. I decided to quit bitching and relax in the sun if it ever came out—I wanted to shake my miserable cold.

AUGUST 18, 1966
ROLLING THUNDER MISSION #93

Our contest in the Pack One Park played smoothly and quietly, but we never found any trucks or ferries along the coast. I used my last flares to scatter our bombs on some suspected storage areas on the beach—I was tired of dropping on the Umpire's deserted truck parks. I might get a bad call from the Umpire, for not following orders, but doubted if he would throw me out of the game. I questioned why our astute planners never discovered any worthy targets for our ordnance at the end of our missions but maybe it was because there were few, if any, important targets in Pack One or Five. I had been telling Wing Intelligence for months that I had seen few targets of consequence. I had only destroyed 19 trucks in 93 missions, and maybe half were decoys.

Mission Results: 0 trucks. (1+15 night)

RTL Summary: 19 trucks, 1 ferry & 1 storage building.

Mission Notes:

-It was extremely difficult to discover trucks at night with high-speed fighters.

-Dropping ordnance on suspected truck parks was a waste of time and money.

I was assigned to man the duty counter at the Squadron until the last bird landed. I was pleased that our new teammates were learning how to compete quickly. I hoped they would safely survive their tour. I talked with our Wing

Intel teammates and learned that no one had discovered any trucks in Pack One tonight.

My Coach ordered me to lead my seventeenth scheduled high PRF Six Pack mission north of Hanoi tomorrow, which was to be expected. I had completed two notably strenuous battles on the Northeast Railroad and understood the ground rules for the treacherous Park. The new Rookies had not accumulated sufficient knowledge to lead a flight to Pack Six, so I had to dig in and take the heat, until they were ready to compete. Nonetheless, I was pleased that I only had seven more contests before I would leave the field for the American League.

I was later told that the distant contest might be canceled—the weather was forecast to become nasty. I was gratified to know that the Umpire could only place me in the lineup for seven more Pack Six contests using the worst case scenario. However, I was really going to be pissed if I had to charge "The Valley of Death" during my final engagement.

Thanks to the Edsel Kid, our flying schedule had rapidly deteriorated—now we arrived for work at 1600 and finished at 0600. The astute Kid ordered the use of only 18 aircraft for two complete squadrons, and it was causing all sorts of problems for our Equipment Managers. I speculated on where this brilliant idea had originated and figured it must have come from some desk bound bean counters.

I was fearful for the Rookies, as they had to compete for a long time against evil skunks that were breeding like crazy. Our Coach had placed additional Rookies in the lineup, but the squadron was still under strength, which indicated that I might be competing every night. I learned that my old roommate, Tom Boyd, and a good friend, Bill Van Patten, would be arriving soon. I hoped they would be assigned to our squadron, so I could fly with them. I wanted to give them a few ideas on how to survive this war.

AUGUST 19, 1966
ROLLING THUNDER MISSION #94

It appeared that the Big Boss had not wanted me to compete in my seventeenth scheduled Six Pack battle tonight as the weather was too wretched to take the field. Nonetheless, I acted as though it was a shame that we were not flying north of Hanoi to hunt for rolling stock on a railroad track. I briefed my teammates for our substitute contest on Pack One field using cluster bombs and rockets. The CBU's could be directed against shy moles hiding in the tall grass, although we could not see them. I told my wingman that I was going to release my CBUs on a straight stretch of the trail, extending south from Mu Gia Pass, if we never found any trucks.

I used my final flares to light up a straight portion of the trail after we ceased hunting for trucks in the Pass. I maneuvered our bird to position for an attack at low level in order to release our bomblets over the road. We flew down the road at an altitude of between three and five hundred feet with an airspeed of 450 knots to drop the bomblets. I wanted to place all the ordnance directly on the small trail so it would reach any vehicles or equipment hidden near the road.

We completed our run over the trail and not one harmful stinker bothered to hurl a fireball while we were under the night-lights. My wingman reported seeing eleven secondary explosions, which indicated to me that we had hit some trucks or gas storage tanks. I instructed my wingman to fire his rockets on the burning fires and then we would head to Home Plate. I told my Rookie GIB that we had helped our teammates in South Vietnam tonight, but I knew it was just a drop in the bucket.

Mission Results: 11 small secondary explosions. (1+15 night)

RTL Summary: 19 trucks, 1 ferry & 1 storage building.

Mission Notes:

-Cluster bombs were a good weapon to use against trucks hiding in the jungle.

The Wing Personnel participants told me that I would get credit for a Permanent Change of Assignment (PCS), although I might not have six months duty time on base before I departed. That meant the Air Force could not say that I had only finished a temporary duty tour and could not be sent back immediately. I had not received my new base assignment, but Paul Blease procured orders to the Air Defense Command, which indicated that maybe I too could get out of the Tactical Air Command. I hoped the Air Force would direct me to fly F-106's at McChord AFB, Washington—it was close to God's Country. I only needed six more missions, and I was gratified to see that I was on the schedule for a contest in the Pack One Park tomorrow night. My old roommate, Tomas, should be arriving in a few days, and it would be interesting to learn what had been taking place in the States.

AUG 20, 1966
ROLLING THUNDER MISSION #95

I was grateful for the opportunity to participate in a fast engagement on the Pack One fields tonight. We were very fortunate to have lifted off the saturated runway, as the weather was too miserable for most night owls. We hunted for slippery moles along the small dirt trail that extended from Mug Gia Pass to Dong

Hoi, but never noticed any movement. The peacefulness of the well-groomed trail never ceased to amaze me, but I speculated that there were many timid moles hiding out of sight in the tall grass. The sinister skunks completely ignored us tonight, but I still kept moving our tail around in case they were lurking in the dark. I used our final flares to light up the coast so we could bomb several suspected storage areas on the beach. I questioned why the Umpire had not called me on the carpet for attacking them—they were not on the Target Master's list of approved targets.

Mission Results: 0 trucks. (1+20 night)

RTL Summary: 19 trucks, 1 ferry & 1 storage building.

Mission Notes: I thought North Vietnam was ferrying supplies down the coast in small dark boats and using beaches for storage sites.

My assignment finally arrived, and I was not pleased! The Air Force ordered me back to George Air Force Base to become an instructor pilot. I had not wanted to return to the high desert, and definitely had no desire to remain in the Tactical Air Command. However, it was logical for the Air Force to use my combat experience to train new aircrews for the missions over here, but I wanted to go back to flying a delta wing aircraft. Some publications indicated that American Airlines was hiring pilots, but I questioned if the Big Boss would sanction this change of fate. I felt that my destiny was to fly fighters from the day I was born. I was also aware that flying airliners would be boring as hell. Maybe I was meant to return to George AFB to instruct new aircrews on how to survive in the war.

I was pleased that my Coach had scheduled me for a distant contest in the Pack Five Park tomorrow night, which might be my last long tail busting mission. It was a more suitable field to compete on—we had a slight possibility of being rescued. I performed my nightly duty at the squadron and had to divert all our airborne teammates to Korat when it started to come down in torrents. I personally never wanted to set foot on Korat again, unless it was on the way to the States. I would have to arise at 1500 hours tomorrow for our contest, as the "Kid" had us on a crazy schedule that was driving every teammate up the wall. I could expect to be in the lineup anytime from 0600 to 1500, and it was all due to a stupid test program. I realized that I had to grit my teeth and continue to play hard!

26

AUGUST 21, 1966
CURTAIN OF FIRE IN THE RED RIVER VALLEY
ROLLING THUNDER MISSION #96

Only three lucky Night Owls had a chance to spread their wings to fly away from their roost, and I was one of them. The weather was unfavorable everywhere except up in the Pack Five Park. We were fragged to start our mole hunt about 30 miles south of the Chinese border and follow a road southeast along a ridge of mountains that extended towards Hanoi. Our Thud teammates used the terrain for protection when they made their runs to Hanoi—the mountains were high with some rising to over five thousand feet.

I was airborne with our two Owls just after sunset, and we flew directly to the KC-135 that was waiting for us near Udorn. As usual, the tanker teammates had their act together—they were on time, on station and loaded with JP-4 for our birds. It had to be monotonous for them to bore holes in the sky waiting for our fighters to join up, but at least they were in a safe area. I enjoyed refueling with them—it was a challenge to link up in a professional manner and refuel without a bobble. The boom operators always seemed to enjoy their profession. They gave us a drink with excellent manners and then sent us on our way with a friendly word—wishing us luck. They were probably thankful that they never had to worry about harmful AAA or SAM sites while carrying all that fuel.

I allowed my Rookie GIB to fly our Phantom before we reached the North Vietnam border, but then it was game time—we had to get ready to compete on a hostile field. The Thuds flew in this region each day and there had to be hundreds of hurtful skunks throwing fireballs at them. I kept our birds tail moving smartly around all night—I was not in favor of being shot down on my 96th mission in Pack Five. It was a long rescue for the Jolly Green Team, and I had no desire to spend a night in a jungle with gigantic green snakes.

We observed the bright lights of Dien Bien Phu for a few minutes before the residents pulled a switch that extinguished every light, at the same instant, which was very impressive. We hunted for evasive moles on the road from south of the Chinese border to Dien Bien Phu with our night-lights, but there was no activity on the trail. I had just deployed our last flares in the Red River Valley when we saw the most astounding sight that I had ever seen! We witnessed a breath-taking occurrence that unveiled an imposing long wall of spectacular red sizzling fireballs. I was overwhelmed by a solid red curtain of bloody fire that erupted from a zillion 37/57mm skunk dens located in the jungle just to the northwest of our bird. The dazzling red fireballs were dramatic! They all peaked at the same time and then arched downward to earth in a brilliant display of color. The wall appeared to extend for over a mile. I was in awe that every gun had been timed to fire at the same second. I questioned how the enemy had managed to perfectly situate hundreds of AAA sites that all fired at the same instant to form an impenetrable wall of deadly fireballs. I would never forget the sight of that solid wall of murderous fireballs that no bird could penetrate without losing its wings.

I immediately radioed my teammates to inquire as to their well being, and if they had ever seen such a sight. My wingman was nearest to the bloody skunk spray, and thought it had come from the area of Thud Ridge. The enemy had evidently closely positioned 37/57mm AAA sites along the mountain ridge, with a system to allow each shooter to fire his weapon at the same instant. I had flown over Thud Ridge during the day and it looked extremely rocky with dense jungle that appeared inaccessible. I thought that it was impossible for even an Idaho mountain goat to climb along the ridges or to move around in the impenetrable jungle. The enemy must have cut trails and hauled the guns up piece by piece or used helicopters to place the weapons.

I had no idea why the wicked skunks had triggered a curtain of bloody fireballs because both of our birds had been flying parallel to the ridge. Maybe God wanted to give me another omen to remember this lethal contest. I questioned how the Thuds were ever going to be able to fly over that ridge and live to tell about. The Target Master needed to order B-52's to bomb that ridge, or more than a few Thuds would be blasted out of the air. However, the Buff Teams had not shown their tails since they bombed Mu Gia Pass four months ago.

We experienced inclement weather all the way to Home Plate. I had another miserable vertigo adventure in the holding pattern and during the penetration. It was pouring down so hard during our approach that the high-pressure air on the windscreen, for blowing the rain away, was useless. I made another high PRF landing, using the marvelous strobe lights to find the runway. It was probably stupid to take chances at this late stage, but I thought that I could land on any runway and in any kind of weather.

Mission Results: 0 trucks. (1+35 night & 1+00 night weather)

RTL Summary: 19 trucks, 1 ferry & 1 storage building.

Mission Notes:

-The enemy had installed a long line of 37/57mm AAA sites on Thud Ridge.

-The Target Master should employ B-52s to eliminate the AAA sites.

-I never spotted any targets of significance in Route Package Five.

I informed our Intelligence team about what the enemy had cooked up for fighters in Pack Five. I felt confidant that the sinister skunks would just wait for a Thud to come flying across that ridge during the day and then they would blast him out of the sky. I requested the Intel participants to call the F-105 bases and let them know about this deadly flak trap in case they were not aware of it. It would be difficult to see the curtain of fire in the daytime.

Ed Collins recovered from a tough mission in Pack Six and was lucky to be alive—he had been sprayed by some loathsome sharp shooting skunks. His tough bird had taken a load of buckshot, but still kept humming, and flew home with numerous holes in its skin. Ed had big balls to complete a hundred missions, and then volunteer to remain for more of these high PRF battles. Ed would need all the luck he could find to finish his additional tour—he was receiving additional deadly exposure time.

AUGUST 22, 1966
ROLLING THUNDER MISSION #97

I was beholden to the 497th for permitting me to fly my 97th mission to Route Package One with a Rookie GIB. I may have been getting a little consideration from the Big Boss—we were one of the few owls that flew in the borderline weather. I saved my last flares to illuminate the beach south of Dong Hoi, as I was convinced the enemy was bringing supplies down the coast in small wooden boats. I had never seen any fishing boats along the coast, but it was extremely difficult to see them at night. It appeared to me that the suspicious looking round spots on the beach might contain supplies covered with camouflage. I directed my flight to drop our bombs on the strange round areas, but we could not assess our damage as the last of our flares had extinguished.

The disgusting stinkers were very active tonight and tried to blast us when we were near Dong Hoi. The enemy must have moved additional AAA sites into Pack One, during the last few months, as the flak was increasing—I felt fortunate that I only needed three more missions. I believed that someday the skunks were going to learn how to direct their spray effectively and that would be bad for the Rookies. We had to make a weather penetration to a wet runway, but we both stopped with no problems.

Mission Results: 0 trucks. (1+15 night & +15 night weather)

RTL Summary: 19 trucks, 1 ferry & 1 storage building.

Mission Notes:

-The Edsel Kid's test was driving me crazy with its unrealistic schedule.

-There were suspicious round areas on the beach near Dong Hoi.

I had not been to sleep for over 30 hours! My lack of rest was a direct result of the unmerciful Kid's astonishing new half-witted program. I was completely exhausted, but I still had trouble sleeping and even felt numb at times. Nevertheless, I realized that I had to dig in and stay on my toes—I had three more battles in this miserable conflict.

J.B. Stone told me that Lt. Tom Boyd had finally arrived on base, but assigned to the day squadron. I was sad that he would not be flying in my squadron. I recalled that it had been my good fortune to meet a number of fighter pilots at George AFB who were single and desired to drive to Los Angles for entertainment whenever possible. Tom was in another squadron, but we had the same interests and decided to rent a new house on the Hesperia Golf Course—about 17 miles from the base. We purchased our own bedroom furniture and each contributed household furnishing to the common areas. We had hoped to be stationed at George AFB for a number of years protecting our country from Russian and China. We never imagined that we would be ordered to attack North Vietnam.

Two other rear seat pilots in the 497th, Ed Collins, and Allen (Crash) Pollard, also enjoyed driving to LA each weekend to party. We loved to frequent the swinging nightspots around Manhattan Beach and enjoyed basking on the delightful beaches. We stayed at the Airport Marina Hotel, where Continental Airlines had their Stewardess training school, which was paradise for a single fighter pilot. I looked forward to locating Tom and discovering what had been going on in the real world. I also needed to warn him about the wicked skunks and moronic ground rules in this league. However, he had to compete from the rear seat and would be at the mercy of his aircraft commander.

AUGUST 23, 1966
ROLLING THUNDER MISSION #98

The weather was miserable tonight, but my Coach allowed me to participate in another Pack One contest with a Rookie GIB. That was exactly where I preferred to complete my remaining engagements. I led my flight directly to the coast, as I wanted the opportunity to fly out over the ocean if we had to eject. I placed our night-lights below the clouds, but there was nary a speeding dark mole in sight on the dirt trails. I then led my teammate to the beach south of Dong Hoi where we dropped our bombs on the suspected storage sites along the shore. I flew multiple bombing attacks under the flares so my Rookie could practice calling the pickle altitude. It was critical for him to experience the shock of coming out of brilliant light into total darkness and the resulting vertigo. We only encountered a few foul skunks that wanted to spray in our direction, but it was enough for my teammate to see some scorching fireballs. Our flight was fortunate in that we returned for a nice normal landing in clear weather.

Mission Results: 0 trucks. (1+15 night)

RTL Summary: 19 trucks, 1 ferry & 1 storage building.

I finally had a chance to talk to my old California roommate, Tomas, and learned that his squadron was sending him to Pack Six tomorrow. This would be his first mission since arriving at Ubon. I was sure the battle around Hanoi would receive his full attention! He indicated that he had been having a great time in LA, but had not yet found the consummate woman to marry. I told Tomas that it had been difficult to say goodbye to my shiny bronze Jag that we had both enjoyed. It had been exhilarating to drive the XKE at speeds up to 125mph on the way to Las Vegas to enjoy the shows. We also managed to lose a few bucks at the craps table, but my betting was constrained—I had a 25-dollar limit on losses. We relived the delightful times at our rental house with numerous parties. We may never again experience the thrilling weekends on Manhattan Beach, or dancing at the many nightclubs in Los Angles, but we had a glorious time while it lasted.

I managed to get a few rays as the sun had come out of hiding, but my joy was short lived—it soon turned to rain. Just two more night battles and it could rain all the time. I would even paddle my tired tail out of here if necessary. My Coach placed me on the schedule for #99. I was gratified that it was not a distant high PRF battle in the Pack Six Park. It was getting harder for me to sleep at night—my back was hurting. I finally decided to roll out of bed after seven hours of sleep. It was time to ride to the Clubhouse for my usual breakfast.

AUGUST 24, 1966
ROLLING THUNDER MISSION #99

I led my flight of Rookie Night Owls to the coast and searched for slippery moles on the trail between Quang Khe and Dong Hoi. I shunned the deadly 85mm skunk den located at Ron Ferry! The deadly skunk was a sneaky straight shooter, and I always made it a point to warn my teammates about the murderous critter. I had learned that the sinister skunk was devious—he never fired unless you made a stupid mistake and flew straight and level. I warned my Rookies that radar guided AAA sites were increasing in Pack One. The big 85mm guns could nail your ass if you were careless. I had no regrets about departing the field for the American League because our field conditions were definitely becoming worse. However, I was concerned for the Rookies. They only had a few experienced Night Owls remaining to teach them how to survive a deadly contest.

The enemy appeared to be sending more supplies south with inexperienced drivers. We discovered two trucks north of Dong Hoi in the open and nailed them with Napalm. It was a good mission for our Rookies. They experienced fighting under flares and knocking two trucks out of the contest. My teammates appeared to be competing in a satisfactory manner under the night-lights. They had not appeared to be bothered by the persistent fireballs.

It was obvious that North Vietnam was increasing their war effort during the last few weeks. I only destroyed 7 trucks during my first 67 missions, but had annihilated 14 trucks during my last 32 missions. The use of napalm and CBUs had certainly assisted. It appeared to me that the enemy had more trucks and were sending additional supplies south.

Mission Results: 2 trucks. (1+15 night)

RTL Summary: 21 trucks, 1 ferry & 1 storage building.

Mission Notes:

-North Vietnam appeared to be driving additional trucks traveling south.

-I had destroyed 14 trucks in my last 32 mission for a 44 percent average.

-Napalm contributed to achieving higher truck kills, but was a nasty war weapon.

I had an argument with Wing Personal. They had not given my port call the attention that I thought it deserved. I wanted to leave ASAP, after I finished my last mission, but they were not concerned about what I wanted. I told them that they would have a furious fighter pilot in their face if I was not on the Freedom Bird by September first.

I decided to unwind after my controversy and went to town with Bill Van Patten, who had arrived with Tom. It was his first time to see the thriving community and I figured that I would see it for the last time. Some of my teammates enjoyed going to the village, but I never felt comfortable there. This would be my second trip to town since I had been here. I hoped no one wanted to eliminate an American fighter pilot tonight.

Bill and I recalled the good times we experienced in Hawaii and Los Angles—life had been sweet in those days. I sure hoped he would survive his 100-mission tour. He had a long way to go and the harmful skunks were breeding like mad.

My little tin can was almost full! I only needed one more lucky coin to conclude my tour. I recalled that I had completed 64 missions extending from June 19 to August 24. I had only flown one day mission during that period. I wondered if 63 night missions in 67 days was a record, but was sure that no one really cared. I learned that my squadron was allowing me to fly my final mission in Pack One, and I greatly appreciated the consideration. I planned to compete in a guarded manner and avoid all the dangerous skunk dens in Pack One.

I researched the military manuals for possible assignments and discovered that the Air Force and Navy had an exchange program with several slots available on each coast for F-4 pilots. I had always wanted to fly off an aircraft carrier—the catapult shot looked like a real kick in the tail.

AUGUST 25, 1966

I wanted to fly tonight but the 497th scheduled me to complete my final mission in Pack One the following night. I had time to visit the library to see what the experts were writing about the conflict and how "we" were winning the war. I always questioned who the "we" people were, as they wrote that "we" were not leaving until the job was finished and "we" would stay for as long as it took. Where did this "we" crap come from—I had never seen any of those "we" people on the schedule to fly north of Hanoi at night. I also doubted if any of them were flying with the Thuds into the biggest flak trap the world had known. It appeared to me that the "we" people were trying to give the impression that they were somehow involved in our life and death struggle.

A noteworthy article in the 19 August TIME referenced a report from Saigon citing Army and Marine Corps studies in the Pentagon. The study concluded that North Vietnam could endure its present rate of losses in the South for another eight years even if our troop level was raised from 292,000 to 750,000. However our National Command Authorities denied any knowledge of these studies and McNamara had not agreed with the conclusions

I considered writing my Congressmen from Idaho about the futility of this war and even offer to provide them with a first hand analysis of our battles. However, I decided that all my efforts would probably be in naught, as our astute politicians would not believe me and probably think that I was not a loyal American supporting his country. I wondered if Congress really believed that a tiny country threatened our Navy. I recalled that I had flown up and down the coast numerous times and had never spied a single enemy combat vessel during day or night missions. I personally believed that North Vietnam never had any combatants that could have threaten our Navy, except for several small PT boats.

27

I was gratified when the 497th assigned me to fly my final mission in Pack One for number 100! I thanked our squadron commander for this consideration. I led my flight to the coast and shied away from all known AAA sites while we hunted for trucks along the coast. I used my last flares to scatter our bombs on suspected storage areas on the beach after we were unsuccessful in discovering any vehicles or ferries. We made several routine passes under the night-lights that allowed the Rookies to practice some easy night attacks before they were sent to compete in the dangerous Six Pack Park.

I enlightened my teammate to the reality that I had only seen one person up close during 100 missions over North Vietnam and 14 over Laos. I related my story about the little fisherman pulling in his net while standing in a small black wooden boat. It seemed strange that he was the only person I had ever seen up close and personal during this war.

None of my teammates seemed to care that I had finally completed my tour when I made my usual sign-in. Rl and Paul were not in the squadron, and I had never taken time to become well acquainted with any of the Rookies. I signed our score book for the last time and thanked my Coach for allowing me to end my competition in Pack One. Then I returned my flight gear to the personal equipment team and thanked them for a job well done. I probably should have been exhilarated that I had survived the conflict, but it seemed like I had accomplished very little. I just rode my bike to the Clubhouse to buy one hundred drinks for anyone in the building.

Mission Results: 0 trucks. (1+20 night)

RTL Summary: 21 trucks, 1 ferry & 1 storage bldg.

Mission Notes:

-My final score against the Mole Team in the Rolling Thunder League was 21 trucks out of 100 events for a 21% average.

The Officers Club was quiet as most of the night contestants were still on the field. I decided to enjoy a few drinks—it might be my last time in our old wooden Clubhouse. I probably should have been jumping with joy after completing my series, but there was no joy in Mudville. The expensive booze seemed to have very little taste to me.

I relaxed with my JD Black whiskey sour and meditated about my tour. I had done my very best to stem the flow of supplies to South Vietnam, but had only destroyed a few trucks and one ferry. Maybe the magazine articles had been correct when they indicated the war could go on for years. It appeared to me that it was impossible to stop the supplies going to South Vietnam. I wondered why only two Generals visited our base, for a few hours, and never talked to our squadron. I questioned if our leaders really knew what was going on, as their comments in the magazines seemed out of touch with reality.

AUGUST 27, 1966

The Base Personnel player, a non-rated Lieutenant, debriefed me and requested my comments about the 114 missions that I had flown. I provided the following observations:

1. I had only observed two targets of significance during my entire tour at Ubon—a ship at Quang Khe, that I missed, and a large truck convoy coming from China, that I could not strike due to restrictive ground rules

2. I had never noticed any targets of importance in Route Packages One or Five.

3. The enemy could drive trucks from western China to South Vietnam, and always be near the jungle for immediate cover.

4. Every resident in North Vietnam appeared to have an automatic weapon to fire.

5. The dirt roads in North Vietnam were always repaired overnight.

6. North Vietnam appeared to be acquiring more trucks and boldly using them.

7. The enemy was substantially expanding their AAA and SAM sites.

8. It appeared that the enemy was ferrying supplies down the coast in small boats

9. In my opinion, F-4C fighters were not suited to hunt trucks because they were fast movers with limited loiter time.

10. I discovered that bombs were worthless for accurately hitting small targets like trucks.

11. I learned the hard way to never fire rockets in heavily defended areas at night.

12. I could not understand why F-4C aircraft were not equipped with radar warning devices as in the B-52 bombers.

I assumed that some of my mission totals might be combat records. I also speculated that I had flown more night missions over North Vietnam than any Air Force F-4 aircraft commander. However, I knew that my striking record and a dollar might get me a beer in a stateside bar. My 31 missions over North Vietnam in July, with 30 at night, might be a monthly record for F-4 drivers, but no one cared. I completed 100 missions over North Vietnam and fourteen mission over Laos from 12 March to 26 August (167 days), which might be another useless record. I recalled that I had completed 54 missions over North Vietnam in 57 days, July 1 to 26 August, with 53 at night. I was convinced that I had earned my extra $390 combat pay—about $3.42 cents a mission.

I was pleased to learn that I would leave Ubon on the 29th for Bangkok and then depart for the States on 1 September at 0100. I would have a few days for sight seeing in Bangkok before departing on a Continental charter flight. However, I was still required to pull squadron duty officer from three to four hours each night, and it was busy tonight as a AAA site knocked down one of our Phantoms. My teammates had been hit in Pack One but the wounded "Hummer" managed to fly out to sea where the crew ejected. I hoped the 85mm AAA site at Ron Ferry had not hit them, as I had warned them about that lethal radar controlled site.

AUGUST 28, 1966

I learned that our downed aircrew was lucky—a Navy helicopter rescued them after a 37/57mm AAA site near the coast had knocked them down. I was not surprised to learn that the downed aircraft commander was the Major that had bitched about the way I flew my bird. I cleared our base by completing the usual paper work and then I took my personal effects to the Transportation section for shipment back to George Air Force Base. I found a Rookie to buy my trusty bike that had served me well—maybe it would bring him luck.

I was scheduled to be on duty for six hours tonight, but I could care less. This Night Owl was flying away tomorrow! It was still pouring, but it no longer bothered me—I was almost home free.

I received word that Captain Kenneth Robinson and Lt. Sammie Hoff were missing in action. This was very distressing to me, as I had flown with both of them during this lethal conflict. It appeared that they had been lost in Pack One during a napalm attack under the flares. I recalled that Ken and I had almost run out of fuel when I was flying in his rear cockpit. I remembered that Sammie had helped me survive a tough high PRF battle in Pack Six with admirable professionalism and courage.

28

AUGUST 29, 1966
DEPARTURE TO THE STATES

I bordered the old C-47 for my departure and realized that I was the only passenger—just like when I arrived almost six months ago. I tried to relax in an old fabric seat for the flight to freedom and reminisced about my tour at Ubon. I recalled that I had asked God to provide "Omens" about this war, and maybe the Big Boss had answered my request.

The most profound omen of my tour was when God made time stand still over the river and the little fisherman had looked me straight in the eye. I was fortunate to have avoided an incredible curtain of bloody fireballs rising from the ground in the Red River Valley. The Big Boss granted me the opportunity to witness thousands of brilliant tracers without being hit. The bloody red tracers coming from the enemy's rapid-fire guns looked like a huge fire-hose discharging a solid stream of red water. God certainly impressed me with St. Elmo's fire—the fiery omen appeared to be beads of red-hot liquid mercury dancing in my cockpit.

God also exposed the beauty of the coastal beaches as the sun slowly surfaced from the Gulf of Tonkin during our early morning missions. I was given the opportunity to witness the splendor of the imposing mountains at sunset, as we returned to Ubon after a watchful night hunting for trucks. I will always remember the clear meandering rivers heading to the ocean, with fishermen in their little black boats. I recalled watching the lush green jungle, that covered the steep rocky mountains in Laos, pass by our bird during our low-level missions through Laos.

The Big Boss also provided painful omens of horror and death that will be retained forever. The deathly sight of burning trucks from my napalm attacks was an ugly reminder of war. I could never forget the sight of thousands of sparklers on the ground, as angry residents fired at our bird with the intent to kill us.

Maybe God also wanted me to feel many extraordinary and intense emotions during my missions. I was allowed to experience the ultimate high during our low-level attack on the Quang Khe Ferry—it was an exhilarating encounter! It would be impossible to ever forget the incomparable thrill of flying on the deck north of Hanoi at night under a full moon and feeling invincible. I was given a moment to feel that I was going to die when the deathly sizzling fireballs tried to converge with our bird over Dong Hoi. God allowed me to feel completely defenseless, as I entered dense weather at night north of Hanoi. Now I completely understood the meaning of "being up shit creek". The unwavering vertigo that I experienced during our landing approaches was impossible to even explain to another human. I was impressed with the gutsy truck driver and the solitary fishermen in their little wooden boats, who were not afraid of deadly Night Owls. However, I was unhappy to have become "The Bad People" to the children, when our noisy Night Owl hunted in the darkness over their country.

God allowed me to comprehend the significance of a "moment in time" during this tour. I watched an 85mm explosive projectiles bursting off my birds wing—only moments from killing us if I had not turned. Bill and I were only a few seconds from death when the bombs lighted the dark mountain walls in Mu Gia Pass, and exploded under our bird due a faulty altimeter. I certainly appreciated our strobe lights during the violent weather—they were a timely lifesaver on many occasions.

There were also feelings of disappointment that will never go away. I was extremely saddened when Rags and Ned were lost during a very hazardous mission. Our leaders disturbed me when they lied to our country about the shortage of ordnance. I was upset when I read the erroneous information in major newsmagazines about the air war over North Vietnam. I was irritated, that we could not attack valid targets, like Haiphong or the convoys coming from China. I was displeased that we had not been trained properly to wage war or provided with warning equipment that was used on other aircraft. I was disturbed that I had seldom helped our troops in South Vietnam, as it was impossible to stop the flow of supplies to the enemy. I was fearful that we had been ordered to compete in deadly battles with unfavorable ground rules and no game plan.

I was pleased with my dedicated teammates during this conflict, as they were remarkable and always participated at the highest level. I was thankful for Bill's support during our many missions in hostile parks, and I enjoyed the camaraderie of my friends. We were extremely lucky to have a Clubhouse with comfort, food, movies, and a game room. I will remember the old wooden church and the torrential rains battering its tin roof.

I will always be thankful to God for riding "shotgun" during many treacherous missions. The Big Boss also saved my tail with many nights of lousy weather over North Vietnam—it might have been impossible to survive seventeen "Charges into the Valley of Death".

I also had time to contemplate about my fellow teammates. I believed that fighter pilots served in the Military because they had a fierce determination to safeguard their country at any cost. They were willing and ready to fight for their country, no matter the danger, and in any part of a hostile world at a moment's notice. Many pilots remained faithful to the Air Force and served past their required commitment, as they wanted to protect our way of life. We all believed that we were the best fliers in the world and could perform any possible air maneuver or ground attack. Confident fighter pilots habitually self-proclaimed that they were the greatest pilots the world had ever known and willing to take on any comers who doubted this declaration. Fighter pilots wagered on every bomb, rocket, or bullet expended during a range mission and had a ready excuse if an event was lost. Fighter pilots are the ultimate risk takers and believe they are invincible—accidents always happen to others.

Many fighter pilots have no desire to live a nine to five existence and would never be content flying any aircraft that was not a combat plane. They could go to work for an airline flying large aluminum people movers with multiple engines for safety if boredom was their life's desire. Fighter pilots are known to be extremely aggressive and willing to fly alone over belligerent territory where capture and torture are a very distinct possible. They feel they can accomplish any assigned mission using their own skill and judgement, as guidance is not needed from some distant target planner sitting at a desk. No one, except other fighter pilots, can ever appreciate their skill, as they are the only ones capable of judging their peers. Fighter pilots will resort to extreme measures to avoid mistakes in the air—they never want to be looked down upon by their peers. They realize that death is always just a few seconds, or a few feet away, and that fear or panic are not an option in the air—there is no time for hesitation during a hypercritical situation. Combat pilots are willing to follow their leader in the air through any peril including heavy flak, and to place their life in the hands of a fellow wingman flying a few feet away. They are aware that even a small error in judgement, while flying during dangerous combat, can result in the death of both of them.

I believe that fighter pilots are embroiled in situations more dangerous than racing cars or playing professional football, but never receive any recognition or adulation from the public. Many are true artists in aerial flight maneuvers, but few outsiders ever come to appreciate their skill and daring in the air. Only a small number people will ever comprehend what makes them tick, unless they are fellow fighter pilots. The only recognition that fighter pilots might receive is some medals that are seldom worn, because they live in a flight suit and normally work twelve-hour days. Combat pilots are well aware that they may be the first to go to a war where they could die, or suffer torture if shot down and captured.

Even in peacetime, fighter pilots receive orders to remote locations far from family and friends, but many non-rated officers never receive a single remote assignment. Fighter pilots realize that a non-rated officer of equal rank is able to retire with the same pay and benefits, although their only risk may just involve getting to and from work. The Air Force never provides fighter pilots with special preferences in basic pay, housing, retirement, or family benefits. They do not receive any extra consideration in the Air Force, except for flight pay, if the required hours are flown each month. However, money is not a factor or many would be flying for the airlines, because the government could never pay them enough to be fired upon, or taken prisoner and tortured. I find it curious that any officer in a combat zone is entitled to sixty five dollars combat pay, even if they are only in the zone for one day.

Fighter pilots are aware that their promotions are uncertain in the Air Force, as their independence and risk-taking characteristics may not be highly desired traits for staff officers. I questioned why combat fighter pilots were never afforded "Spot" promotions such as those allotted to peacetime bomber pilots. Many fighter pilots have a passion for aircraft and women, as both are beautiful stream-lined objects with exquisite curves and designs. However, many women are bored with aerial talk and flying hands unless they too are creatures of the air, which is why many fighter pilots date stewardesses. They realize that marriage will be diffi-cult—many women will never understand that fighter pilots have a notable desire for independence and excitement.

History indicates that the Air Force seldom defends fighter pilots when they make an error in judgement, and seldom hesitates to take away their wings. Fighter pilots are known to have some characteristics the Air Force does not con-done during peacetime, but those imperfections might be meaningful in a war. Nevertheless, it is obvious that some fighter pilots have an irresistible urge to fly as fast and low as possible, even when not authorized by their commanders. Some have been known to buzz their hometown during a cross-country flight, although it could end their military career. A highly motivated fighter pilot might consider any fighter, encountered in the air, as fair game for practicing an aerial attack. A few might even be tempted to fly in the Grand Canyon, and under bridges when-ever they thought they could get away with it. I believe that fighter pilots are a strange breed of bird that desires to defend their country at any cost, although they may never receive any recognition. I have no doubt that Great Britain treasured their fighter pilots during WWII and maybe our country might appreciate us sometime in the future.

I decided to end my fighter pilot career and depart the Air Force as soon as possible after returning to the States, unless the Big Boss allowed me to obtain a Navy Exchange position. Obtaining this assignment would be my final determinate as to whether I had always been "meant" to fly fighters.

Epilogue

SEPT 1, 1966 TO JULY 12, 1968
GEORGE AIR FORCE BASE, CALIFORNIA

I instructed and evaluated replacement pilots in all phases of F4C operations. I was assigned two students during each training course and instructed 12 hours a day. I also flew functional control flights, as the squadron maintenance test pilot on weekends. I remained in the military past my one-year commitment to help new aircrews going to the war. I felt that I could teach them how to survive over North Vietnam. However, I decided to leave the military if I was not selected for a Navy Exchange Tour.

JULY 13 TO JULY 12 1971
FIGHTER SQUADRON 101 DET OCEAN
NAVAL AIR STATION OCEANA
VIRGINIA BEACH, VIRGINIA

It appeared that the Big Boss wanted me to remain in the military—I was selected to fly with the U.S. Navy as an Exchange Officer. I instructed in conventional weapons delivery, formations and aerial refueling using the F4B & J aircraft. I also directed the training of staff and replacement crews; prepared lecture material; prepared training checklists, and updated all changes to flight manuals. I was the first Air Force pilot to land on the aircraft carrier John F. Kennedy, where I completed day and night carrier qualifications. I was selected to attend the F-4 Tactical Manual Conference and contributed improvements to the sections on Night Attack and Armed Reconnaissance. The Navy agreed that rockets should not be fired in highly defended areas at night and placed a warning note in their manual. My Navy Skipper, Commander Pete Booth, promoted me to hold the position of Detachment Operations Officer and selected me to attend the "Top Gun" Fighter Weapons Course at NAS Miramar in San Diego, California. I was the first USAF pilot to attend the course and possibly the only Air Force F-4 pilot to graduate from the school. I was honored when my Skipper wrote that he would accept my transfer to the U.S. Navy at anytime, now or in the future.

JULY 13, 1971 TO JULY 2, 1973
426 TACTICAL FIGHTER SQUADRON
LUKE AFB, ARIZONA

I returned to Air Force duty as an F-4 instructor pilot for combat crew training in day and night missions. I held the position of Flight Commander and maintained a combat capable status.

JULY 3, 1973 TO AUGUST 3, 1974
35TH TACTICAL FIGHTER SQUADRON
KUNSAN AB, KOREA

I maintained combat ready status in the F4D to perform assigned unit missions. I maintained proficiency in nuclear and conventional weapons delivery, aerial combat tactics and ground attack. I was named the squadron Top Gun for two quarters of the year that I was stationed at Kunsan.

AUGUST 4, 1974 TO JUNE 2, 1975
58 TAC FIGHTER WING
LUKE AFB, ARIZONA

I performed duties as an instructor pilot in the F-4 Central Instructor School. I was selected as a Detachment Air Operations Officer for the first visual air to ground and air to air simulators. I developed project plans and test procedures; monitored the collection of test data, analyzed results, prepared test reports, and scheduled aircrews for participation in the two advanced simulators.

JUNE 2, 1975 TO NOVEMBER 2, 1976
HEADQUARTERS AIRSOUTH
NAPLES, ITALY (NATO)

I was selected for a notable assignment to a Naples, Italy working for NATO—my twelve-hour work days finally ended. It appeared that my flying days was over, but I was excited to receive such a greatly favored assignment. I again worked for my old Wing Commander from Ubon who was now a Lt. General and Commander of Air South and 16th Air Force. I was responsible for establishing nuclear policy guidance, doctrine, employment plans, and weapons requirements for NATO strike units within the Southern Region. I received outstanding efficiency reports and General Wilson recommended me for accelerated promotion. However, it appeared that the Big Boss was not finished with my destiny as General Wilson arranged for me to command the 614th Tactical Fighter Squadron in Torrejon, Spain. It was a distinct honor to be selected for this command—there were only three American fighter squadrons located in Southern Europe.

NOVEMBER 1, 1976 TO 1 AUGUST 1978
614TH TACTICAL FIGHTER SQUADRON
TORREJON AB, SPAIN (USAFE)

I was responsible for 47 F-4D aircrew members and 11 enlisted personnel in the 614th TFS. I was also responsible for the squadron's wartime mobility mission to two NATO forward operating bases. It was a demanding mission for my aircrews, as we had to allot our time between Spain, Turkey and Italy. I was extremely proud of my teammates, as we received an "outstanding" rating during Operational Readiness Inspections. It was exciting to get a flight in an F-15 against Navy F-14 Tom Cats from the aircraft carrier, America, that my old Navy Skipper commanded.

AUGUST 2, 1978 TO AUGUST 3, 1981
JOINT CHIEFS OF STAFF
THE PENTAGON,
WASHINGTON D.C.

Major General Yancey assisted in my assignment to the J3 OJCS as an Action Officer. I was designated as a member of the JCS Response Cell and JCS Crisis Action Team. I coordinated reports for the JCS and the Secretary of Defense, with the Joint Staff, OSD, and State Department. I prepared and gave briefings on the JCS Crisis Action System to US and foreign officials. I also prepared military options for decision by the National Command Authorities and operational messages for decision implementation. I felt honored to have received outstanding efficiency reports from Major General James E. Dalton, USA, Lt. General Philip C. Gast, USMC, and Rear Admiral Thomas C. Watson, USN.

AUGUST 4 1981 TO JULY 1, 1984
HEADQUARTERS 12TH AIR FORCE
BERGSTROM AFB, TEXAS

I decided to retire early and was allowed to select my final assignment. I selected Bergstrom AFB in Austin, Texas as the Eanes School District had an excellent school system. God was kind to me as I was blessed with three wonderful children who are now medical doctors. Andrew graduated from the Naval Academy and Tulane Medical School—he is now a Navy Emergency Room Doctor with the rank of Commander. Charles graduated from Duke and Tulane Medical School in the top 10% of his class—he is currently an Air Force Radiologist with the rank of Lt. Colonel. Ashley graduated from the University of Texas and Southwestern Medical School—she was Phi Beta Phi in academics, and helped Texas win two National Championships in Tennis.

MY FINAL AIRCRAFT FLYING HOURS

F102 732
   F-4C&D 2003
   F-4B&J 591
   T-33 362
   Student 261
   Combat 165
   Instructor 1119

Names, Acronyms, and Terms

AAA—antiaircraft artillery.
AC—aircraft commander (F-4 front cockpit).
AC-47—"Spooky" gunship armed with three 7.62mm gattling guns.
AFB—air force base.
AGL—above ground level.
Aim-9—"Sidewinder" infrared air to air missile.
Aim-7—"Sparrow" radar guided air to air missile.
Aircraft Arresting Gear—device used to engage hook equipped aircraft to stop forward momentum of a routine or emergency landing or aborted takeoff.
Armed reconnaissance—missions flown against specified areas hunting for enemy targets.
Atoll—Russian infrared air-to-air missile.

B-4—military green canvas suitcase.
B-52—USAF high altitude bomber than could carry 84 500-pound bombs internal and 24 external. Armed with four tail guns.
B-66—"Douglas Destroyer" tactical twin engine light bomber.
Barrel Roll—military code name for flight operations in Laos.
Big Boss—God
Bird Dog—forward air controller in small maneuverable single engine plane.

C-47—"Gooney Bird" twin engine prop cargo aircraft.
C-130—Lockheed Martin "Hercules" cargo aircraft with four turbo props.
CBU-24—cluster bomb units (rearward dispenser—600 golf ball size bomblets/300 steel pellets each).
Clubhouse—Officers Club located at Ubon, Thailand.
Commander 7th Air Force—Headquarters Seventh Air Force (PACAF) at Tan Son Nhut Airbase, Saigon.

DShK M 1938—dual purpose 12.7 machinegun, 600 rounds per minute, green tracers, up to 3,000'.
Dien Bien Phu—town located in Route Package V.

293

Dong Hoi—town located near coast approximately 24 miles north of DMZ in Route Package One.

DMZ—the 1954 Geneva Conference divided Vietnam by establishing a six-mile wide demilitarized zone separating North Vietnam from South Vietnam along 17th parallel.

Dragon's Jaw Bridge—bridge in North Vietnam situated between Vinh and Hanoi.

Duffel bag—green canvas bag issued to military personnel.

EB-66—electronic counter measures (ECM) aircraft.

Edsel Kid—Robert Strange McNamara

F-102—Convair "Delta Dagger" supersonic all-weather jet interceptor.

F-105—Republic "Thunderchief" fighter-bomber.

F-106—"Delta Dart" mach II jet interceptor.

F-4—McDonnell Douglas "Phantom II" twin engine supersonic multipurpose all weather jet fighter.

FAC—forward air controller. Pilot who controls fighter aircraft against specified targets.

Fire bombs—cylindrical thin-skinned aluminum tanks for carrying napalm.

Flak—the bursting shells fired from antiaircraft artillery.

FNG-f—ing new guy.

Frag Order—defined operational missions for the next 24 hours; received by Teletype.

G-pressure—the force exerted upon an aircrew member and aircraft by gravity.

Gattling gun—six barrel gun that fired 20mm ammunition consisting of either high explosive incendiary (HEI) or armor piercing incendiary (API) bullets.

GCA—ground controlled approach for landing aircraft.

GIB—guy in back (rear cockpit of F-4).

Guard Channel—243.0 megacycles on all radios for emergency transmissions.

Gunship—aircraft equipped with rapid firing guns.

HH-3—Sikorsky twin engine helicopter "Jolly Green" used for combat rescue missions.

Haiphong—port located on coast in North Vietnam (Route Package 6B).

Hanoi—Capital of North Vietnam.

Ho Chi Minh Trail—series of trails winding through Laos and North Vietnam leading to South Vietnam.

Home Plate—Ubon Airfield.

Hootches—wooden buildings used for sleeping quarters.

Hummer—Speeding object that may or may not be under control.

JCS—Joint Chiefs of Staff.

K-2B—green military flight suit for aircrews.

Karst—limestone outcropping.

Kbar—military combat knife.

KC-135—Boeing "Stratotanker" air refueling with four jet engines capable of off loading 200,000# of fuel.

Kep—North Vietnam airfield located northeast of Hanoi.

Khaki 1505's—sand colored military short sleeved uniforms.

LAU-3—rocket dispenser (disposable) carrying 19 rockets.

Lowering device—150+ feet of thin nylon strapping attached to a lowering device.

Mach I—designated as the speed of sound.

Martin Baker MK. H-7—rocket ejection seat.

MiG—name for Russian built fighter aircraft developed by designers Mikoyan & Gurevich.

MiG 21—Mikoyan/Gurevich "Fishbed".

MiG 17—Mikoyan/Gurevich "Fresco".

MiGCAP—combat air patrol to defend against enemy MiGs.

Mk 82—500# general-purpose (GP) bomb.

Mk 83—1000# general-purpose (GP) bomb.

Mk 117—750# general-purpose (GP) bomb.

Moles—slang for trucks.

Molehill—slang for truck park.

Mu Gia Pass—steep pass on Laos/North Vietnam border in Route Package 1.

Napalm—mixture of gasoline & M-4 thickener that adheres to target & burns for 15-20 seconds with temperatures up to 1400 degrees F.

Northeast & Northwest Railroad—two rail lines leading from Hanoi northeast and northwest toward China's Kwangsi and Yunnan Provinces.

O-1—" Bird Dog" Cessna twin place all metal aircraft with tandem seating capable of 100 knots.

PE—Personal Equipment

Pickle—slang for pushing a red button located on the aircraft's control stick to release ordnance.

Pipper—illuminated dot on pilot's gun sight for expending ordnance or firing gun.

Piss—slang for flak to include tracers.

PRF—pulse rate frequency.

Pylon—position located under aircraft's wing where ordnance or fuel tanks could be carried.

Quang Khe Ferry and Naval Complex—located between Dong Hoi and Ron Ferry on coast.

RF-101—McDonnell "Voodoo" photo reconnaissance single engine jet.

Recce.—Reconnaissance.

Rockets—2.75" folding fin aerial rockets (FFAR)

Rolling Thunder—code name of US air campaign against North Vietnam starting March 2, 1965.

Ron Ferry—ferry located approximately 60 miles north of DMZ near coast in Route Package 1.

ROTC—Reserve Officer Training Corp.

Route Package—geographical division of North Vietnam into seven areas for U.S. Air Force, Navy, and Army air operations.

Route Package I—area extending approximately 65 miles north of DMZ slightly north of Ron Ferry; then west to Laos just north of Mu Gia Pass (assigned to all military operations).

Route Package II—area located north of RPII & assigned to Navy.

Route Package III—area located north of RPII & assigned to Navy.

Route Package IV—area located north of RP III & assigned to Navy.

Route Package V—area located in northwest North Vietnam and assigned to Air Force.

Route Package VI (A)—a pie shaped area directly north of Hanoi that extends east to the northeast railroad and assigned to the U.S. Air Force.

Route Package VI (B)—a pie shaped area east of Hanoi extending from northeast railroad to coast & assigned to the U.S. Navy.

RTL—Rolling Thunder League

SA-2—surface to air missile (SAM) consisting of 6 launchers placed in a star pattern.

SAC—Strategic Air Command. Bomber branch of the U.S. Air Force.

SAM—surface-to-air missile.

Samlars—three wheeled pedal cycles with pedicab driver.

Scramble—a military order directing aircraft to become airborne within five minutes followed by mission instructions.

Shrapnel—shell fragments from any high-explosive shell.

Skunk or Stinker—slang for antiaircraft gun emplacements.

SOS—Squadron Officers School.

SUU-16—20mm gattling gun with 6 barrels that fire up to 6000 rounds per minute with a 1200 round capacity.

Su-23-2—twin 23mm gun, 1000 rounds per minute each barrel, up to 10,000'.

SUU-25—flare dispenser.

T-33A—two seat version of Lockheed F-80 Shooting Star—nicknamed "T-Bird".

TAC—Tactical Air Command. Fighter branch of the U.S. Air Force.

TACAN—electronic air navigation system that provides a continuous indication of bearing & distance (slant range) from the aircraft to the station.

Takhlie—Thailand airbase located approximately 380 miles west of Ubon.

Target Master—President Johnson

Tchepone—(Sepone) town on Ho Chi Minh Trail located in eastern Laos near South Vietnam border.

TFS—tactical fighter squadron.

TFW—tactical fighter wing with a complement of three fighter squadrons.

Thud—slang name for F-105 fighter.

Thud Ridge—series of hills located between the Red & Black Rivers in Route Package Five.

Tracers—military round that leaves a visible trail as it travels.

Ubon—Royal Thai Air Force Base located in Eastern Thailand.
Udorn—Royal Thai Air Force Base located north of Ubon near Laos's border.
Umpire—slang for Headquarters Seventh Air Force located in Saigon.
Vertigo—the sensation of dizziness and the feeling that oneself or one's environment is whirling about—a confused, disoriented state of mind.
Vinh—North Vietnam city located on coast in Rout e Package II.
Willy Pete—marking rocket (2.75").

100mm gun—largest AAA weapon, 12 tons, and crew of seven, 15-20 rounds a minute, up to 45,000'.
355th Tactical Fighter Wing-F-105 wing located at Takhli.
388th Tactical Fighter Wing-F-105 wing located Korat.
433rd Tactical Fighter Squadron-8th TFW F-4 squadron located at Ubon.
497th Tactical Fighter Squadron-8th TFW squadron located at Ubon.
555th Tactical Fighter Squadron-8th TFW squadron located at Udorn

978-0-595-41676-9
0-595-41676-4

CPSIA information can be obtained
at www.ICGtesting.com
Printed in the USA
FSHW011635210319
56553FS